THE SECRETS
of JESUIT
BREADMAKING

—

AMDG

Dear Doreen and Mark,

With prayerful best wishes,

[signature] SJ

THE SECRETS of JESUIT BREADMAKING

—

*Recipes and traditions from
Jesuit bakers around the world*

BROTHER RICK CURRY, S.J.

HarperPerennial
A Division of HarperCollins*Publishers*

HarperCollins books may be purchased for educational, business, or sales promotional use. For information please write: Special Markets Department, HarperCollins Publishers, Inc., 10 East 53rd Street, New York, NY 10022.

FIRST EDITION

Designed by Joel Avirom

Library of Congress Cataloging-in-Publication Data

Curry, Rick, 1943–
     The secrets of Jesuit breadmaking / Brother Rick Curry, S.J.—
1st ed.
        p.   cm.
     Includes index.
     ISBN 0-06-095118-4
     1. Bread.   I. Title.
TX769.C85   1995
641.8'15—dc20   95-15424

95 96 97 98 99 DT/RRD 10 9 8 7 6 5 4 3 2

Ad Majorem Dei Gloriam

*To my sister, Denise Curry, S.N.D.de N.,
who continues to inspire me by her life
of enthusiastic service to others.*

Ah! qu-il est bon le bon Dieu.

Contents

FOREWORD

It may be that there is no great difference between talking about victuals and talking about religions. In nearly all faiths, the divinity is made present in what we ingest. In fact, no one would deny that an obligatory rite of almost every religion is the moment of eating or drinking with the deity, eating and drinking in honor of the deity, or eating and drinking the deity himself or herself. In some measure, the profound meaning of nourishment has to do with our thirst for eternity as it is encoded in our daily sustenance. That may be why almost all our gods have chosen to leave a sign of their presence in foodstuffs. In this sense, we eat and drink for life, and in order to have life. In enjoying our food, we experience flashes of eternal life. The act of eating is not merely fundamental in itself; so, too, is the ceremony of preparing and sharing it. The ritual ceremony that takes place around the table is an act of profound and ancient religious significance. It is not gratuituous, therefore, that some religions use the evocation of the Supper, or the fraternal gathering around the Table, to symbolize their most important Mysteries. How, then, could the preparation of bread *not* have special meaning? In Christian cultures, the presence of the bread recalls the passion, death, and resurrection of the Son of God, whose body, as described by the celebrated Mexican baroque poet Sor Juana Ines de la Cruz, "in its niveous manifestation, avails itself of the grain of the wheat, which is transformed into His flesh." Dividing the bread was the perfect sign for the resurrection of the Messiah. Through the ritual of communion, the absent Master, in the form of bread and wine, returned to nourish his disciples spiritually and materially. That is why religious communities have always valued the importance of the partaking of food and drink, and have considered it a sacrament, the actual presence of God among man, and have developed subtle and wondrous methods to symbolize the many ways in which they may affect the loving act of preparing nourishment for the pleasure of their brothers. In this book will be found recipes for breadmaking from a variety of Jesuit communities, collected by a very dear friend of mine, Rick Curry. And even for those of us who are not religious, I believe none will find it strange to believe that through the aromas and savors of the food we share with our fellow beings, and the substantial presence of the divinity contained within it, we humans may, day after day, enjoy a small taste of Paradise.

Laura Esquivel
Mexico City, D.F.
December 1994

ACKNOWLEDGMENTS

S t. Ignatius of Loyola taught us that the beginning of any prayer is the acknowledgment of all the gifts God has given us. In that spirit I would like to begin this book with thanking some of the people who made it a reality. My only regret is that so many more of my friends who put up with my projects for years will go unmentioned. My only consolation is that they know who they are and they know I am grateful.

Firstly, to my Provincial of the Maryland Province of the Society of Jesus, Rev. Edward Glynn, S.J., who not only gave me permission to write this book, but also generously allowed its proceeds to go to the National Theatre Workshop of the Handicapped.

My thanks also go to Rev. Joseph A. O'Hare, S.J., Rev. John D. Alexander, S.J., and Rev. Kenneth J. Boller, S.J., whose friendship and wise counsel have encouraged me to pursue this project; to Rev. John W. Donohue, S.J., of *America* magazine, who so generously edited my work and kept me from errors of faith and morals; to Rev. Vincent T. O'Keefe, S.J., of New York and Brother Rafael Garcia Bandera, S.J., from Spain, who mapped out my European tour and opened for me the doors that led to richness of Jesuit lore, and to Brother Robert J. Fitzgerald, S.J., of St. Joseph's University, Philadelphia, who by his fraternal friendship and baking skills has kept me close to the hearth on many levels. Finally, a collective shout of thanks to Brother John B. Hollywood, S.J., Brother James A. Horan, S.J., Brother John J. McLane, S.J., Rev. Salvador Jordan, S.J., and Brother James C. Lemon, S.J., who heroically put up with me as a novice and gave me a love for manual labor.

I owe special gratitude to Mary Johnson of *McCalls*, who insisted that I do this book when others were not so enthusiastic.

Books take time and if it were not for the generosity of Edward Nicoll, of Waterhouse Securities, Inc., who arranged funding for my indispensable assistant, Christopher Banks, I could not have been free to do this work. Office details at the National Theatre Workshop of the Handicapped were further lightened by Bobbi Wailes, my able assistant.

Robert Lipsyte of the *New York Times* deserves much of the credit for the publication of this book. It was he who on my behalf called Wendy Wolf of HarperCollins. Wendy then promoted the project and enlisted Patty Ryan to hold my hand and walk me through the work of writing. Hugh Van Dusen of Harper-Collins put on the final touches.

Technical assistance was given to me by Brother Gilbert J. Scott, S.J., who patiently exhumed material from the New York Jesuit Archives. James J. McGuire, of Mayer, Brown and Platt, used his astute lawyer skills on my behalf and Michael Hogan, another lawyer friend, added a lyrical quality to the manuscript.

Not enough can be said about the leadership that Robert F. Sennott, Jr., as chairman of the board, brings to the National Theatre Workshop of the Handi-capped, nor about the skill of all the students and staff of the workshop who sliced, diced, baked, and sampled all the breads in this book.

I must also thank Laura Esquivel, whose friendship greatly encouraged me. Through her introduction I met Thomas Colchie, who as my agent guided me calmly through the sometimes turbulent waters of publication.

The last thank you is to all the Jesuit Brothers who have gone before me and on whose shoulders I so proudly stand.

March 19, 1995
Feast of Saint Joseph

LOYOLA SHIELD

*The Jesuit symbol for hospitality
depicts two wolves licking a
boiling cooking pot.*

INTRODUCTION

Jesuits are best known as priests and as educators, but the Society of Jesus also includes those who are called Brothers, of which I am one. We Brothers are full Jesuits, but we are not ordained to the priesthood. Traditionally, we have served the Church through temporal activities and practical actions. We call this "service without power."

The Jesuit order was founded by St. Ignatius of Loyola in 1534 and recognized by Pope Paul III in 1540. In its early history, Jesuit Brothers distinguished themselves in many fields. They were architects, builders, painters, musicians, linguists, and physicians, to name a few professions. Then the order was suppressed from 1773 to 1814. (The history of that dispute is complicated, but I don't think it's self-serving to say that the achievements and prestige of the Jesuits caused a good deal of jealousy within the Church. In addition, the Jesuits were in the vanguard of the Counter-Reformation, and in that role they became a favorite target of anticlerical and antipapal forces outside the Church.)

After the Society was reinstated in 1814, a new tradition took hold: Most of the Brothers became artisans. Part of the mission of the Second Vatican Council was to return the various orders back to their historic missions. Jesuit Brothers were therefore encouraged to obtain advanced degrees. The fact that I am both a baker and a teacher reflects the influence of both pre- and post-Vatican II thinking upon my training as a Jesuit Brother.

I was introduced to the subculture of the Jesuits in the fall of 1961, when I left my home in Philadelphia to enter the novitiate of St. Isaac Jogues in Wernersville, Pennsylvania. My goal all along was to become a Brother, not a priest, and I went to the novitiate to pray, to learn, and to prepare myself for the work that Brothers did in those pre-Vatican II days—artisanship and craftsmanship.

With the novice scholastics—those students studying for the priesthood—I shared the classes on the Jesuit life and constitutions, Scripture, and the theology of the Christian life. But while the novice scholastics were studying Greek and Latin, we prospective Brothers were instructed in the various trades.

Actually, my first assignment at Wernersville was dusting the back stairs because the Superiors wanted to keep me isolated. By nature, I'm very talkative. They figured—correctly—that temptation to break silence would be much less for me if I were off by myself. Then I moved to the kitchen, peeling potatoes and the like. Eventually I was apprenticed as a baker in the mornings and as a tailor in the afternoons.

I was thrilled to think that I was going to learn how to sew. But Brother John B. Hollywood, S.J., to whom I was apprenticed, was quite irate when I appeared in his tailor shop. To his credit, I never knew about his anger until twenty years later, when he finally felt he could tell me of his reaction upon meeting me. You see, he had known he was assigned a new novice to train, but he had not been told that this novice had only one arm. With his help, I became an accomplished helper.

My entry into the bakery was less dramatic. When I met Brother Walter Dragansky, S.J., he told me simply to read the recipe and make the corn bread. Thus began my instruction in the sacred art of bread baking and the secrets of Jesuit bread baking.

Although the work of the Brothers was less academic, some of the priests-in-training were rather envious of our assignments. After I had spent a particularly hot and exhausting summer day in the novitiate's bakery, John O'Donnell, a scholastic novice, complained to me that while he had spent the day in the unfulfilling task of learning one more Greek verb, my assignment of baking bread brought joy to hungry Jesuits. Jesuits are sometimes referred to as the Marines of the Church. This remark by John O'Donnell was an early lesson for me that Ignatius's army, like any other, travels on its stomach.

As things turned out, I became neither a tailor nor a chef, although I have never stopped baking bread for my community, wherever it might be. After leaving Wernersville, I studied at Xavier University in Cincinnati and St. Joseph's College (now University) in Philadelphia. I then went on to take an M.A. in theater arts at

Villanova University. In 1975, I was assigned by my Jesuit superior to begin a doctoral program in theater at New York University. While developing a dissertation subject, I became interested in providing training in the theater arts for persons with disabilities, and I soon began the National Theatre Workshop of the Handicapped on a modest basis in a SoHo loft. Now I direct this workshop, teach classes there and also at Fairfield University, and bake bread.

But back to bread and my training as a Jesuit Brother. I was not at the novitiate in order to learn how to dust the stairs, alter a cassock, or make corn bread. I was there in order to learn to pray, and to learn to serve others in the ambience of prayer. St. Ignatius believed that the authentic search for God must pass through one's ordinary life. He prescribed for Jesuits—as well as others who take religion seriously—a daily spiritual exercise called the Examen of Conscience. Simply put, this is prayer spent in checking one's progress toward a greater union with God and better service to others. Ignatius was actually prescribing an ongoing self-examination, what he called a discernment of spirits.

When I make bread, I make an Examen of Conscience. After reading the recipe, I take a deep breath, relax, and recall that I am in God's presence. I recall the last twenty-four hours and name the good things that have come into my life, and I thank God for them. After the dough has been mixed and begins to rise, I reflect on how I have participated in this new life, and I beg God to show me how I am growing more alive in my spiritual life. I examine what my recent actions, omissions, thoughts, and desires tell me about my relationship to God and myself and others in God. I examine how I have dealt with my family and coworkers. Have I spent any time in the last twenty-four hours doing something generous for another? Do I harbor resentment? Have I held my tongue? Have I prayed for another's needs? Has my conversation been hurtful? Am I part of the problem or part of the solution? Have I been kind? Have I remembered that God is lovingly watching over me?

When this evaluation is completed, I take what I have learned about myself and place it in God's understanding hands. I bring to Him the larger needs that I feel at the moment. I speak to Him as to a friend who delights in my company and understands and loves me. I talk to God about my fears, hopes, and joys. I ask God to let me be open to life and love. And when the smell of fresh-baked bread fills my kitchen, I let my spirit be filled with gratitude and praise for God and for all the things in my life. I thank God for the gift of bread and the gift of life.

In the pre-Freudian era of the sixteenth century, making an Examen of Conscience was rather revolutionary. It was even more revolutionary because it was an *individual* spiritual exercise. Ignatius believed that individuals had to find the path to God in the way that suited them best, and he fought to release Jesuits from the required coming together five times a day for prayer. Ignatius taught his Jesuits to pray on their own. The conversation with God was to be intimate, conducted in the language of the heart. If this prayer did not lead to the service of others, then it was a false prayer. Accordingly, Ignatius's first job, coming even before preaching, was to commandeer every resource that he had to feed the poor. He systematically went around to the rich and begged bread in a rather great spirit of courageous confrontation, and he was unwilling to take no for an answer. He had his companions do the same. The first house of the Jesuits in Rome, which was connected to Our Lady of the Della Strada Chapel, became a bread distribution center.

As we near the end of the twentieth century, most of us are well practiced in self-examination. Perhaps being asked to make an Examen while we are baking bread does not seem very radical. Radical or not, I consider it to be one of the secrets of Jesuit breadmaking.

Every once in a while I have to remind myself that there was a time when I didn't make bread, but I also have to remind myself that I've been making bread for only about thirty years, and many, many bakers have gone before me. Because bread has been such an important staple throughout the ages, it is not surprising that Jesus used it to symbolize his body and his life to his followers.

The early residents of Egypt and Mesopotamia ate wheat, but not as delicious leavened bread. Instead, grains of wild wheat were spread over stones and dehusked and eaten "as is": hard and gritty. Eventually it was discovered that mixing and beating the dehusked grain with water would produce a palatable gruel that could then be baked over hot stones. These were the earliest flatbreads (a category of breads that is still eaten around the world, by the way; the tortilla, made from corn, is a form of flatbread). Then around 2600 B.C., Egyptian bakers made the discovery that if this wheat-and-water mixture were not baked immediately, it would bubble into a fermentation, and this swollen dough would yield a delicious raised bread. That was the momentous discovery of leavening. Egyptians became quite expert.

The flour mill was invented in Mesopotamia around 800 B.C. By 300 B.C. leavening was not just left to "chance" fermentation. Yeast was collected from beer sediment and then stocked.

Leavened bread was introduced to Greece around 400 B.C., and bread very quickly became a great social divide. The rich ate white bread and the poor ate a grittier type of wheat, a rather coarse unleavened bread.

The Romans lived by bread. Baking was a great social gathering. There would be common bake ovens in the town rather than individual ovens in the home. The women made up the dough at home, then brought it to the professional bakers at the communal ovens. These loaves were the standard size that we use today.

The technique of bread baking stayed pretty much the same from the Middle Ages until the nineteenth century. Most bread was baked at home or in the village ovens, but with the Industrial Revolution, cities and populations grew and specialized bakeries began to industrialize the baking of bread for the masses. Jesuits, however, have continued baking bread the way they have since the days of Ignatius.

A LITTLE FLOUR AND WATER

Each time I bake bread, I'm reminded of the simplicity of mixing unrelated ingredients that are then transformed into the most wonderful delight. It all seems so perfect and so easy. A little flour and water and a few other wholesome ingredients make an infinite number of breads. But putting these wholesome ingredients together with *understanding*—that's the axiom of success for bread baking. I'll share with you what I have learned from the Jesuits and other fellow bakers about these ingredients.

FLOUR

Grains of wheat are technically called wheat berries. Flour is produced by grinding these wheat berries into a fine meal. The ground wheat is then processed into a number of different flours: whole wheat, bread flour, bleached and unbleached all-purpose flour, pastry flour, cake flour, and whole wheat pastry flour. (By the way, wheat flour is the most common flour used for breadmaking because it is the only one that can be used to make leavened bread. Without going too deeply into the chemistry of the process, suffice it to say that only wheat flour contains sufficient amounts of the protein that converts into the gluten that provides rising dough with its elastic frame.) Among the other flours are buckwheat, millet, barley, brown rice, and soy. These are often used to flavor breads and can usually be found in natural food stores or a bakery supply house.

In the "old days"—thirty years ago—recipes sometimes called for "hard" flour or "soft" flour. This nomenclature has gone out of style. You won't find any sack of flour in the store labeled "hard" or "soft." But when I was a beginner, I would stand in front of the flour shelves and endlessly read labels to try to figure out what was a soft flour and what was a hard flour. My label-reading was to no avail. Eventually I learned that hard flour is milled from hard wheats, which are high in protein (high in gluten) and good for baking products that require a strong structure such as bread. Bread flour is a hard flour. Soft flour is milled from soft wheats, which are lower in protein and more suitable for pastries. But rest assured, I do not use these terms in this book. None of these recipes will send you searching for flours with names not on the labels..

Most of the recipes call for white or whole wheat flour. If white is called for, I recommend using unbleached, although some very wise bakers say that any white flour, even bleached and enriched, will do fine. Some of the recipes specify bread flour. However, if bread flour is not available, you usually can buy gluten at a health food store and add a tablespoon of it to regular all-purpose flour. Or simply use the flour that you have.

With whole wheat flour, I think stone-ground whole wheat flour is better for bread baking. I think it produces a finer texture and a lighter loaf than regular whole wheat flour. Unlike any other flour, whole wheat flour is processed with fat and, unless it is kept cool, it will spoil. I keep mine in the refrigerator.

In both prayer life and in baking, I get very uncomfortable with what I call prayer fascists and food fascists. In bread baking, there are people who refuse to use white flour, or who won't use any flour that they haven't ground themselves.

Prayer fascists are those who think there is only one way to pray, only one way to find God, and of course it's always their way. But St. Ignatius taught us that all paths lead to God, and history teaches us that all flours can lead to delicious and nourishing bread.

Graham flour is named after its first proponent, Sylvester Graham, a nineteenth-century Presbyterian preacher and vegetarian who was one of the first individuals to advocate a strict dietary regimen, and also one of the first to link good food to spiritual health. Graham flour is an unsifted, sometimes unbleached, coarsely ground whole wheat flour—raw stuff, basically the same as whole wheat flour but with a slightly different taste.

Rye flour has very little gluten in it, and therefore it's rarely used by itself. It's usually mixed with white or whole wheat flour. If you use it alone, your bread will be very heavy and dense. Rye flour is susceptible to ergot, a fungus that can cause hallucinations when tainted grain is eaten. In 1951 in Pont-St. Esprit (named after the Holy Spirit), France, ergot found its way into the local bread. People and animals were running around hallucinating before the problem was discovered and remedied. The FDA keeps our supply of rye ergot-free. However, if you are having hallucinations in prayer, check out your rye bread.

WATER OR MILK

Water is an often ignored ingredient in cooking, but for making bread it is one of the essentials. Liquids create the texture of bread. For the small amount of water that you are going to be using in breadmaking, I would encourage you to use bottled spring water. It's very accessible now and if you're suspicious about your tap water, I would get a couple of gallons of natural spring water and enjoy it in your cooking. Water is used not only in the dough. If you want a nice crispy brown crust, mist your loaves just before baking until they're really wet.

Some recipes call for milk as the moistening ingredient, or for a combination of milk and water. Milk produces a richer and more tender loaf that has a less grainy taste. I recommend using only fresh milk. I think bread made with powdered milk has less flavor. Most of the recipes that call for milk specify scalded milk. Milk is scalded when bubbles start to form around the edges of the pan. Then it must be cooled before adding to the other ingredients. Before pasteurized milk, bread recipes called for scalding milk to kill enzymes that were harmful to the yeast. With pasteurized milk there is no need to scald milk, so I don't. But since yeast does like a warm environment, I usually heat it slightly.

A few recipes, especially biscuit recipes, call for buttermilk. If you don't have any on hand, you can always "sour" skim milk by adding one tablespoon of lemon juice per cup of milk.

YEAST

In England and Wales and Scotland and Ireland, when I asked the Brothers for bread recipes, they immediately thought I was asking about Irish soda bread—a quick bread made without yeast. They didn't think that Americans were interested in old-style European yeast breads. But we are. At least I am.

Yeast is a living plant and needs suitable conditions to survive. It needs moisture, food to form the sugar starches, and a little warmth. It eats sugar and forms carbon dioxide and alcohol. The gas that it releases during fermentation makes the dough rise. Yeast also works on the gluten in the flour to develop flavor and texture.

Yeast can be bought either fresh or dried, and either kind can be used with equally good results. The general rule of substitution is simple: Use half the amount of dried yeast to fresh yeast; or, looking at it the other way, twice as much fresh yeast as dried yeast. The recipes in this book call for active dry yeast. If you prefer fresh yeast, double the amount specified.

Fresh yeast is crumbly and has a fawn color. Well-wrapped, it can keep for three weeks in the refrigerator and for several months in the freezer. But if you're going to use fresh yeast, why not use it *fresh*?

I always use active dry yeast because it's more convenient—no muss, no fuss—and it stores well in the refrigerator. You can buy it in large jars or in little packets. One packet is about 2¼ teaspoons, and many of the recipes in this book call for that amount. A jar of yeast is cheaper than the packets, but the quantity you buy will depend on how often you are going to bake bread. Keep all your yeast in the refrigerator, where it can stay dry and cool.

In one respect, the European Brothers who assumed that I as an American was looking for yeast-free quick breads were correct. Seeing a recipe that calls for yeast is enough to strike trepidation in the heart of many potential bread bakers. They feel that this recipe will take too much time, while what they want in life is instant gratification and huge success. This approach will bruise the bread and defeat our whole spiritual journey. If you are intimidated by the thought of yeast, pray for courage and proceed. You can make yeast your friend.

SUGAR

A little sugar added to a bread dough accelerates the action of the yeast. But too much will kill the yeast. Sugar obviously adds sweetness, but it also makes the texture of the bread more tender by softening the gluten. In addition, it adds color and gives the bread a browner crust. Many recipes specify honey and molasses instead of sugar. These sweeteners give a distinctive taste to breads and can be substituted for sugar.

FAT

Butter, vegetable shortening, and oils are used in the dough to enrich it and to make it more tender and flavorful. The dough is coated with oil while it rises to retain its moisture and keep a crust from forming, and the surface of bread, brushed with butter before it bakes, will have a softer and browner crust. A little butter brushed on the top after baking also will soften the crust. And, of course, some kind of fat is necessary in the preparation of loaf pans and baking sheets. (For pan preparation, I generally use vegetable shortening.)

I use olive oil whenever I'm making Italian bread because of the taste it imparts. I like to use walnut oil for the same reason. Brother Fitzgerald uses only safflower oil, and he taught me what a versatile oil this can be.

I love using butter because it makes a luxurious loaf of bread, but I'm also well aware of the health consequences. I guess it's a trade-off. You can buy salted butter or sweet, unsalted butter. The recipes in this book assume you are using sweet butter. If you use salted butter, reduce the amount of salt in the recipe.

We used a lot of butter in our baking at the novitiate in Wernersville. We procured it in fifty-pound bricks! With a rather sophisticated series of wires, we would then cut the brick into serviceable sizes for baking and for serving at meals. Cutting the butter was one of my jobs. Although it was a very difficult job to cut this butter with the wire, particularly since I have only one arm, I always tried to be as adroit as possible. One morning while I was working on this chore, old Brother Dickson, S.J., came over to my station. He often came to the bakery on his coffee break to ask us how we were doing. He had taken a particular liking to me and without fail asked me if I was happy in my vocation and in what I was doing. When he asked me on this particular day if I was happy in my vocation, I answered, "Yes." He then asked me if I was happy in what I was doing. With perhaps a slight tone of irritation in my voice I said, "Cutting butter? I'm not particularly happy cutting butter." He was unfazed and simply replied, "Oh Brother Curry, the Little Flower St. Theresa of Lisieux says you must find happiness in the little things, not in the great things."

Now I often ask myself, "Am I happy cutting butter?"

EGGS

Eggs do a couple of things for bread. Used in the dough, they contribute to the leavening process. They also add flavor and color. Used as a glaze, commonly called an egg wash, they give the surface a golden color and make the crust more tender. Brioche, with its golden brown outside and soft yellow inside, is a perfect example of delicious results from using egg in bread.

OTHER INGREDIENTS

Salt is used in most recipes. Mostly it adds flavor, but it also has some control over the dough. Salt strengthens the gluten. Dough made without salt rises faster. Too much salt can kill the yeast entirely.

Jesuits use spices, herbs, nuts, and fruits in their breads with regularity. It's always great fun to add any kind of fruit to a regular bread. It just makes it a festival bread.

Toward the end of Lent, the Brother baker would start adding some raisins or nuts to the bread to wake up our taste buds, to let us know that spring was coming, that Easter was coming, that the world of fasting would soon be over. Take heart! So I always think of raisins and nuts in a bread as giving courage.

When I was in the bakery at Wernersville, I shared the responsibilities of the bakery with a fellow novice, Brother Salvador R. Jordan, S.J. Brother Jordan was born in Puerto Rico and he favored vivid coloring dyes for the icing of feast day cakes. We followed the liturgical calendar and celebrated special occasions, as best as we could, with foods that reflected those feast days. I remember smothering a cake with jelly beans at Easter. I also remember the unfortunate green corn bread that we served on the feast of St. Patrick. With these mistakes we learned another of St. Ignatius's fundamental beliefs: moderation in all things. The older Brothers quickly advised us that this also was a secret of Jesuit breadmaking. They introduced us to the art of restraint.

MAKING BREAD

It was clear from the very establishment of the Jesuits that Ignatius wanted you to be good at what you did. He certainly wanted people to be excellent bakers. Father Nadal, an early Jesuit, put this attitude clearly in his exhortation at Alcala in 1561 when he said, "The Society wants men who are as accomplished as possible in every discipline that helps it in its purpose. Do not be satisfied with doing it halfway."

I learned how to bake bread the same way that I learned how to pray—through practice. Certainly a Jesuit is mandated to pray daily, as are all Christians. I decided to make bread baking as systematized as I made my prayer life. I also decided that I would try to bake bread every day. In graduate school, my assignment was to finish my doctorate, but I still baked bread daily. When I moved into the community, I was not assigned to the kitchen but I still baked bread each night.

Many people feel they don't have time to make bread. But you don't have to devote three or four hours to a loaf of bread. You work on the bread for ten minutes and then let it go for an hour and a half. You come back to work on it for ten or fifteen minutes longer and then leave it to itself for another length of time. You put it in the oven, let it bake, take it out of the oven, and let it cool. I like to think of making bread as an ongoing relationship, because what I'm making is a living thing, and like other living things, it can in fact be left alone at times to grow on its own.

When I first began to bake I really didn't think that I was ever going to be able to accomplish anything. The baked goods served to us looked so wondrous and so out of reach, I thought I would never be able to match them. But out of necessity I had to dive in and do the job. The Brothers let me know that what we're talking about here is some water and some flour and some heat. Just go and do it and learn by doing.

A point of Jesuit pedagogy that's very much overlooked today, I believe, is the question of repetition. The Jesuits believe that something is learned by repeating it over and over and over again. And the *ratio studiorum*—the Jesuit code of methodology and curriculum—recommends *repeticio* as a very definite form of learning. At Wernersville, we made seven different kinds of bread on a weekly basis. I made those seven breads over and over and over again, learning more and more about each bread each time I repeated the process.

A PLACE TO WORK—A PLACE TO PRAY

Ignatius's advice on the approach to prayer was to find space, give time, make it your time, enjoy it, and reflect upon it. The first thing that I do when I begin to bake is take a deep breath and place myself in the presence of God and let Him know that I know that I'm engaged in a wonderful, sacred activity. This is my own personal time and this is my own personal space and this is something that I enjoy. I'm participating in a life-giving and a pleasure-giving product.

When Ignatius taught the Jesuits to pray, he insisted that they be comfortable. They could pray sitting, lying down, standing, kneeling, or in any other position where they were at ease. Obviously, you can take this approach into your kitchen and make yourself comfortable while you bake bread. You can create an environment for yourself in which you feel relaxed and can enjoy the process. You can feel good as you make something good.

You don't have to have a dream kitchen to make a great loaf of bread. Find some free counter space or a table on which you can put out all of your ingredients and still have some room in which to mix them together and to throw some flour around to knead the dough. For me, free counter space means cleaning all the obstacles away from it. When I was at Xavier University in Cincinnati, I took a creative writing course and Mr. Feldhouse, an extraordinary teacher of writing, said, "Don't encumber yourself by small pieces of paper. Get large pieces of paper and write all over them and *clear off* your desk."

I say, *clear off* your work space!

I urge you to pay attention to the height of your counter or table. Find the best height for your size. Working at one that is too high or too low can put stress on your back and turn an enjoyable activity into a painful one. I'm six feet tall, and my good friend Kirk Moore built me a butcher block table forty-eight inches high, the perfect height for me. He finds it a bit excessive when I claim that this gift has changed my life, but if you've ever struggled with lower back pain, you'll agree this claim is only a slight exaggeration. I also have a small step stool handy, should I need more height and leverage over the dough. If you're stuck with a counter that is too high for you, raise yourself by standing on a step stool or even on a phone book. Or if your counter is too low, do your mixing and kneading on a board that has been raised by a phone book.

SACRED TOOLS

The Rule of St. Benedict reminds us to regard all utensils of the monastery as if they were sacred vessels of the altar. One of the rules of the kitchen at Wernersville was that if we dropped a spoon, for example, we had to bend down and kiss it. We learned to respect our tools. They had to last so they had to be taken care of. The Brothers taught us to clean our utensils as we used them. We couldn't let them pile up until the end. At the end of a long day of baking and cooking, all those utensils piled up waiting to be washed and scrubbed would have been quite a daunting sight.

In my early days in Jesuit bakeries, I was always amazed to see what little equipment the brothers had and the exquisite foods they were able to achieve with them. In fact, I believe there is a correlation. I absolutely believe in keeping the breadmaking utensils simple. Sophisticated machinery can detract from your learning the basics of good breadmaking. You need only a bowl, a spoon, a measuring cup, an oven, and a little peace and quiet.

There seems to be very strong agreement that the best pans for baking are the dark ones. And this is true. These pans conduct the heat much faster and give a very even rise. However, perfectly good bread can be baked in the light silver aluminum pans. My friend Ted Koehler in Maine insists that Irish soda bread can be baked only in a glass Pyrex loaf pan. He exaggerates, of course, because Pyrex pans did not exist until this century, but the point is well taken. I personally like terra cotta loaf pans. It's a personal choice. Test different pans on your own, remembering that they will give different results.

If there's one little point of luxury that I have allowed myself, it's a good ceramic mixing bowl. I think that the atmosphere of bread baking should be that of warmth, and a ceramic bowl is able to retain the heat and thus creates a womb, a matrix out of which the dough can begin to live and thrive. If it's cold in my kitchen and I think my ceramic bowl is too cold to make the dough in, I run the bowl under hot water to take the chill off. So if you're going to treat yourself to any new equipment for baking bread, treat yourself to a nice six- to eight-quart ceramic bowl. And that's your bowl for baking.

I prefer to use wooden spoons, which I carve myself, but lots of good bread has been mixed with whatever could be found in the utensil drawer. And several years ago I discovered what is called a Danish whisk. It's a rather odd-looking utensil, but it's very strong and it now often replaces my wooden spoon.

SAY WHAT YOU ARE GOING TO TEACH

A very strong part of the Jesuit pedagogical method is saying what you are going to teach. It's the specific preparation to bring clarity to your lecture. In baking bread, this preparation is reading the recipe—saying what the ingredients are, saying how you are going to put them together, and saying how long the dough rises, at what temperature, and how long it bakes.

I read the recipe from start to finish so there will be no surprises. I read it once, say it once, without doing anything. I'm just absorbing the information about what is expected. Then I reread the recipe, say it once again, and get out all the ingredients and place them on the table in front of me. I put each ingredient to my right. When I have added it to the dough, I move its container to my left. That way, I never have any doubt about what I have added and what remains to be added.

PUTTING IT ALL TOGETHER

Ingredients can be put together in a lot of ways to make a loaf of bread. A lot depends on what kind of bread you are making—a yeast bread, a quick bread, or a sourdough bread. Even with similar types of bread, the steps involved to produce a delicious slice of bread can vary from recipe to recipe.

But a word of caution about the *amounts* of ingredients you put together:

Follow the recipes as exactly as you can and be as accurate as you can in your measurements. Don't be cavalier about the quarter-teaspoons and the quarter cups.

If you think you need to make some adjustments in the measurements, if you think the bread is too dry, too gooey, or too salty, make the adjustment after you've made that bread several times. Making adjustments can be tricky. Flour responds very much to the weather. If there is moisture in the air, it's going to go right into the flour. The flour will be heavier and you will need less of it and less water, too. And don't be surprised if on some days you can add as much as two more cups of flour than is called for in the recipe.

The amount of flour that actually ends up in your bread also depends on how you measure it. If you scoop it directly out of a bag where the flour is well packed, you will introduce more flour into your dough than if you loosen up the flour before you measure. The difference in the amount of flour you use with these two ways of measuring can vary as much as a quarter-cup. To provide some consistency, I use a stainless steel bowl and pour the approximate amount of flour that I am going to use into this bowl and fluff it up a little bit with a wooden spoon. Then I scoop into this flour for my measurements. This is the "1 cup of flour" I list in the recipes in this book. If you use another system, take note.

With yeast breads, there are two common methods for putting the ingredients together. One I call the "straight dough" method, the other the "sponge" method. With the straight dough method, you simply mix the ingredients, knead the dough, let it rise, then bake. The sponge method involves a preliminary step. The yeast is first blended with parts of the liquid and flour and, perhaps, a little sugar. This soft batter is set aside and allowed to ferment for at least two to three hours, sometimes up to twelve hours, until it puffs up, becomes bubbly, and looks like a sponge. This sponge is then mixed with the rest of the ingredients and you proceed as in the straight dough method.

Many breads produced from a heavy dough, one with proportionally a lot of flour or loaded with fruits or nuts, start with a sponge because it's a very simple way to give a heavy dough mixture a jump start in the rising stage. Breads that start with a sponge are also usually tangier in taste because of the extra fermentation involved with using the sponge. For example, sourdough breads, which we'll talk about specifically later, always start with a sponge.

With either the straight dough method or the sponge method, you need to activate the yeast. This means combining it with some warm water and maybe a little sugar and letting it stand for about five minutes until it becomes foamy or bubbly. I have my own technique for activating the yeast. I pour the warm water into a bowl and then sprinkle the yeast over it. I try to make certain that all the yeast particles are wet, and I do this with my hand. Most bakers probably use spoons to do the stirring, but with my fingers I can actually feel when all the yeast is no longer gritty, completely dissolved.

Most of the recipes in this book instruct you to add the rest of the ingredients gradually to the activated yeast, and to beat the dough for a given amount of time. This beating is what I call the first mix and it takes a good eight to ten minutes. You can beat the dough by hand or with an electric mixer with a paddle attachment. If you do it by hand, beat vigorously. It's tiring, I know, but it's also the only way the gluten will get activated. When you start beating the dough, the consistency will be like a batter, but as you continue to beat and gradually add flour— I usually add about ½ cup at a time—the dough will start to come together, leaving the sides of the bowl. At this point the dough is ready to knead.

IS IT SOUP YET?

Brother Horan used to tell me that it's not soup yet. He meant that when you're cooking some soup, it's not really soup until the ingredients start to come together, thicken, and then take on a life of their own. Then, and only then, is it soup. He explained that the same principle applies to bread during the first kneading of the dough. That kneading is what brings all the ingredients together and gives the dough a life of its own. It is what makes the bread *bread*. Kneading develops the elastic gluten and distributes the ingredients. Without a good kneading, your bread won't rise sufficiently and will have a poor texture.

Certainly one of the secrets of Jesuit breadmaking is the secret of any breadmaking, and it is precisely this step—kneading. Never scrimp on the kneading. Spend time with it. Don't be afraid of it. Enjoy it.

You can knead bread with one hand or with two hands or with an electric mixer that has a dough hook. St. Ignatius said that all creatures are indifferent. He meant that how we use them determines whether they are good or evil. I believe that an electric mixer is one of those indifferent creatures. It's how you use it. Earlier I advocated simplicity in the kitchen, but I also acknowledge that an electric mixer has been good for my breadmaking, saving me time and saving my back.

But how *exactly* should you knead bread? Over the years I've discovered that kneading the dough is a very personal thing. There isn't just one and only one right way to do it and you'll develop your own technique. But the first step is to turn the dough out onto a lightly floured surface. Then you begin pulling and stretching the dough, turning and folding the dough into itself. Get into a rhythm of folding and pushing. I think a common mistake new bakers make is that if the dough is sticky while they're kneading, they add too much flour at a time. Just sprinkle a small amount on the dough whenever you feel it getting too sticky.

Whether you use your hands or a machine to knead the dough is not as important as how long you knead it. You have to knead dough anywhere from six to fifteen minutes. Most dough starts to come together in eight to twelve minutes. I think people are more apt to *under*knead the dough than to *over*knead it. Dough looks as if it is coming together after four or five minutes, but don't be fooled. You really want to knead it for eight to ten minutes. You might want to clock yourself and be certain that you're kneading the dough long enough. When you see little bubbles appear, then you know you're in great shape. The dough will be smooth and elastic.

Many people think that kneading is the hard work of breadmaking. Yes, it is work, but I find it to be most pleasurable. I like spending time with the dough. Even when I initially mix the dough with the dough hook, I knead it by hand for the last minute or two. I want some direct contact with the dough. I like to be involved manually in the process and I want to get a real feel for the dough. I want to feel the smooth and silky texture with my own hand. If you find that your kneading seems like drudgery, be patient and realize that you're one with this bread. You will eventually find the rhythm of this ancient craft. That's the kind of centering you need for your soul.

DOUBLED IN BULK

When I've finished kneading the bread, I place it back in the ceramic bowl in which I have poured about 1 tablespoon of oil. I turn the dough over to make sure it is lightly coated on all sides with oil, cover the bowl with plastic wrap to keep it moist, and let it rise in a warm, draft-free place. To create a warm place, I turn on my electric oven for five minutes, set at only 200 degrees. If you have a gas oven with a pilot, you can let the dough rise in there without even heating the oven.

The beginning baker is always very anxious that the bread is not rising or is not rising fast enough. Your dough doesn't rise as if you were blowing air into a balloon. There's something going on that's growing, but it's like life, it grows subtly, sometimes you're not aware of it. Let the dough bide its own time, then return in an hour and—Oh my heavens, look at that, it has in fact doubled in bulk.

By all means, be patient. Again, this is something repetition is going to teach you. If you're not certain that the dough has doubled in size, test the dough by sticking two fingers into it. If the dough doesn't spring back, your dough has risen enough.

Father John LaRocca, S.J., came under my tutelage one Christmas holiday in New York to learn Italian bread baking for his weekly dinner for his students at Xavier University. Shortly after he returned to Cincinnati, Father LaRocca faxed me a frantic message: "Bread not rising!" My reply: "Keep it warm and be patient."

His bread was not rising because his kitchen was cold. Normal rising times are calculated for an ambient temperature of 90 to 95 degrees. The dough will rise if the temperature is less—it will just take longer. In fact, there is another whole school of thought about rising. This second school believes in a slow rise at a very cool temperature. A few of the recipes in this book call for letting bread rise in the refrigerator for ten to twelve hours. A slow rise gives a tangy flavor to bread. Father LaRocca's bread was rising slowly simply because of the temperature in his kitchen. (Jesuit priests are not excessive in their correspondence with other Jesuits or in their patience. When I received no further faxes, I knew his bread was a success.)

You don't want to put your bread in too hot an environment because it will rise too quickly, which will affect the texture. But if your bread has risen too quickly, remember that the dough is still living. It is not terminally ill. It has life and it will rebound. Just punch it down, flatten it out, knead it again, and put it in a cooler environment for a second rise. In fact, some bakers like two and three rises as a matter of course. Multiple risings add flavor to the bread and give it great texture.

PUNCHING DOWN THE DOUGH

After the dough has risen completely, punch it down to remove the air bubbles. I think it's important to have respect for what you are doing, so when I punch the dough, I don't make an angry pugilistic punch. I just press my fist into the dough to remove the air bubbles from it and let it collapse. I like to show respect for this food that I am going to be blessing and eating. It's going to be something sacred.

SECOND KNEADING

Breads that are going to be baked in loaf pans call for a short second kneading after the dough has been punched down. This kneading on your lightly floured work surface needs to be gentle and only for about two minutes—just long enough to get rid of all the air bubbles. This second kneading distributes the trapped carbon monoxide more evenly and gets the gluten activated again.

At the conclusion of this kneading, I fold the dough into itself and shape it to conform to the bread pan, where it is immediately placed. (With free-form loaves, I mold them into round or torpedo shapes, braid them, or do whatever the recipe calls for.)

THE FINAL RISE

For the second and final rise, the dough is in the bread pan. At this stage, I'm careful not to let the bread rise too much. You just want to see it creeping up the edges of the pan. This rise will be about half the length of the first rise. If it rises too long, the bread will collapse and go flat. During this rising, I cover the loaves with a tea towel to keep them moist. Plastic wrap at this point will impede the rising.

PREPARING YOUR PANS

Most recipes will instruct you to prepare whatever loaf pans, muffin tins, or baking sheets are called for before you punch down the dough, or while the dough is resting. As I said earlier, I like to prepare the pans at the very beginning. Regardless of when you decide to grease them, do it well. I grease my pans with vegetable shortening, or if I feel a moment of great largesse, I do it with butter. I'm really very generous with the greasing of the pans because I don't want to put all this work into the bread and then have it stick to the pan. Most of the time I line my baking sheets with kitchen parchment, but greasing them and sprinkling on a little cornmeal works just as well.

RESTING THE DOUGH

If your recipe doesn't call for a second kneading, it probably will call for letting the dough rest for about ten minutes after you punch it down. Resting the dough relaxes the gluten, which makes the dough more manageable and easier to shape into free-form loaves.

SLASHING

I make my slashes with a serrated knife, but a razor blade works well, too. I make them about half an inch deep. If my bread calls for poppy or sesame seeds on top, I make the slashes after applying them.

BAKING

Magic and spiritual things happen during baking. If you're lucky enough to have an oven with a glass door, you can watch some of this process. When a fully risen bread is first put into a hot oven (make sure your oven is fully preheated unless the recipe specifies otherwise), it gives an initial rise that is called the oven spring. Then it will fall down and then slowly rise again. This you can see. What you cannot see is the yeast being killed or the alcohol that was produced in the fermentation evaporate. You also won't be able to see the gluten coagulate and form the structure of the bread, the grains burst open, or the starch turn into sugar, but this is what's happening as your bread becomes golden brown and your kitchen is filled with smells that create consolation and great warmth.

TESTING FOR DONENESS

You'll be able to see and smell if your bread is burning, so your main concern will be if it has baked *sufficiently*. There are several ways to test whether the bread is done. You can take one of the pans out of the oven, take the bread out of the pan, and with your fingertips or knuckles, thump it on the bottom. If it has a hollow sound, it's done. Of course, learning to identify this "hollow sound" requires trial and error and repetition. Another surefire way to determine doneness is to take an instant-read thermometer and stick it in the bottom. If it reads 190 degrees, your bread is done. Baguettes are done at about 200 degrees, but baguettes cook so quickly—in about twenty minutes—that I've never felt the need to test for their doneness. Most quick breads can be tested by inserting a toothpick into the center of the loaf. If it comes out clean, the bread is done. Try not to open the oven door continually to check on your bread because an awful lot of heat does escape from the oven by just opening the door. And never open the oven door until the bread has been in there for at least twenty minutes, unless the recipe directs you otherwise.

WHEN CAN I EAT IT?

Most people want to eat bread the moment it comes out of the oven, but in the novitiate I learned quickly that the Brothers were very insistent that the bread cool thoroughly. This cooling also allows moisture to evaporate, which would otherwise soften the crust, improves the texture of the bread, and enhances the flavor. So take the bread out of the oven, remove it from the pans, and let it cool on a wire rack. When the time comes, slice gently, and preferably with a serrated knife. Also, if you rest the loaf on its side while you slice, it will cut much easier and there will be fewer crumbs spilled.

REFLECTION

Just as saying what you are going to teach is an important step in Jesuit pedagogy, so is saying what you have just taught. Just as reading and thinking about the whole recipe is an important step prior to beginning baking, looking at the finished product and reviewing your baking is an important final step. This review is often totally ignored once the bread is out of the oven, but it's important.

To say that I taught it, I write notes and comments on my recipes. If I don't want to write in my book, I simply notate a copy of the recipe. (One of the rules of the Jesuits that I found particularly difficult, not to say almost abhorrent, was the prohibition against writing in our books. We had to keep the textbooks as clean as possible because we passed them on to the Brothers behind us. It was very exciting when we were allowed to buy our own books and make them our own, with as many annotations as we wanted. Likewise, make your recipes your own.)

However your bread turns out, make note of it. If your bread was not a complete success, compare your comments with my "what went wrong and what to do about it" list.

PROBLEM	REASON OR SOLUTION
Bread is overly brown on top but inside is just right.	Try covering loosely with foil for last 10 to 15 minutes of cooking.
Loaf is cracked.	It will taste good anyway. This happens even to experienced bakers, and no one has yet devised a way to prevent it.
Loaf is dry.	You used too little liquid, too much flour, or baked too long.
Dough doesn't rise or bread is flat.	The water for the yeast was too hot or too cold. It needs to be 105 to 115 degrees. Try testing the water with an instant-read thermometer until you can feel the right temperature. Also, your bowl could have been too cold. Make sure your yeast foams in the bowl. If it doesn't, discard it and start over.
Bread has gooey streaks.	The second rising was probably too long and dough collapsed in oven. As a general rule, the second rise should be about one half of first rise.
Bread is full of holes.	Dough was overkneaded or allowed to rise too long. But if you like the bread like this, fine. Some people do.

PROBLEM	REASON OR SOLUTION
Bread is lumpy, hard mixed with gooey lumps.	Dough was not mixed sufficiently before kneading.
Bread turns moldy in fewer than five days.	It probably was not allowed to cool completely before being wrapped. Wrap in paper, or freeze, wrapped in plastic wrap or aluminum foil.
Top is nicely browned but sides and bottom are pale and soft.	Take bread out of pan and place directly on rack for last 10 to 15 minutes of baking.
Top of loaf is sunken rather than nicely rounded and crumb tastes soggy.	Dough was insufficiently kneaded or there was too much liquid. Ten minutes of kneading is not too much for bread.
Loaf is shapeless	Breads baked on baking pans instead of in loaf pans need a fairly dense loaf to hold up. Check recipes to see which breads are suited to being baked on pans. Also, a ring from a springform pan can contain a free form loaf during second rising.
Dough took exceptionally long time to rise.	The rising environment is probably not warm enough.
Bread is soggy.	Bread did not bake long enough. Resist the temptation to take bread from oven the moment it starts smelling wonderful. Cutting into hot loaf can also cause deflation.

PROBLEM	REASON OR SOLUTION
Loaf is uneven	Oven may not be level. Experiment with different ways of placing bread. Get to know your oven. Even very good ones have cold and hot spots in them.
Bread doesn't look store bought.	There's nothing wrong with it! There's a charm that comes out of your own oven because it's authentically yours.

Part of my reflection is also spiritual. I look back and thank God for this wondrous thing that has happened. I thank myself and give myself credit for the work I've done creating this staff of life. I look back. I celebrate.

THE EXTRA STEP

A portion of the breads that we made at Wernersville was always given to the poor in the neighborhood. There was a large wicker basket where we put the breads of the day. Anyone from the village was welcome to take the breads. When they did so, they always left a personal note—a thank-you note. That was one of our little contacts with the outside world, and a precious one, knowing that someone out there was very grateful for the breads that we baked. I still always give away part, if not most, of the bread I make. You might want to make it a practice, too.

In America, every time I was at a Jesuit Brothers' conference or any other Jesuit function, I would make gathering recipes part of my agenda. Once word got around about what I was doing, Brothers started coming to me with their recipes. It was all rather straightforward. And of course, many recipes came to me through family and friends.

But gathering recipes in Europe was a different story. First of all I had to make connections and I am deeply indebted to Brother Bandera, who knew or knew of most of the European Brother bakers. He enthusiastically sent me in their direction.

But I also experienced another problem with the Brother bakers in Europe. Time and time again when I would ask them to give me some of their recipes, their first reaction was really very standoffish, because except for some very specific holiday breads or quick breads, they usually didn't have their recipes written down. They made up recipes by the seat of their pants and by weights, not by measurement. In giving me their recipes, they would talk about getting together some yeast, some water, all-purpose flour, a little salt, shaping it into loaves, letting it rise, and baking it. Nothing more. It was so simple to them I know they wondered why I was even asking. So I had to spend a lot of time asking them to be more specific, and gradually I was able to get these recipes down to some form where we could handle them in our own kitchen.

And, of course, many of these recipes are from Wernersville, which no longer exists as I knew it, which touches on the main reason for my gathering all these recipes. In the kitchen at Wernersville, we had a large loose-leaf binder that contained all of our bread recipes. Actually, we had only about twenty recipes, many of which are in this book. And in typical novitiate style, this binder was kept *chained* to the shelf over the mixing table. But besides these twenty recipes, the binder contained the rules for the Brother baker and the calendar for the first-, second-, and third-class feast days. As well, every recipe was filled with generations of copious notes from Brothers past regarding the preparation of the recipes and when they had been served. It was really a journal of the bakery.

ADVENT

Dearest Lord, teach me to be generous.

Teach me to serve thee as thou deservest;

To give and not to count the cost;

To fight and not to heed the wounds;

To toil and not to seek reward,

Save that of knowing that

I do thy will, O God.

—St. Ignatius of Loyola (*1491–1556*)

Advent, which stretches across the month (including four Sundays) before Christmas, is a time when we prepare for the great celebration of Christmas, when we accept the gift of God in the Christ child. It is also a time that people pray for refugees and for the homeless, since that certainly was what Mary and Joseph were.

Advent in the novitiate was not as severe a time as Lent, but the Novice Master did recommend that we give up something. In the Jesuit community—as in the rest of the neighborhood—there's an air of real anticipation all during the month. It's also a time people think about returning home for the holidays, but we were allowed to see our parents only four times a year, and it might not include Christmas, so the novices were given lots of busywork to combat homesickness. When I was in my first year, I noticed a certain amount of frenzy, but if any first-year man asked or inquired about it, he was graciously told it was a secundi secret—a secret of a second-year man. You would know only after you had been there a year. I think it was a way to motivate us; if we persevered for a year, all truth would come to us—or at least the second-year men acted as if they had all truth.

I think of fall and Advent as a continuum. Fall is the time when the luxuries and beauties of summer are stripped away; a more austere time of the year is about to take its place. Advent makes the bridge from autumn to winter. The breads included in this section are breads that can be served throughout the fall as well as during Advent itself.

STEAM POWER

*M*any people maintain that you can't make *real* French bread without steam inside your oven. I think I spent much more of my youth as a Jesuit trying to create steam while baking than I did at any other task. But when I visited the Poilâne bakery in Paris, I realized they had an automatic system building up steam in a whole separate section of the oven and then pumping it inside the stove, and that I could never duplicate the effect in my home oven. A kitchen oven just doesn't have that much heat. Putting a pan of water under your bread in order to create steam creates a nice illusion, but it doesn't help cook the bread any better.

Noble Masi, my instructor chef at the Culinary Institute of America in Hyde Park, New York (the former site of a Jesuit novitiate, St. Andrews), taught me an alternative to steam. Using a plant sprayer, spray the bread with plain white vinegar right before you put it in the oven and again after you've baked it for ten minutes. The acid in the vinegar gives the bread just the right crisping kick.

French Bread

Brother Dennis Lonergan, S.J., spent most of his life cooking for Jesuits and thought that how you baked bread was more important than what you put into it. He also believed in the proper rhythm of baking: He was a master at using the heat of his wood-burning oven efficiently, baking those items that needed the most heat early in the morning and those that took much less heat, such as pies and cakes, at the end of the day.

> 1 package active dry yeast (see note)
> 1¼ cups warm water
> 2 teaspoons salt
> 3 to 3½ cups unbleached all-purpose flour
> Vinegar

Combine the yeast and ¼ cup of the water in a large mixing bowl, stirring until dissolved. Set aside for 5 minutes.

Add the remaining ¾ cup of water, salt, and 2 cups of the flour and beat vigorously for 3 minutes. Beat for another 5 minutes, continuing to add the remaining flour until the dough begins to pull away from the sides of the bowl.

Turn out on a lightly floured surface. Knead for 8 to 10 minutes, until dough is smooth and elastic, adding flour as necessary to prevent stickiness.

Lightly oil a large bowl. Place dough in bowl and turn to coat on all sides. Cover with plastic wrap and let rise in the refrigerator for 10 to 12 hours or overnight.

Let dough come to room temperature. Preheat the oven to 450 degrees.

Turn out again. Divide into thirds, shape into baguettes, and place in trays.

Cover with a tea towel and let rise until doubled in bulk—about 20 minutes. Spray with vinegar. I sometimes throw poppy seeds on the baguettes at this point.

(continued)

Make the seven traditional slashes in each baguette. (I don't know why there are seven, but authentic French baguettes all have that many.)

Bake for 20 minutes, until golden brown, spraying again with vinegar after 10 minutes of baking. Transfer to wire racks to cool for at least an hour.

NOTE: One school of thought says you don't add sugar to French bread and another school says you add a little sugar to get the yeast activated. I don't use sugar in my French bread recipe.

VARIATION

There are six or seven different ways to present French bread: baguettes, rolls, the *épi* (sheaf of wheat), daisy form, heart-shaped, the corona, the ring shape, and the *pan de mie*.

Often I divide this bread into twenty-four sections instead of three, roll them into tight little balls, and let them have the second rise. Right before I put them in the oven, I slash them, spray them again with vinegar, and throw poppy seeds or sesame seeds on them. They bake into luscious, really chewy dinner rolls.

YIELD: *Three baguettes*

FEASTS

—

*T*he Church, in all her wisdom, has always been careful that throughout the year she dotted her calendar with festive days. These are days to celebrate great people who have gone before us, marked with that sign of faith to show us the way. For every feast day we always had a special Mass and a very special meal.

Preparing and eating particular foods with particular feasts and holidays helps set those days apart for everyone.

The Church also understood human nature very well and realized that the enjoyment of the feast could be heightened through anticipation, and the vigil the day and night before marks the official anticipation of the feast. A vigil and its accompanying preparations don't have to mean a solemn watch from a pew. Think about planning the menu, inviting the guests, choosing recipes, gathering ingredients, putting them together, all as part of the enjoyment of the feast.

At the center of every celebration of a Jesuit feast was the meal. The refectory (dining room) would be filled with about 125 young men, scholastics and young Brothers, and then about 40 older people, the older Brothers and the priests. The meal began with a very short Gospel passage reading, after which the rector, in a very loud voice, would give the *deo gratias*, a Latin term meaning thanks be to God. When the *deo gratias* was given, the entire dining room erupted in a great roar of male voices as we broke silence and responded, *"Semper deo gratias et mariæ."* The feast had begun.

Potato Bread

The job of cleaning potatoes is known as *tubera*, the Latin word for potato. Potatoes and potato water give moisture to bread. The classic recipe for potato bread uses fresh mashed potatoes and some of the water they were cooked in. This is a Wernersville recipe.

> *1 medium baking potato, peeled and coarsely chopped*
> *3 tablespoons butter*
> *2 tablespoons sugar*
> *1 teaspoon salt*
> *1 cup skim or whole milk*
> *1 package active dry yeast*
> *6 cups unbleached all-purpose flour*

Boil the potato for 15 to 20 minutes, until it's very tender. Drain the potato but reserve the potato water and let it cool.

Combine the potato, butter, sugar, and salt. Mix thoroughly. Gradually add 3 tablespoons of the milk and beat until the mixture is very smoothly puréed. Blend in the remaining milk.

Combine the yeast and ¾ cup of the potato water in a large bowl, stirring until yeast is dissolved. Set aside for 5 minutes.

Stir in the potato mixture. Beat vigorously for 10 minutes, gradually adding 3 cups of the flour. Continue to beat and add flour until dough begins to pull away from the sides of the bowl.

Turn out on a lightly floured surface. Knead the dough for 5 to 8 minutes, until it's smooth and elastic, adding flour as necessary to prevent the dough from sticking.

Lightly oil a large bowl. Place dough in bowl, turning the ball over to coat completely. Cover with plastic wrap and let rise in a warm, draft-free place until doubled in bulk—about 1 hour.

Grease two 9 × 5-inch loaf pans.

Punch down the dough. Divide in half, shape into loaves, and put in the pans. Cover with a tea towel and let rise again until doubled in bulk—40 to 45 minutes.

Preheat the oven to 375 degrees. Dust loaves slightly with flour before you bake (this gives them a more rustic look).

Bake for about 40 minutes, until they are well browned. Transfer to a wire rack to cool.

VARIATION

I often divide the dough into six parts and put three parts right next to each other in the loaf pan. The loaves look like three little mountains. You can also tear off a section of the loaf and put the rest in the refrigerator or freezer. I think a three-part loaf is more attractive.

YIELD: Two loaves

Date and Walnut Bread

This recipe comes by way of Brother Fenton Melias, who was a merchant marine before he entered the Jesuits. He served as a Jesuit in the Pacific Northwest, including a year in Alaska. He was trained as a cook and a baker and always gave this recipe as a gift to his friends and fellow Jesuits.

> ½ cup vegetable shortening
> 1½ cups boiling water
> 1½ cups coarsely chopped dates
> 4 eggs, beaten
> 1½ teaspoons vanilla extract
> 2 cups sugar
> 3 cups unbleached all-purpose flour
> 3 teaspoons baking soda
> ½ teaspoon salt
> 2 cups chopped walnuts

Combine the vegetable shortening, water, and dates in a large bowl. Let cool for about 30 minutes.

Preheat the oven to 325 degrees. Generously grease two 9 × 5-inch loaf pans.

Add the eggs, vanilla, and sugar to the date mixture. Stir in the flour, baking soda, salt, and walnuts, mixing just enough to moisten.

Spoon the mixture into the pans. Let it settle for about 10 minutes before baking. Bake for about 1 hour. Test with a toothpick for doneness. Cool in the pans on a wire rack for about 10 minutes. Remove from the pans and finish cooling. (See note.)

NOTE: These loaves are much better served 24 hours later. So after they have cooled, Brother Melias suggests that you wrap them in aluminum foil and put them in the refrigerator. If you wrap them in both foil and plastic wrap, they can easily keep in the refrigerator for a good week.

YIELD: Two loaves

BROTHER KIMURA

—

Brother Leonard Kimura, Martyr of Japan (1575–1619), was a cook, a baker, and the first Jesuit Brother martyr. His was an old family of Christians in Japan; his grandfather was baptized by St. Francis Xavier. When missionaries were banned in Japan in 1614, he stayed and lived as a fugitive. He was captured in 1616 with some other men who were suspected friars, but at the time of his capture he was not suspected of being a Jesuit. When asked if he knew the whereabouts of a Jesuit priest he replied, "I know one Jesuit, he is a Brother and not a priest. I am the Brother." Because of his admission, he was sent to prison and burned at the stake. The feast of Brother Kimura is observed on November 18.

Poppy Seed Braid Loaf

I never remember eating any kind of food with poppy seeds until I entered the novitiate. I love to use them now and think they make any bread festive. Brother Jack McLane, who brought great zest to the culinary arts at Wernersville, introduced us to this bread.

1 tablespoon active dry yeast
1 cup warm water
1 teaspoon sugar
1 egg, beaten
¼ cup vegetable oil
1 teaspoon salt
4 to 5 cups bread flour
Cornmeal
Milk
Poppy seeds

Combine the yeast and water in a large bowl. Add the sugar and stir until dissolved. Set aside for 5 minutes.

Stir in the egg, oil, and salt. Beat for 10 minutes, gradually adding flour until the dough begins to pull away from the sides of the bowl.

Turn out on a lightly floured surface. Knead for 8 to 10 minutes, until dough is smooth and elastic, adding flour as necessary to prevent stickiness.

Lightly oil a large bowl. Place dough in bowl and turn to coat on all sides. Cover loosely with a damp cloth and let rise in a warm, draft-free place until doubled in bulk—about 1½ hours.

Grease a baking sheet and sprinkle with cornmeal or line it with kitchen parchment.

Punch down the dough. Turn out on a lightly floured surface and gently knead for 2 minutes. Divide into three equal pieces and roll each piece into a 15-inch-long rope. Braid the ropes, handling them very gently. Pulling on the ropes will make the loaf flat instead of round and plump.

Place both of your hands under the loaf and lift gently onto the baking sheet. Cover loosely again with a damp tea towel and let rise until doubled in bulk—about 30 minutes.

Preheat the oven to 425 degrees. Brush the loaf with milk and sprinkle generously with poppy seeds. Bake about 25 minutes, or until golden. Transfer to a wire rack to cool.

YIELD: One loaf

Mountain laurel is the state flower of Pennsylvania. On one of our three major work holidays at Wernersville, we would go up into the mountains and pick laurel, but only after a lecture on how to tell the difference between male and female laurel. (We were allowed to pick only the male laurel.) The actual date of this holiday varied year to year and was a well-kept secret. Only the Brothers in the kitchen were given any kind of advance notice, and that because we had to prepare a picnic for this mountain holiday. After our expedition, and throughout the rest of Advent, we spent every night after dinner outside in the freezing cold weaving laurel into garlands.

SPECIAL MEALS
—

FIRST-CLASS FEASTS

BREAKFAST as usual.

DINNER: Oysters or other shellfish are added, olives and celery, and an additional meat course is served, usually consisting of fowl or some other choice meat.

Drinks are served ordinarily at dinner, except that a wine of better quality is added towards the end of the meal.

Dessert: Fruit, two kinds of sweet dessert, cheese, coffee, and a cordial.

SUPPER is served in the usual way.

SECOND-CLASS FEASTS

At dinner, the usual courses are served, but better in quality than usual; cake or some other sweet dish is added to the usual dessert, and a wine of good quality.

—*Custom Book of the American Assistancy of the Society of Jesus*

Buttermilk Biscuits

Once in Cincinnati, I and other junior Brothers were invited to the family estate and horse farm of Brother Brutus Clay, a Jesuit Brother from Kentucky who had been stationed for years at our headquarters in Rome. His mother, Mrs. Clay, a grand southern lady, presented us with a lovely outdoor feast of southern fried chicken and buttermilk biscuits. I was able to slip into the kitchen and talk to the cook, who gave me this recipe and much sage advice about baking biscuits.

> 2 cups unbleached all-purpose flour
> 1 tablespoon baking powder
> ¼ teaspoon baking soda
> ½ teaspoon salt
> 1 tablespoon sugar
> ⅓ cup vegetable shortening
> 1 cup buttermilk

Preheat the oven to 450 degrees. Sift the flour, baking powder, baking soda, salt, and sugar into a medium bowl. Using a pastry blender or your fingers, cut in the vegetable shortening until the mixture resembles coarse crumbs. Add the buttermilk. Stir quickly until the dough is soft and follows the fork around the bowl.

Turn out onto a lightly floured surface and knead gently for 10 to 12 minutes, adding flour as necessary.

Roll the dough until it is ¼ inch thick. With a floured biscuit cutter, cut straight down into the dough. (The cook insisted on this. He explained that twisting the cutter seals the ends of the biscuits, which impedes proper rising.)

Place biscuits 1 inch apart on an ungreased baking sheet. Bake for 12 to 15 minutes, until light golden brown.

YIELD: Twelve to fifteen biscuits

ST. ALPHONSUS RODRIGUEZ

—

St. Alphonsus Rodriguez (1533–1617) is the patron Saint of Jesuit Brothers. He was born in Segovia in Spain, was married and had two children. His wife and children died during an epidemic. He applied to the Society of Jesus but was rejected time and time again because they thought he was too old. His perseverance was so strong that the Provincial finally relented, although he said he couldn't accept him as a candidate but he could accept him as a Saint. Rodriguez was thirty-five years old when he entered the Society of Jesus and proved to be a master spiritual director.

He had been a wool merchant and brought his business expertise into the Society. But he was so astute in directing people in regard to the spiritual life that he was made porter at the college in Majorca and became a great favorite of the people on the island. He would try to see Jesus in every person; for example, every time there was a knock at his door he would say, "I'm coming, Lord." When he died the Society of Jesus and the Church weren't particularly eager to canonize him. But there was such a groundswell of support by the people of Majorca that the Society was pressured into seeking his cause for canonization.

St. Alphonsus Rodriguez's Raisin Bread

The feast of St. Alphonsus Rodriguez is on Halloween, October 31. I was introduced to this bread at my first party at the Frascati at Wernersville, which was a dual celebration of Halloween and the Feast of St. Alphonsus.

FOR THE BREAD

1½ teaspoons salt

½ cup sugar

¼ pound (1 stick) butter, melted

1 cup milk, scalded

2 tablespoons active dry yeast

¼ cup warm water

2 eggs

1 teaspoon grated orange peel

1 teaspoon ginger (preferably freshly grated)

1½ cups raisins

5¼ to 6 cups sifted unbleached all-purpose flour

FOR THE ORANGE NUT GLAZE

1 cup confectioners' sugar, sifted

2 teaspoons butter, softened

½ cup finely cupped walnuts

2 to 4 tablespoons orange juice

Combine the salt, sugar, and butter in a large bowl. Add the milk and blend. Cool to lukewarm.

(continued)

Combine the yeast and water in a small bowl, stirring until the yeast is dissolved. Beat vigorously for about 5 minutes. Beat in the eggs, orange peel, ginger, raisins, and ¼ cup of the flour. Beat for another 5 minutes, gradually adding flour until the dough begins to pull away from the sides of the bowl.

Turn out on a lightly floured surface. Knead for 8 to 10 minutes, until dough is smooth and elastic, adding flour as necessary to prevent stickiness.

Lightly oil a large bowl. Place dough in bowl and turn to coat on all sides. Cover with plastic wrap and let rise in a warm, draft-free place until doubled in bulk—about 1¼ hours.

Grease two 9 × 5-inch loaf pans.

Punch down the dough. Cover with a tea towel and let rest about 15 minutes. Divide in half, shape into loaves, and place in the pans. Make three ¼-inch-deep diagonal slashes across the top of each loaf. Cover and let rise about 1 hour.

Preheat the oven to 375 degrees. To make the glaze, blend the confectioners' sugar, butter, and walnuts. Add the orange juice and mix thoroughly. Brush the glaze on the loaves. Bake for 40 to 50 minutes.

YIELD: Two loaves

A LESSON FOR ST. IGNATIUS
—

The initial joint objective of Ignatius and his men was to get to Jerusalem to defend the Holy Land. Every time they tried to get there, however, they were stopped by wars, by storms or canceled passages, by something. Ignatius was openly frustrated and disappointed by his failures. Pope Paul III saw his failures differently and admonished him for his shortsightedness, saying, "Rome could be your Jerusalem." Ignatius took this admonishment to heart and realized that the mission that one has is often right in one's own home.

Rick's Cranberry-Walnut Buttermilk Loaf

This is a recipe I perfected, while studying at the Culinary Institute of America, as a birthday present for my friend Father Ken Boller, who's allergic to eggs.

I felt right at home at the C.I.A. because the students' dining room was in the old chapel of St. Andrews. It was a beautiful room with many stained-glass windows, depicting a variety of scenes. One of the students asked me to explain who all these men in the windows were. I laughed to myself but gladly informed him that they were all Ignatius. This student's confusion was understandable because the scenes represented Ignatius's life from birth to death and in every window he was dressed in something different—from armor, to a cassock, to vestments. Anyone would be confused.

FOR THE STARTER

½ teaspoon active dry yeast
¾ cup water
¾ cup unbleached all-purpose flour
¾ cup whole wheat flour

FOR THE BREAD

1½ cups water
½ cup fresh orange juice
½ teaspoon active dry yeast
5½ cups whole wheat flour
1½ cups buttermilk
2 tablespoons honey
1 tablespoon sea salt

1 cup chopped walnuts
3 cups chopped cranberries
Cornmeal

To make the starter, combine the yeast and water in a medium bowl, stirring until yeast is dissolved. Set aside for 5 minutes. Add the all-purpose flour and whole wheat flour. Beat the starter until it has the consistency of a thick batter. Scrape down the bowl, cover with plastic wrap, and let stand in a warm, draft-free place for 2 to 10 hours. The starter needs to be soupy and bubbly.

To make the bread dough, scrape the starter into a 6-quart bowl. Add the water, orange juice, and yeast. Stir until it's mixed thoroughly and slightly foamy. Add 2 cups of the whole wheat flour, buttermilk, and honey. Mix thoroughly. Add the salt and enough of the remaining flour to make a thick mass. The dough will be difficult to stir.

Turn out on a lightly floured surface. Knead for 8 to 10 minutes, until dough is smooth and elastic, adding flour as necessary to prevent stickiness. Gradually knead in the walnuts and the cranberries until the dough is soft and smooth—about 5 minutes. Shape into a ball, cover with a tea towel, and let rest for 10 minutes.

Lightly oil a large bowl. Place dough in bowl and turn to coat on all sides. Cover with plastic wrap and let rise in a warm, draft-free place until doubled in bulk—about 1¼ hours.

Sprinkle a wood peel with cornmeal.

Punch down the dough. Turn out again and divide in half. Flatten each piece with the heel of your hand, using firm direct strokes. Shape each piece into a tight ball and place on the peel. Cover with a tea towel and let rise until doubled in bulk—1¼ to 2 hours.

Preheat the oven to 450 degrees. Lightly dust a baking stone with cornmeal.

Slide loaves gently onto the baking stone. Bake for 2 minutes and then mist with water. After 20 minutes, reduce the oven temperature to 400 degrees and mist again with water. Let bake for another 15 or 20 minutes. Place on a wire rack to cool.

YIELD: Two loaves

ST. RÉNÉ GOUPIL

—

St. Réné Goupil (1607–1642) was the first of the eight North American martyrs to die for the faith and be canonized. He entered the novitiate in Paris and was accepted for the Huron mission. He was sent to New France in 1640, where he was assigned to a hospital in Quebec. Trained as a barber, blood letter, and doctor, he ministered to the French settlers, until Father Isaac Jogues selected him to work with the Algonquin Indians in their own territory. As he traveled up the St. Lawrence River to his destination, his flotilla was ambushed by about seventy Mohawks on the warpath. They were taken captive, beaten, and tortured. Brother Goupil was held prisoner and taken to Auriesville, in what is now New York state, where he was tomahawked to death on September 29, 1642. He was canonized on June 29, 1930.

Pan de Sal

This bread is from the Ateneo de Manila, a Jesuit school in the Philippines. The recipe is more than 150 years old and is served on the Bethlehem breakfast days, which are the nine days before Christmas.

> *1 tablespoon vegetable shortening*
> *1 tablespoon salt*
> *1 tablespoon sugar*
> *1 cup boiling water*
> *1 tablespoon active dry yeast*
> *1 cup warm water*
> *4 cups unbleached all-purpose flour*
> *4 ounces plain crackers (40 crackers), crumbled*

Combine the shortening, salt, sugar, and boiling water in a large mixing bowl. Stir and set aside to cool.

Combine the yeast and the warm water in a small bowl, stirring until yeast is dissolved. Set aside for 5 minutes. Gradually mix in the flour to make a dough.

Turn out on a lightly floured surface. Knead for 8 to 10 minutes, until dough is smooth and elastic, adding flour as necessary to prevent stickiness. Return it to the bowl. Cover with plastic wrap and let rise in a warm place until doubled in bulk—about 45 minutes.

Preheat the oven to 425 degrees. Flour two baking sheets.

Gently knead the dough again. Divide into 16 pieces and shape into buns. Roll the pieces in the cracker crumbs and place on the baking sheets, spread well apart. Cover and let rise about 20 minutes. Bake for 15 minutes. Transfer to a wire rack to cool.

YIELD: Sixteen buns

Apricot, Orange, Cranberry Bread

This is the best all-time apricot, orange, cranberry bread. At Christmastime, the disabled students at our workshop bake at least four hundred loaves of this bread, which we sell to help support the workshop and give to friends and supporters of the workshop.

My aunt Winifred Curry traveled a lot and we had an agreement that if she encountered a recipe she thought I would like, she would do her best to get it for me. She considered getting this recipe a real coup. I thank my aunt and an anonymous chef on the *Queen Elizabeth II* for this recipe.

> 3½ cups unbleached all-purpose flour
> 1½ teaspoons baking powder
> 1 teaspoon baking soda
> 1 teaspoon salt
> ¼ pound (1 stick) butter
> 1 cup sugar
> 1 tablespoon plus 1 teaspoon freshly grated orange zest
> 2 large eggs
> ⅔ cup orange juice
> ⅔ cup milk
> ⅔ cup finely chopped apricots
> ⅔ cup chopped walnuts
> 3 cups cranberries, picked over and chopped in a blender

Sift together the flour, baking powder, baking soda, and salt.
Cream the butter and sugar in a large bowl. Beat in the orange zest and eggs,

one at a time. Add the orange juice and milk and beat until mixed thoroughly. It will appear curdled.

Add the flour mixture and beat until it is just moistened. Stir in the apricots, walnuts, and cranberries.

Place baking rack in middle of the oven. Preheat the oven to 350 degrees. Butter and flour five 5¾ × 2¼-inch loaf pans.

Pour batter into the pans. Bake for 45 minutes. Test for doneness with a toothpick. Remove the bread from the pans, transfer to a wire rack, and let them cool on their sides.

(These breads, wrapped well in aluminum foil and plastic wrap, keep for one week in the refrigerator or frozen for a month.)

YIELD: Five small loaves

A blessing should precede the meal and a thanksgiving come after it, and all ought to recite with proper devotion and reverence.

—*Common Book of Rules*

BROTHER BENNY

—

Brother Biniakiewicz (a.k.a. Brother Benny) was the assistant to Holy Trinity Parish at Georgetown in Washington, D.C., and when he retired he was sent to Wernersville, where I met him. Every afternoon he worked in the tailor shop. When I was assigned there as a tailor, his job was to sew interfacing in the collars of the cassocks to strengthen them. He did this faithfully for hours.

Brother Benny was an old-style eastern European Brother, born in Posen, Germany. He came to Buffalo at the age of four. He had great charm and great humor and always encouraged me. (Among other things, he told me to grow up!) He had a wonderful laugh and was built like Santa Claus—his whole body shook when he laughed. His all-time favorite food was sweet potatoes. He actually never saw any value in the regular white potatoes and sometimes denied their existence.

Sweet Potato Bread

Brother Benny's mother passed this recipe down to him as a young boy and he gave it to me. It's very moist and very delicious.

1½ cups scalded milk

2 tablespoons sugar

⅜ pound (1½ sticks) butter, softened, plus additional, melted, for glazing

1 tablespoon salt

1 cup mashed sweet potatoes, unsalted

2 tablespoons active dry yeast

½ cup warm water

8 cups unbleached all-purpose flour

2 cups raisins, soaked in water and drained

Cornmeal

¼ cup sugar

2 teaspoons ground cinnamon

Combine the scalded milk, sugar, ¼ pound (1 stick) butter, and the salt. Stir until butter melts. Add the sweet potatoes and mix thoroughly. Cool to lukewarm.

Combine the yeast and water in a large bowl, stirring until yeast is dissolved. Set aside for 5 minutes.

Add the milk mixture and 4 cups of the flour to the yeast. Beat vigorously for 5 minutes. Stir in the raisins. Beat for another 5 minutes, gradually adding flour until the dough begins to pull away from the sides of the bowl.

Turn out on a lightly floured surface. Knead for 8 to 10 minutes, until dough is smooth and elastic, adding flour as necessary to prevent stickiness.

Lightly oil a large bowl. Place dough in bowl and turn to coat on all sides.

(continued)

Cover with plastic wrap and let rise in a warm, draft-free place until doubled in bulk—about 1¼ hours.

Grease a baking sheet and sprinkle with cornmeal or line one with kitchen parchment.

Punch down the dough. Turn out again and divide in half. Roll each portion out into a 10 × 12-inch rectangle. Spread 2 tablespoons butter on each rectangle.

Stir together the sugar and cinnamon and sprinkle half of it on each rectangle. Starting with the narrow side, roll the dough like a jelly roll and pinch the ends together. Place the seam side down on the baking sheet. Brush the top with melted butter. Cover with a tea towel and let rise until doubled in bulk—about 30 minutes.

Preheat the oven to 375 degrees. Bake for 35 to 40 minutes, until loaves are golden brown. Transfer to a wire rack to cool.

YIELD: Two loaves

On Thanksgiving, we novices were given the day off, but because we thought we had become so important to the running of the operation, we couldn't imagine how this feast was going to be prepared without us. The answer was that the senior Brothers from the other branches of the house, the shoemaker, the carpenter, the Brothers who ran the laundry, the Brothers who were the librarians—everyone—came together to help the senior Brothers in the kitchen prepare this magnificent meal.

After a wonderful day of touch football and exhilarating autumn weather, we gathered in the dining room where a golden turkey sat on every table, waiting to be carved. (Normally the platters were prepared in the kitchen.) Whoever was sitting at the head of the table had the honor.

Most of the novices were surprised by the serving of sauerkraut with this otherwise traditional Thanksgiving feast. But a Jesuit tradition is to conform to the customs of the place where you live. Wernersville is in Pennsylvania Dutch country and a tradition of the Pennsylvania Dutch is to balance sweet and sour. Following that custom, we had sauerkraut with our sweet cranberry sauce.

Mincemeat Bread

Because we didn't eat meat on Fridays, we could never have Thanksgiving leftovers until the Saturday after Thanksgiving. Brother Dragansky would scarf up the mincemeat on Thanksgiving, turn it into mincemeat bread on Friday, and put it under lock and key until the 4 o'clock *haustus* on Saturday.

> 2 cups unbleached all-purpose flour
> 3 teaspoons baking powder
> ½ teaspoon baking soda
> ½ teaspoon salt
> 5⅓ tablespoons butter
> ¾ cup molasses
> 1 egg
> ¾ cup mincemeat
> ¼ cup whole wheat flour
> ⅔ cup milk

Preheat the oven to 375 degrees. Grease two 9 × 5-inch loaf pans.

Combine the all-purpose flour, baking powder, baking soda, and salt.

In a large bowl, beat the butter, molasses, and egg until well blended. Add the mincemeat and whole wheat flour. Alternately add the milk and the all-purpose flour mixture to the butter mixture. Pour into the pans and bake for 30 to 35 minutes. Test for doneness with a toothpick. Invert the pans on a wire rack and let cool.

YIELD: Two loaves

CORN BREAD

Thou openest thy hand, O Lord,

the earth is filled with good;

teach us with grateful hearts to take

from Thee our daily food.

orn bread, *panem aurelium*, is a Jesuit staple. I considered it a privilege to rise at 5:00 A.M. to light the ovens and bake the corn bread. I loved the quiet of the empty bakery in the early morning and reveled in the luscious smell as the corn bread rose in the brick-lined oven In these comforting mornings I got my first glimpse of what the older Brothers called "spiritual consolation."

Each kitchen has its own flavorful version to which that community's novices generally become quite attached. They then hold that recipe as the criterion for all corn breads. The Maryland Province Jesuits had a very strong feeling about the corn bread recipes at Wernersville, and of course the only corn bread that meant anything at all to the southern Jesuits was the one served at Grand Coteau in Louisiana. The Jesuits in the Missouri Province maintained theirs was the best because they were from the great corn country and therefore knew more about corn bread than anyone else. I guess a Jesuit's attachment to a particular corn bread is not unlike the feeling some young husbands have toward their mother's cooking. Nothing less will do.

But memories play tricks when it comes to culinary delights. If I were to give some of my Brothers the exact corn bread recipe they were raised on, so to speak, it would be sure to disappoint. The memory of *their* corn bread is really a memory of their Jesuit youth. No corn bread recipe can capture that; the same all too often holds true for your mother's meat loaf recipe.

This section is a corn bread festival of recipes given to me by Brothers throughout the country. Naturally, each thinks his is the best (you'll notice the first is the recipe I had at Wernersville), but you be the judge.

Wernersville Corn Bread

At Wernersville, corn bread appeared on the breakfast table three times a week. The three-inch-high slices were accompanied by butter and maple syrup and were usually served with eggs and bacon or even beef stew. On Fridays and meatless weekdays in Lent, we got baked beans sweetened with brown sugar. The leftover corn bread was served with jelly at *haustus*—a Latin term describing a four o'clock snack that was "always eaten in silence" according to the rule.

> 1¼ cups yellow cornmeal
> ¾ cup unbleached all-purpose flour
> ¼ cup sugar
> 4 teaspoons baking powder
> ½ teaspoon salt
> 2 eggs, lightly beaten
> 1¼ cups milk
> ½ cup vegetable oil

Preheat the oven to 425 degrees. Grease a 9 × 5-inch loaf or 8-inch square pan.

Sift together the cornmeal, flour, sugar, baking powder, and salt into a large bowl.

In a medium bowl, mix the eggs, milk, and oil until smooth. Add the milk mixture to the cornmeal mixture, stirring just enough to incorporate and moisten all the ingredients.

Pour the batter into the pan. Bake for about 25 minutes, until golden brown. Test with a toothpick for doneness. Cool the bread in its pan on a wire rack. Cut into squares and serve.

YIELD: Four to six servings

ST. FRANCIS XAVIER

—

Francis Xavier (1506–1552) was the greatest missionary that the Church has known since apostolic times and is considered one of the founding fathers of the Society of Jesus. He was born in Navarro, Spain, and went to the University of Paris. He, Peter Faber, and Ignatius all lived in the same house. Ignatius tried to persuade both of them to join him and won Peter Faber over easily. Francis Xavier proved more difficult, but eventually he succumbed and pledged his loyalty in 1534.

He was the first missionary from the Society of Jesus sent to India. He proselytized thousands of people and left his mark of Christianity. He then went to Japan and received permission from the emperor to proselytize there, but his sight was always set on China. As he was attempting to reach mainland China in 1552, he was taken ill and died. In 1927 Pope Pius XI declared Francis Xavier the patron of the missions.

JESUITS AND SCHOOLS

—

Jesuits today are widely known as educators, but Ignatius was initially reluctant to have the order establish schools. The first school, the Collegio di San Nicola, officially opened in Mecina in 1548, and others in Ferrara, Florence, Venice, Padua, Naples, Bologna, and Rome were started shortly thereafter. These colleges became the principal centers for all Jesuit ministries. In 1789 the first Jesuit university in the United States, Georgetown, was founded. Today there are 28 Jesuit colleges and universities and 45 prep schools. Worldwide, there are 190 colleges and universities, 385 secondary schools, 28 primary schools, and 47 technical schools. And we have begun to open grammar schools for the poor in the inner cities. Jesuits try to go where they are needed and we think quality primary education is necessary in our inner cities.

Green Chili Corn Bread

This recipe comes from a Franciscan Brother from Mexico.

1 cup yellow cornmeal
1 cup flour
2 tablespoons sugar
1 teaspoon baking powder
¼ teaspoon salt
½ cup shredded cheddar cheese
2 tablespoons vegetable shortening
1 small onion, finely chopped
¼ teaspoon ground cumin
2 tablespoons butter
1 can (4 ounces) diced chilies
1 egg
1 cup milk

Preheat the oven to 425 degrees. Grease an 8-inch square pan.

Sift the cornmeal, flour, sugar, baking powder, and salt into a large bowl. Mix in the cheese.

Heat the vegetable shortening in a medium frying pan over moderate heat. Add the onion and cook, stirring occasionally, until soft and lightly brown. Stir in the cumin. Add the butter and stir until it melts. Mix in the chilies and remove from the heat.

In a medium bowl, beat the egg and milk. Stir in the onion mixture. Add the egg mixture to the cornmeal mixture and stir just until the dry ingredients are moistened. Spread into the pan. Bake about 25 minutes, until the top is golden brown. Cut into squares and serve warm.

YIELD: Four to six servings

Sweet Potato Corn Bread

Northern and northeastern American Jesuits are more reluctant to talk about food—I guess it was from our Irish American, somewhat Jansenistic, background. But our southern Brothers rattle on about food with passion. This is a recipe for southern sweet potato corn bread that I was served in New Orleans at Loyola University, courtesy of Brother Terry Todd and the Loyola chef.

> ¾ pound sweet potatoes, peeled and cut into chunks
>   (2 or 3 medium potatoes)
> ¾ cup yellow cornmeal
> 2 tablespoons unbleached all-purpose flour
> 1 tablespoon baking powder
> ¾ teaspoon salt
> ½ teaspoon baking soda
> ¼ teaspoon freshly ground black pepper
> ¼ teaspoon nutmeg
> 1 egg
> ¾ cup buttermilk
> 3 tablespoons butter

Bring the potatoes to a boil, covered with water, in a medium saucepan. Reduce the heat to low and simmer for about 20 minutes, until tender. Drain thoroughly and press through a strainer into a bowl. Set aside to cool slightly.

Preheat the oven to 400 degrees.

Sift together the cornmeal, flour, baking powder, salt, baking soda, pepper, and nutmeg.

Add the egg and buttermilk to the sweet potato purée. Mix until well blended.

In an 8- or 9-inch ovenproof skillet, heat the butter until just sizzling—about 2 minutes. Swirl the butter in the pan to coat it well. Pour any excess butter into the sweet potato mixture.

Quickly add the cornmeal mixture to the sweet potato mixture and stir until blended. Pour the batter into the skillet.

Bake for 20 or 30 minutes, until lightly golden and the corn bread has pulled away from the sides of the pan. Remove from the oven and cut into wedges. Serve hot.

YIELD Six to eight servings

Now that I am about to eat, O great Spirit, give my thanks to the beasts and birds whom You have provided for my hunger, and pray delivery of my sorrow that living things must make a sacrifice for my comfort and well-being. Let the feather of corn spring up in its time and let it not wither but make full grains for the fires of our cooking pots, now that I am about to eat.

—A Native American grace from the Lama Foundation,
San Cristobal, New Mexico

Basic Corn Bread

Brother Terry Todd gave me this recipe also. He's a boat builder from New Orleans who currently serves in Pohnpei in Micronesia. He works at PATS (Pohnpei Agricultural and Trade School), where he is a counselor and in charge of the physical plant. But this corn bread recipe is so basic that every Jesuit Brother I talked to had used it or knew of it. I could even get a consensus on this one: both southern and northern Brothers admitted that it was a pretty good recipe.

> *1 cup cornmeal, sifted*
> *1 teaspoon baking powder*
> *1 teaspoon sugar*
> *2 cups milk*
> *3 eggs*

Preheat the oven to 350 degrees. Grease an 8-inch square baking dish.

Mix the cornmeal, baking powder, and sugar. Beat the milk and eggs together and add them to the dry ingredients.

Pour the batter into the baking dish. Bake for 30 minutes. Test for doneness with a toothpick. Serve with butter.

YIELD: Sixteen two-inch-square slices

Corn bread isn't just an American obsession. I was in the dining room one day at the Farm Street Church in London and Father Bernard Hall began quizzing me about corn bread. He is a tall and distinguished looking gentleman—the kind that was born to rule. "You know, it's supposed to have amazing powers," he told me. "When I was in Rome, a Jesuit from the States, Father Dan McGuire, maintained that corn bread had saved his vocation. As a novice, he had thought about leaving the order. He confided this fact to a fellow novice and the fellow novice said, 'Well, that would be very sad if you would leave, but why don't you wait until tomorrow; we're going to have corn bread in the morning.' He waited, and he's been with the Jesuits ever since. Corn bread had great staying powers and persuasion and perseverance."

All are diligently to acquire a more perfect acquaintance and experience in the regular household duties. In addition, those whom Superiors have selected to learn some particular trade or craft, should so perfect themselves in it to the best of their ability that, by always setting as their goal the greater glory of God, Our Creator and Lord, they will be as good as, or better than, competent lay-workers, and give as much edification to others by their professional skill as by the example of their life.

—Common Rules of the Brothers

Southern Corn Bread Muffins

These corn bread muffins were served to me at Spring Hill College in Mobile, Alabama. They were delicious, but the weather was so humid that the pages of the speech I was giving stuck together!

> 1 cup flour
> 2 cups yellow cornmeal
> ⅓ cup sugar
> 4 teaspoons baking powder
> 1 teaspoon salt
> 1 egg
> 1 cup milk
> ⅓ cup vegetable shortening, melted

Preheat the oven to 400 degrees. Grease a 12-tin muffin pan or an 8-inch square baking pan

Sift the flour, cornmeal, sugar, baking powder, and salt into a large bowl. Combine the egg, milk, and vegetable shortening and add to the flour mixture. Stir only until moistened.

Pour into muffin tins or pan. Bake for 20 to 25 minutes. Serve hot with butter and syrup.

YIELD: Twelve muffins

RULES

8

—

Likewise they should understand that they may not lend, borrow, or dispose of anything in the house unless the superior knows it and consents.

Maple Corn Bread

Brother P. J. Maurer, S.J., was a classmate of mine with enormous spirit, but also real common sense. He also had a sweet tooth and put maple syrup in his corn bread. He told me that this was the "way" they made corn bread in his home state of Indiana.

⅔ cup yellow cornmeal
1⅓ cups flour
1 tablespoon baking powder
½ teaspoon salt
⅓ cup maple syrup
½ cup vegetable shortening, melted and cooled
2 eggs, beaten

Preheat the oven to 425 degrees. Grease a 9-inch square cake pan.

Sift together the cornmeal, flour, baking powder, and salt. Add the syrup, vegetable shortening, and eggs. Stir until well mixed but do not beat. Pour into the pan and bake for 25 minutes.

YIELD: Six servings

Bran Corn Bread

I made this corn bread for Father John Donohue's Golden Jubilee Breakfast. Father Donohue is an associate editor of *America* magazine and an avid reader. Even in his seventies, he likes to stay abreast of current ideas. When oat bran became the nutritional rage, Father Donohue conscientiously added it to his diet and asked me to concoct a corn bread with bran especially for him.

> ½ cup vegetable shortening
>
> ½ cup sugar
>
> 2 eggs, well beaten
>
> 1½ cups bran cereal
>
> ½ cup milk
>
> 1 cup unbleached all-purpose flour
>
> ½ cup yellow cornmeal
>
> 3 teaspoons baking powder
>
> ½ teaspoon salt

Preheat the oven to 400 degrees. Grease an 8-inch square pan

Cream the vegetable shortening and sugar. Add the eggs.

Add the bran to the milk and let stand for about 5 minutes.

Sift together the flour, cornmeal, baking powder, and salt. Add the flour mixture to the shortening mixture. Add bran and mix thoroughly.

Bake for 25 to 30 minutes. Serve with butter.

YIELD: Six servings

My province of Jesuits, the Maryland Province, arrived in colonial times in Mary Land. These early Jesuit Brothers were circuit riders, following priests to see what the people needed and how we best could establish the health of the Catholic community in America. They traveled with johnnycakes (from "journey cakes"), an old form of corn bread that could be baked very quickly and was sturdy enough to carry in their backpacks.

Corn is indigenous to the American continent, and baking with it celebrates our heritage in so many ways. When you bake these johnnycakes, think of the shoulders of the great Jesuits we stand upon.

Johnnycakes

Baltimore is a southern city in many ways, so I was not at all surprised when Brother Fee of Loyola College in Baltimore had a southern recipe to give me.

1 cup yellow cornmeal
1 cup flour
3 teaspoons baking powder
½ cup sugar
1 cup milk
2 egg yolks, beaten
3 tablespoons vegetable shortening, melted
2 egg whites, stiffly beaten

Preheat the oven to 350 degrees. Grease an 8-inch square pan.

Sift the cornmeal, flour, baking powder, and sugar. Add the milk, egg yolks, and melted vegetable shortening. Fold in the egg whites.

Pour the batter into the pan. Bake for 20 minutes.

YIELD: Six to eight cakes

CHRISTMAS

*W*e cannot love God
unless we love each other,
and to love each other we
must know each other in
the breaking of bread and
we are not alone any more . . .
heaven is a banquet and
life is a banquet, too, even
with a crust, where there is companionship.
Love comes with community.

—DOROTHY DAY

Christmas celebrates the gift of Christ to the world, and we celebrate often by gift giving among ourselves. It's also a time for gathering around home, for many, for reunion with families that are increasingly strewn around the world. Although isolated behind the novitiate walls, our prayer was for every family throughout the world to experience the joy of God's gift of the Christ child.

For people who are away from home—especially if it's for the first time—Christmas can be emotionally trying. It seems to me that the Jesuits address this in the very best possible way. On Christmas Eve, the first-year men were assembled for night prayer at our regular time and then sent off to bed. We were awakened about 11:30 by voices, and when we looked outside our doorless bedroom cubicles, we began to see movement of light. We heard voices. Groups of Jesuits in their black cassocks and their white surplices and their stocking feet, holding candles as they moved up and down the corridors, singing absolutely exquisitely in four-part harmony.

A few groggy and half-asleep Brothers thought they were in Heaven. And in a heavenly manner, one of these men with candles would come in and say "get dressed and come to Chapel." Very quickly we arose, put on our cassocks, and ran down to the chapel we had left just three hours before. In those short three hours, the chapel had been transformed in magnificent decoration. The laurel we had spent every night of Advent weaving now hung all over the candlelit chapel. The choir sang Christmas carol after Christmas carol until we celebrated the midnight Mass.

From Christmas to New Year's Day, we followed the villa or vacation schedule. St. Ignatius believed in a balance between work and rest, and Christmas was a time for rest. During this week, our Novice Master tried to instill in us the importance of taking breaks from our work. We had snacks during the day, we could listen to music, and we could take all-day walks. Every evening at five we went into the chapel to hear our magnificent choir sing instead of the afternoon meditation. And at dinner we could talk. When it came to food at Christmas, we had the opportunity to learn about gluttony or moderation. The breads in this section are representative of the breads that would be out for us to eat all day long if we so desired. Some of us so desired!

But during this week, we also were to get to know the person of Christ and to celebrate his arrival. And for me there certainly was a sense of fullness in my life. Jesus had come.

Christmas Morning Bread

½ cup vegetable shortening

¾ cup sugar

3 eggs

½ cup mashed bananas

½ cup orange juice

2½ cups sifted unbleached all-purpose flour

4 teaspoons baking powder

¾ teaspoon salt

1½ cups chopped dried apricots

½ cup raisins

¾ cup chopped nuts

Cream the shortening in a large bowl. Add the sugar and beat until light and fluffy. Add the eggs one at a time, beating well after each addition.

Combine the bananas and the orange juice in a small bowl.

Sift the flour with the baking powder and salt in another bowl. Mix in the apricots, raisins, and nuts. Add the flour mixture and banana mixture alternately to the shortening mixture.

Preheat the oven to 350 degrees. Grease and line with greased wax paper a 9 × 5-inch loaf pan (see note). Pour batter into pan.

Bake for 1 hour. Cool for about 20 minutes in the pan. Turn out on a wire rack to finish cooling.

NOTE: The easiest way to prepare the wax paper lining is to cut a piece of wax paper the size of the bottom of the pan. Grease the pan, place the wax paper in the pan, and then grease the paper.

YIELD: One loaf

ST. IGNATIUS AND THE JEWS
—

*T*he history of the Society of Jesus and St. Ignatius of Loyola is inextricably linked with members of the Jewish faith. When the Society of Jesus was founded there was an enormous amount of anti-Semitism. Ignatius stood singularly by himself as a head of a religious order that accepted Jewish converts, which was totally against the practice at the time. He was persecuted for it but stood his ground. Several prominent members of the early society were formerly of the Jewish faith and brought many of their customs, especially eating customs, to the community.

On several occasions Ignatius expressed the wish to be of Jewish blood so that he could be the same race as Christ. (He left his Spanish Brothers astounded if not shocked at this.) He encouraged the Jesuits to become well-versed in Hebrew and some in the Old Testament to understand that we are all spiritual Semites and that Christians were continuing with Jewish law. He set up houses where persons who wanted to become Christians could be housed, fed, and instructed until their baptism. And the Jesuits gladly accepted opportunities to preach formally to the Jewish community.

Challah

Father Myer Toby, a Jewish convert, taught me how to bake challah. Apart from its religious associations, I think that it goes remarkably well with a lot of meals. You can braid challah in three-, four-, five-, or six-rope loaves.

FOR THE BREAD

> 2 packages active dry yeast
>
> 2¾ cups warm water
>
> ½ cup plus ½ teaspoon sugar
>
> 7½ cups unbleached all-purpose flour
>
> ½ cup vegetable oil
>
> 1½ tablespoons salt
>
> 2 eggs
>
> Cornmeal

FOR THE GLAZE

> ½ cup water
>
> 1 egg
>
> ¼ cup poppy or sesame seeds

Combine the yeast and ½ cup of the water in a small bowl. Add ½ teaspoon sugar and 1 tablespoon of the flour. Set aside for 5 minutes.

In a large bowl, combine 5 cups of the flour with about 2¼ cups of the warm water, the oil, the remaining ½ cup of the sugar, salt, and 2 eggs. Mix thoroughly. Add the yeast mixture. Beat for 10 minutes, gradually adding flour until the dough begins to pull away from the sides of the bowl.

Turn out on a lightly floured surface. Knead for 8 to 10 minutes, until dough is smooth and elastic, adding flour as necessary to prevent stickiness.

(continued)

Lightly oil a large bowl. Place dough in bowl and turn to coat on all sides. Cover with plastic wrap and let rise in a warm, draft-free place until doubled in bulk—45 minutes to an hour.

Grease a baking sheet and sprinkle with cornmeal or line one with kitchen parchment.

Punch down the dough. Turn out again. Work in more flour until dough is not sticky. Divide into 6 pieces and roll each piece into a 10-inch rope. For each loaf, take three strands, fold the ends under on one end, braid loosely. and tuck ends under each other.

Place diagonally on the baking sheet. Cover with a tea towel and let rise until doubled in bulk—about 1 hour.

Preheat the oven to 350 degrees.

To make the glaze, combine the water and egg. Brush carefully over tops of braids and sprinkle with poppy or sesame seeds.

Bake for 35 to 45 minutes. Transfer to a wire rack to cool.

YIELD: Two loaves

ST. PETER CANISIUS
—

St. Peter Canisius (1521–1597) was a renowned theologian, preacher, and administrator, who restored Catholicism to Germany. He was a founder of many schools. His last years were spent preaching in the Church of St. Nicholas (Santa Claus) in Fribourg, Switzerland. So great was his devotion to the Incarnation that it was only fitting that he be buried in Fribourg in the Church of St. Nicholas on December 21, just four days short of Christmas.

THE SECRETS OF JESUIT BREADMAKING

St. Peter Canisius's Stollen

Brother Tony Kreutzjans was a carpenter who loved to eat. His parents were from Germany and introduced me to many German traditions. I went with Tony to a function of the Kolping Society, a philanthropic Catholic organization of Germans, of which he was a very active member, and was served this wonderful stollen.

> 1 tablespoon active dry yeast
> ¼ cup warm water
> 1 cup milk, scalded
> ¼ pound (1 stick) butter
> ¼ cup sugar
> 1 teaspoon salt
> ¼ teaspoon ground cardamom
> 4 to 4½ cups unbleached all-purpose flour
> 1 egg, slightly beaten
> 1 cup raisins
> ¼ cup currants
> ¼ cup chopped walnuts
> ¼ cup chopped dried apricots
> 2 tablespoons grated orange peel
> 1 tablespoon grated lemon peel
> ¼ cup sliced almonds
> Cornmeal for dusting

FOR THE GLAZE

> 1 cup confectioners' sugar
> 2 tablespoons hot water
> 1 teaspoon butter

(continued)

Combine the yeast and water in a small bowl, stirring until yeast is dissolved. Set aside for 5 minutes.

Combine the milk, butter, sugar, salt, and cardamom in a bowl and cool to lukewarm. Stir in 2 cups of the flour and beat well. Add the yeast mixture and egg. Stir in the raisins, currants, walnuts, apricots, grated orange peel, grated lemon peel, and almonds. Beat for 10 minutes, gradually adding the remaining flour until the dough begins to pull away from the sides of the bowl.

Turn out on a lightly floured surface. Knead for 8 to 10 minutes, until dough is smooth and elastic, adding flour as necessary to prevent stickiness.

Lightly oil a large bowl. Place dough in bowl and turn to coat on all sides. Cover with plastic wrap and let rise in a warm, draft-free place until doubled in bulk—about 1¾ hours.

Grease a baking sheet and sprinkle with cornmeal or line one with kitchen parchment.

Punch down the dough. Turn out again on a lightly floured surface. Divide into 3 equal pieces. Cover with a tea towel and let rest 10 minutes. Roll each portion into a 10 × 6-inch rectangle. Fold the long side over to within an inch of the opposite side. Fold the remaining side over and seal. Place on the baking sheet, cover, and let rise again until doubled in bulk—probably for over an hour.

To make the glaze, combine the sugar, hot water, and butter in a bowl and mix well.

Preheat the oven to 375 degrees. Bake for 15 to 20 minutes, or until golden brown. Brush loaves with glaze while warm.

VARIATION

You can also decorate the stollen with holly leaves and berries from citron and bits of cut-up candied cherries.

YIELD: Three loaves

RULES

I

---

*T*he daily hour for rising is 5:00 A.M. or 5:30, or some other hour as determined by the provincial for each house. The caller opens the door of each room, but without looking in, says *Benedicamus Domino*, and waits until he hears the response *Deo gratias* (unless some other salutation and response are customary in the province). A quarter of an hour later, he visits the rooms again; however, this second visit may be omitted where superiors take care that all make the visit to the Blessed Sacrament before meditation (*reg. excit.* I; *A.R.* VII, 583).

The custom may be kept which exists in some provinces, whereby the community is permitted to rise one-half hour later on the weekly vacation day.

One who for any reason has not risen at the assigned time without having previously obtained permission, should report the matter to the minister or to the superior.

—*Custom Book of the American Assistancy of the Society of Jesus*

DECKING THE HALLS

—

A curious note went up on the board in Wernersville around December 1, asking us to save the inner cardboard lining of the toilet paper rolls. Of course as very obedient novices we did, with no idea why. After midnight Mass on Christmas Eve it became clear.

We were brought into the dining room, which was brightly lit. The older Brothers had turned our toilet paper rolls into electric candlesticks and put them on the end of umbrella skeletons. Suspended from the ceiling over each table, they became magnificent chandeliers. The entire dining room, which was a rather barren affair during the year, had been transformed into something quite magical.

The tables were filled with every kind of quick bread imaginable—from walnut breads to cranberry loaves to orange loaves. There was a nonalcoholic eggnog and tons and tons of hot chocolate. After an appropriate amount of time for stuffing ourselves, a bell was rung and we went back to bed. When we awakened on Christmas, we had the regular order, but all day long the quick breads and wonderful sweets and Christmas loaves were out and at any time of the day we could celebrate the birth of our Lord.

Brother Leikus's Oatmeal Quick Bread

We had so much oatmeal at breakfast in the winter it's a wonder *all* the bread didn't have some in it.

> 1 cup unbleached all-purpose flour
> ½ cup whole wheat flour
> 1 teaspoon baking powder
> 1 teaspoon baking soda
> 1½ teaspoons salt
> 1 teaspoon ground cinnamon
> ¾ cup brown sugar
> 2 eggs, beaten
> 1 cup applesauce
> 1 cup rolled oats
> 1 cup raisins
> ¼ cup oil (Brother prefers safflower oil)

Sift together the all-purpose flour, whole wheat flour, baking powder, baking soda, salt, and cinnamon in a medium bowl.

Mix the brown sugar, eggs, applesauce, and rolled oats in a large bowl. Add the raisins and oil. Stir in the flour mixture and mix only until moistened.

Preheat the oven to 350 degrees. Lightly grease one 9 × 5-inch loaf pan. Pour dough into loaf pan and bake for 1 hour.

YIELD: One loaf

Cinnamon Raisin Walnut Bread

This is one of mine from my days at the Culinary Institute.

8 cups bread flour or unbleached all-purpose flour
½ cup wheat bran
½ cup raisins, soaked in water for 10 minutes and drained
1 cup chopped walnuts
1 cup brown sugar
2½ tablespoons active dry yeast
2 tablespoons sea salt
1 tablespoon ground cinnamon
1 cup buttermilk
1 to 1½ cups water

Combine the flour, wheat bran, raisins, walnuts, brown sugar, yeast, salt, and cinnamon in a large bowl. Add the buttermilk and water, reserving some of the water for adjustments during kneading. Beat vigorously for 10 minutes, until the dough begins to pull away from the sides of the bowl, adding water as necessary.

Turn out on a lightly floured surface and knead until dough is tacky but not sticky—10 to 12 minutes.

Lightly oil a large bowl. Place dough in bowl and turn to coat on all sides. Cover with plastic wrap and let rise in a warm, draft-free place until doubled in bulk—about 1½ hours.

Grease two 9 × 5-inch loaf pans.

Punch down the dough. Divide in half, shape into 2 loaves, and place in pans. Cover with a tea towel and let rise again until doubled in bulk—about 45 minutes.

Preheat the oven to 350 degrees. Bake for 45 minutes. Transfer to a wire rack to cool.

VARIATION

I sometimes make five or six demi-loaves with this recipe. They will need to bake only 30 minutes.

YIELD: Two loaves

𝓟anettone means "little loaf" and is synonymous with Christmas in Italy. It originated in Milan and its dome shape is in honor of the Duomo at the Cathedral of the Lombardian Kings. Traditionally, the children of Milan leave a bowl of panettone soaked in water on the windowsills for the camels that carried people bearing gifts to the Christ child, just as American children leave cookies and milk for Santa Claus.

Christmas Panettone

Come December, the Italian bakeries in my neighborhood in New York are filled with this Italian Christmas bread. A former assistant at the Theatre Workshop, Louis LoRe, persuaded his mother, Mary LoRe, to share this family recipe with me.

FOR THE BREAD

 2 tablespoons active dry yeast

 ¾ cup warm water

 ½ cup honey

 3 cups unbleached all-purpose flour

 ½ teaspoon salt

 Zest of 1 lemon

 ¾ cup oil

 2 eggs

 2 tablespoons lemon juice

 ½ cup wheat germ

 1 cup raisins or currants

 ½ cup chopped dried apricots

 ½ cup chopped nuts (optional, but walnuts can be
  very nice)

FOR THE GLAZE

 1 egg, beaten

 2 tablespoons orange juice

 1 tablespoon honey

Combine the yeast and water in a large bowl. Add the honey and stir until dissolved. Set aside for 5 minutes.

Mix 2 cups of the flour, salt, and lemon zest in a large bowl. Add the yeast mixture and mix well. Beat vigorously for 10 minutes, gradually adding 1 cup of the flour. Beat in oil, eggs, and lemon juice until smooth. Beat in the wheat germ. Stir in the raisins or currants, apricots, and nuts.

Turn out on a lightly floured surface. Knead for 8 to 10 minutes, until dough is smooth and elastic, adding flour as necessary to prevent stickiness.

Lightly oil a large bowl. Place dough in bowl and turn to coat on all sides. Cover with plastic wrap and let rise in a warm, draft-free place until doubled in bulk—a good 1½ hours.

Punch down dough. Knead gently in the bowl for about 2 minutes.

Grease two 2-quart molds or four 1-quart molds (see note).

Divide the dough and roll each piece gently into a thick sausage shape. Fit it around the center post of the mold or simply into the pan. The dough should fill a mold or pan less than halfway. Cover with a towel and let rise until doubled in bulk—45 to 60 minutes.

Begin baking in a cold oven set at 375 degrees. The small molds will take 30 to 35 minutes and the larger molds will take 40 to 45 minutes. Test for doneness with a toothpick. Turn out molds immediately and transfer to a wire rack to cool.

For the glaze, mix the egg, orange juice, and honey. (Or mix the egg with 1 tablespoon water.) Brush on loaves while they are warm.

NOTE: The only iffy thing about making this wonderful Italian fruit bread is finding a proper mold. If you can't find a plain slanted panettone mold, you can use a Bundt mold, charlotte mold, turk's-head mold, or even a coffee can. And you can always just shape the dough into a free-form loaf.

YIELD: Two large loaves or four small ones

Christmas Morning Cinnamon Buns

Philadelphians claim cinnamon rolls as their own. Brother Fitzgerald was such a loyal Philadelphian that he wouldn't dream of serving anything but cinnamon rolls or buns on Christmas morning.

½ cup vegetable shortening
2 cups milk, scalded
2 eggs, beaten
1 teaspoon salt
1 cup plus 1 tablespoon sugar
1 cup mashed potatoes, unsalted
2 tablespoons active dry yeast
½ cup lukewarm water
7 cups unbleached all-purpose flour
1 cup raisins
1 cup chopped walnuts
4 tablespoons butter, softened
½ teaspoon ground cinnamon

Dissolve the vegetable shortening in the milk in a bowl and cool to lukewarm. Stir in the eggs, salt, 1 cup sugar, and potatoes.

Dissolve the yeast in lukewarm water and stir into the potato mixture. Stir in the flour, raisins, and nuts. Mix thoroughly for 5 minutes. Cover with plastic wrap and let rise in a warm, draft-free place for 1 hour.

Turn out onto a lightly floured surface. Roll into a ½-inch-thick rectangle and spread with the butter. Sprinkle with the 1 remaining tablespoon sugar and the cinnamon. Roll like a jelly roll and slice. Place slices flat in a 12 X 8-inch Pyrex baking dish. Cover with a tea towel and let rise until doubled in bulk—about 30 minutes.

Preheat the oven to 350 degrees. Bake for 30 to 35 minutes, until golden brown. Transfer to a wire rack to cool.

YIELD: Twelve buns

*Lord our God
You invite us
to the banquet of your wisdom,
give us for nourishment
both the bread of the earth
and your living word.
Bless this meal,
and grant us entry to Your banquet.*

—FROM A TABLE PRAYER
BY M. O. BOUYER

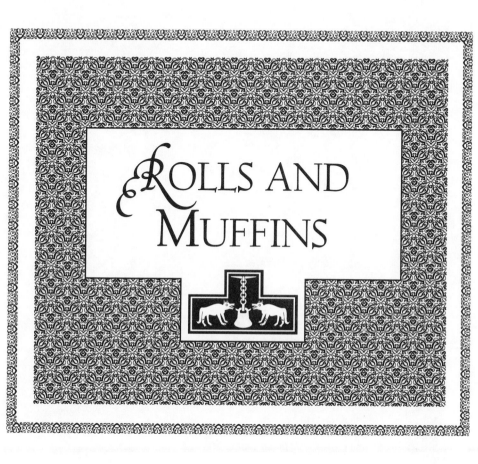

ROLLS AND MUFFINS

Blessed are you

o Lord our God

eternal King,

Who feeds the whole world

with your goodness,

with grace, with loving kindness,

with tender mercy

You give food to all flesh,

for your loving kindness endures forever.

Through your great goodness,

Food has never failed us,

O may it not fail us forever,

for your name's sake, since you

nourish and sustain all living things

and do good to all,

and provide food for all your creatures

whom you have created.

Blessed are you, O Lord,

who gives food to all.

—HEBREW BERAKHAH (BLESSING)

Rolls are usually served in a large Jesuit community only on special occasions. Making rolls for 125 men takes an enormous amount of time and labor. When we made them at Wernersville, we were forced to shut down most of the other baking operations for that day. Also, eating individual rolls doesn't have the sense of community as sharing a loaf of bread. Loaves were our ordinary, everyday food—rolls were reserved for guests. *Hospites venit: Christo Venit* means when guests come, Christ comes—anything special was for guests.

Here are our basic dinner roll recipes. Nothing fancy, but all worthy of being served to your most special guests.

This ornate seal is and has been the official symbol of the Society of Jesus since the time of Ignatius. The three letters in the center are the first three letters of the word "Jesus" in Greek—iota, eta, and sigma. The cross centered above the letters is, of course, the central symbol to the life and mission of Christ. The three nails in the inner circle represent the nails with which the Savior was fastened to the cross. Here they are imbedded in a heart as a symbol of the Lord's true humanity.

In 1991, Father Thomas Lucas, S.J., and a team of historical restorers unbricked a fresco of the seal in the private chapel and conference room at the residence St. Ignatius used in Rome from 1544 until his death in 1556. The fresco dates from about 1600.

Health Buns

In 1969 after Vatican II, we held Santa Clara II, a revolutionary national Jesuit Brothers' conference at Santa Clara University in California. It was there that we moved into the twentieth century and where Brother Cook gave me this recipe.

> 1 tablespoon active dry yeast
> 4 tablespoons butter, melted
> 2 cups lukewarm skim milk
> 1 tablespoon corn syrup
> 2 tablespoons molasses
> 2 teaspoons salt
> 2½ cups whole wheat flour
> 3 to 3½ cups unbleached all-purpose flour
> 1¾ cups graham flour
> Cornmeal

Combine the yeast, butter, and skim milk in a large bowl and stir until yeast is dissolved.

Add the corn syrup, molasses, and salt. Gradually add the whole wheat flour, 2¾ cups of the all-purpose flour, and the graham flour, beating until the dough pulls away from the sides of the bowl—about 10 minutes.

Turn out on a lightly floured surface. Knead for 8 to 10 minutes, until dough is smooth and elastic, adding flour as necessary to prevent stickiness.

Lightly oil a large bowl. Place dough in the bowl and turn to coat on all sides. Cover with plastic wrap and let rise in a warm, draft-free place until doubled in bulk—about 1 hour.

Grease a baking sheet and sprinkle with cornmeal or line one with kitchen parchment.

(continued)

Turn out again and gently knead for about 2 minutes. Divide into 20 pieces, shape into oblong buns, and place on the baking sheet. Cover with a tea towel and let rise until doubled in bulk—about 30 minutes.

Preheat the oven to 400 degrees. Bake for 10 to 15 minutes. Transfer to a wire rack to cool.

YIELD: Twenty buns

I think I may have lived with a saint. When I was a novice, we received news that Bobby Kennedy had swapped a Jesuit, who had been caught behind the Iron Curtain, arrested, and imprisoned in Siberia, for a husband and wife Soviet spy team, who had been captured in Washington, D.C. The liberated Jesuit, Father Walter Ciszek, landed on our doorstep fresh from the Siberian gulag. While he was there, he wrote a wonderful book called *With God in Russia* about his experiences in Russia. He felt great love for the Russian people and he held no resentment that I could see against the Soviet government that had so cruelly imprisoned him. His cause for his canonization is being promoted because he was such an exemplary man—so faithful during great deprivation.

One-Bowl Hard Rolls

Carter Atkins, chef at America House in the 1980s, gave me this recipe. I loved to watch him cook because he was so efficient.

FOR THE ROLLS

4½ to 5½ cups unbleached all-purpose flour
2 tablespoons sugar
1 teaspoon salt
1 tablespoon active dry yeast
4 tablespoons butter, softened
1½ cups warm water
1 egg white
Cornmeal

FOR THE GLAZE

½ cup water
1 teaspoon cornstarch
Poppy seeds

Combine 1⅓ cups of the flour, the sugar, salt, and yeast in a large bowl. Mix thoroughly. Cut in the butter.

Gradually add the water to the flour mixture and beat for 5 minutes. Add the egg white. Beat for another 5 minutes, adding flour until the dough begins to pull away from the sides of the bowl.

Turn out on a lightly floured surface. Knead for 8 to 10 minutes, until dough is smooth and elastic, adding flour as necessary to prevent stickiness.

Lightly oil a large bowl. Place dough in the bowl and turn to coat on all sides. Cover with plastic wrap and let rise in a warm, draft-free place until doubled in bulk—about 45 minutes.

(continued)

Grease a baking sheet and sprinkle with cornmeal or line with kitchen parchment.

Punch down the dough. Turn out again, cover with a tea towel, and let rest for 10 minutes. Divide in half and shape into two 9-inch rolls. Cut each roll into nine 1-inch pieces and form each into a small ball. Place on the baking sheet, about 3 inches apart. Cover with a tea towel and let rise until doubled in bulk—another 45 minutes.

Preheat the oven to 450 degrees.

To make the glaze, mix the water and cornstarch in a saucepan. Bring to a boil. Cool slightly before brushing on rolls. Slit tops in a crisscross fashion. Sprinkle with poppy seeds.

Bake for about 15 minutes. Transfer to a wire rack to cool.

YIELD: Eighteen rolls

RULES OF THE COOK

—

1. He must observe cleanliness in his own person, clothes, and in all things relating to his office, and see that others observe the same.

2. In regard to quality and quantity of food, he must carry out wishes of the Superior, according as the matter shall be explained to him in detail by the Minister.

3. He must take particular care that all the food is served well and with some suitable variety: and he must observe even greater care when sick or convalescent are to be served.

THE SECRETS OF JESUIT BREADMAKING

4. When he cuts up and apportions meat, fish, or other food intended for the table, he must on no account touch it with his fingers, but use a fork or knife for the purpose.

5. All dishes must be ready in good time, and the second table must not receive less attention than the first.

6. He shall allow nobody, except the Infirmarian only to cook and prepare food for any special person, nor do the like himself, without permission.

7. He must be very careful not to burn more fuel than is necessary; and he will exercise the same economy in the use of other things, in order that nothing may be wasted as becomes Religious Poverty.

8. Whatever is over from the table and returned to him should be saved for the use of the Community, or for the poor from outside as the Superior may direct.

9. Let him keep written down in a book a list of things he has for use in the kitchen.

10. If he has assistants, he must take care to edify them by word and example, especially if they are Novices.

—*Custom Book of the American Assistancy of the Society of Jesus*

Basic Refrigerator Rolls

Brother Maurer learned to make these rolls under the tutelage of Sister Jeanette Marie, S.C., the head dietitian at Good Samaritan Hospital in Cincinnati. I know hospital food has a deservedly bad reputation, but these rolls are an exception.

2 cups boiling water
½ cup vegetable shortening
½ cup sugar
1 tablespoon salt
2 tablespoons active dry yeast
½ cup warm water
6 cups unbleached all-purpose flour
Cornmeal

Mix the boiling water, vegetable shortening, sugar, and salt in a large bowl and cool to lukewarm. In a small bowl, dissolve the yeast in the warm water. Add to the shortening mixture. Beat for 10 minutes, gradually adding flour until the dough begins to pull away from the sides of the bowl.

Lightly oil a large bowl. Place dough in the bowl and turn to coat on all sides. Cover with plastic wrap and let rise in a warm, draft-free place until doubled in bulk—about 1½ hours.

Punch down the dough. Cover with plastic wrap and place in the refrigerator until ready to bake.

Grease a baking sheet and sprinkle with cornmeal or line one with kitchen parchment.

Turn out onto a lightly floured surface. Roll out to a ¼-inch thickness. Cut with a floured biscuit cutter. Shape each piece into a ball and place on the baking sheet. Let rise until doubled in bulk—about 45 minutes.

THE SECRETS OF JESUIT BREADMAKING

Preheat the oven to 400 degrees. Bake for 15 minutes. Transfer to a wire rack to cool.

YIELD: About 2½ dozen

GIUSEPPE CASTIGLIONE

Giuseppe Castiglione was born in Milan on July 19, 1688. In 1707, at the tender age of 19, he entered the Society of Jesus. This young novice made a specific choice to become a Brother so that he could paint and use painting as his chief apostolate.

He wanted to serve in China and arrived in Macao in July 1715, where he became a favorite of the emperor. He was able to introduce three-dimensional art to what was a two-dimensional tradition in China. To demonstrate to Chinese artists how this was possible, he painted a hundred horses in various positions. This famous painting of these horses is in the National Museum in Taiwan.

Yeast Rolls

Ialways take these rolls as a gift when I'm invited out to dinner. Father Ken Boller's family in New York is my second family and I spend many Sundays and feast day dinners at his mother's house in Woodside, Queens. One Sunday, his nephew Vincent, age twelve, remarked that he was surprised that I had baked the rolls and said, "I thought they were real."

1 tablespoon active dry yeast
¼ cup sugar
1¼ cups warm water
1 teaspoon salt
1½ tablespoons vegetable shortening
1 egg, beaten
4 cups unbleached all-purpose flour
Cornmeal

Combine the yeast, ½ teaspoon sugar, and ¼ cup lukewarm water in a large bowl. Set aside for 5 minutes.

Add the remaining sugar and water, the salt, vegetable shortening, and egg. Mix well. Beat vigorously for 10 minutes, gradually adding about 3 cups of the flour, until the dough begins to pull away from the sides of the bowl.

Turn out on a lightly floured surface. Knead for 8 to 10 minutes, until dough is smooth and elastic, adding flour as necessary to prevent stickiness.

Place in refrigerator for at least 2 hours.

Grease a baking sheet and sprinkle with cornmeal or line one with kitchen parchment.

Divide into 18 pieces, shape into rolls, and place on the baking sheet. Cover with a tea towel and let rise until doubled in bulk—about 1½ hours.

Preheat the oven to 425 degrees. Bake 12 to 15 minutes, until brown. Transfer to a wire rack to cool.

YIELD: Eighteen rolls

ANDREA DAL POZZO

—

Brother Andrea dal Pozzo (1647–1709) was a painter, architect, and theorist. He executed trompe l'oeil paintings for many Italian churches, his greatest and best-known being in Sant' Ignazio in Rome, one of the most important of the Jesuit churches.

The original design for Sant' Ignazio included a dome over the crossing. But neighboring Dominicans feared that the dome would rob their library of all natural light. Their valid concern was addressed by commissioning Pozzo to paint a dome. Several architects, fooled by the painting, commented that the construction was not solid enough. Pozzo anonymously defended his work replying, "A certain painter with whom I am very intimate has solemnly sworn to me that he will bear all damages and charges if the bearing stones ever break and the poor columns come tumbling down."

Parker House Rolls

I had the privilege of serving these rolls to Lena Horne at America House. Ms. Horne and her daughter and son-in-law were invited for dinner by the Superior, and when the cook became ill, I volunteered to substitute for him. I felt like an understudy who'd been waiting in the wings to go onstage and come back a star. Ms. Horne was lavish in her praise.

2½ to 3½ cups flour
¼ cup sugar
½ teaspoon salt
1 tablespoon active dry yeast
5 tablespoons butter, softened
⅔ cup warm water
1 egg, at room temperature
Cornmeal
¼ pound (1 stick) butter, melted

Combine ¾ cup of the flour, the sugar, salt, and yeast in a large bowl. Cut in the softened butter. Add the water gradually and beat for 5 minutes. Add the egg. Beat for 10 minutes, gradually adding flour until the dough begins to pull away from the sides of the bowl.

Turn out on a lightly floured surface. Knead for 8 to 10 minutes, until dough is smooth and elastic, adding flour as necessary to prevent stickiness.

Lightly oil a large bowl. Place dough in the bowl and turn to coat on all sides. Cover with plastic wrap and let rise in a warm, draft-free place until doubled in bulk—about 1 hour.

Grease a baking sheet and sprinkle with cornmeal or line one with kitchen parchment.

Turn out again on a lightly floured surface. Divide in half, roll each half into ¼-inch-thick circles. Cut into rounds, using a 2½-inch floured biscuit cutter. To make the traditional Parker House shape, use the dull edge of a knife to crease the top of each round a little off center. Brush each round with the melted butter to within ¼ inch of the edge. Pull the larger side over the smaller side so the edges just meet and pinch well with fingers to seal.

Place on the baking sheet so that the rolls are almost touching. Cover with a tea towel and let rise until doubled in bulk—about 1 hour.

Preheat the oven to 400 degrees. Brush the rolls again with melted butter. Bake for 10 to 15 minutes. Transfer to wire racks to cool.

YIELD: *Two to three dozen rolls*

Fresh Potato Rolls

Brother Lou Mauro of St. Peter's in Jersey City shared this recipe with me.

> *1 tablespoon active dry yeast*
> *½ cup warm water*
> *⅔ cup milk, scalded*
> *½ cup vegetable shortening*
> *1 cup fresh hot mashed potatoes, unsalted*
> *⅓ cup sugar*
> *2 teaspoons salt*
> *3 large eggs, lightly beaten*
> *6½ cups unbleached all-purpose flour*
> *3 tablespoons butter, melted*

Combine the yeast and water in a small bowl, stirring until yeast is dissolved. Set aside for 5 minutes.

Combine the milk, vegetable shortening, potatoes, sugar, and salt in a large bowl. Cool until lukewarm. Add the yeast and eggs.

Beat vigorously for 10 minutes, gradually adding about 1½ cups of the flour until the dough begins to pull away from the sides of the bowl.

Cover with plastic wrap, let rise in a warm, draft-free place until doubled in bulk—about 1 hour.

Turn out on a lightly floured surface. Knead for 8 to 10 minutes, until dough is smooth and elastic, adding flour as necessary to prevent stickiness.

Lightly oil a large bowl. Place dough in the bowl and turn to coat on all sides. Cover with plastic wrap and refrigerate 10 to 12 hours or overnight.

Grease and lightly flour muffin tins or prepare a baking sheet with grease and cornmeal or kitchen parchment.

Shape into small balls.

Place on the baking sheet or in muffin pan. Brush with melted butter. Cover with a tea towel and let rise until doubled in bulk—1¼ hours.

Preheat the oven to 325 degrees. Bake for 20 minutes. Transfer to a wire rack to cool.

YIELD: Forty medium rolls

*L*ove consists in sharing
what one has
and what one is
with those one loves.
Love ought to show itself in deeds
more than in words.

—*St. Ignatius of Loyola*

Onion Rolls

The dry cellar flooded at Wernersville and all the onions we had stored got wet. Knowing that they would rot if we didn't use them very quickly, everything that was cooked for a short period had onions. The bread was no exception. We concocted this recipe during this minor crisis and it was good enough to become part of the permanent file. Now when I make these rolls, however, I use dried onion flakes.

> *3 tablespoons dried onion flakes, or ½ cup chopped onions*
> *1 cup boiling water*
> *4 tablespoons butter, softened*
> *1½ teaspoons salt*
> *2 tablespoons sugar*
> *⅛ teaspoon ground ginger*
> *¼ cup warm water*
> *1 tablespoon active dry yeast*
> *1 egg*
> *2 tablespoons dried dill weed*
> *3 cups flour*

Combine the onion flakes and the boiling water. Cover and let stand for 15 minutes.

Place the butter, salt, and sugar in a large bowl.

Drain the onion flakes and reserve the liquid. Bring the reserved liquid to a boil and pour over butter mixture. Stir until dissolved. Cool to lukewarm.

Combine the ginger, warm water, and yeast and stir until yeast is dissolved. Add to the butter mixture. Beat in the egg, onion, and dill weed. Beat for 10 minutes, gradually adding the flour until the dough begins to pull away from the sides of the bowl.

Lightly oil a large bowl. Place dough in the bowl and turn to coat on all sides. Cover with plastic wrap and refrigerate until chilled—15 to 30 minutes.

Grease a twelve-muffin tin.

Punch down the dough. Fill the muffin tin one third full. Cover with a tea towel and let rise for 30 minutes.

Preheat the oven to 300 degrees. Bake for 12 minutes, until golden brown. Transfer to a wire rack to cool.

YIELD: Twelve rolls

*T*he anonymity of Jesuit Brothers is always a great source of humility for me. Very few people, even within the Catholic world, know that Jesuits have Brothers as well as priests. Father Leo Daly was going to offer Mass at a convent of the nuns and he invited me to attend. I was told to meet him there after my class at NYU. I rang the doorbell and the window in the door opened with a nun's face in it. She said, "Yes?" I said, "I'm Brother Curry and I'm here for Mass."

This is in a rather tough section of New York and she leaned out rather cautiously and said, "What kind of Brother are you?" I said, "I'm a Jesuit Brother." She slammed the window shut yelling "Jesuits don't have Brothers!" Well, I rang the doorbell again and said, "Sister, I am a Jesuit, I'm a Jesuit Brother, I'm a friend of Father Leo Daly, and he's invited me to come to your Mass. Could you please tell Father Daly that I'm downstairs?"

A couple of minutes later the door opened very gingerly and a very shy and apologetic Sister was there and said, "Oh, Brother, please come in."

During the Mass at the prayer of the faithful, this Sister in a loud, clear voice said, "And I would like to pray for an increase in Jesuit Brothers' vocations."

LENT

*F*aithful God
let this table be a

sign of tomorrow's hope

already here, when with

the world which hungers

for your justice and peace,

we shall come together

singing your name

as our very own.

—FATHER JOHN GUILIANI,
THE BENEDICTINE GRANGE,
WEST REDDING, CONNECTICUT

Lent is an austere time: forty days of fasting and preparation for the highest of holy days—Easter. However, excessive self-imposed penances were not acceptable to Ignatius. He felt that discipline was found in our work. So during Lent, our Novice Master was very concerned that we learn to regulate our austerity and most eager to reinforce in us *moderation in all things*. We had to discuss with him what we were giving up for Lent and get his permission to do so.

Lent was also a time when we seriously looked at Christ's life and Joseph Fitzmyer, S.J., a famous theologian, came to Wernersville to teach us during Lent. We studied the Old and New Testaments. We took a look at the Gospels for the first time. We studied the mystery of the Mass and the gift Christ gave to his heavenly Father.

For me, the real penance of Lent was the seemingly never-ending forty days of sameness broken only by St. Joseph's Day, Lætare Sunday, and the human touch that the older Brothers gave to this serious time.

For all participants, Lent is an excellent time of reflection and review—recalling what is precious and meaningful in both spiritual and concrete terms, and what each of us means by the words sacrifice and penance, which have resonance for all, in or out of the church.

We Jesuits take fasting very seriously and in our houses, even with the new leniency, the Father General recommends that we have as many meatless meals as possible. At Wernersville, Brother Horan challenged himself not to repeat one single lunch for the forty lunches of Lent, which included coming up with as many different breads to supplement meatless meals. When we began adding little pieces of fruit or pieces of nut or coconut to the breads, we knew that the forty days of Lent were winding down and Easter would be here soon. A sign of hope came from the bakery.

The breads in this section are mostly hearty breads, which helped supplement a meatless menu. There are a few but very important feast days during Lent so a few special breads are also included.

BROTHER GOODMAN

Brother Matthew Goodman, S.J.—universally known as Benny—has one of the highest profiles of any Jesuit because he is the porter of one of the most frequently visited Jesuit houses in the world, Farm Street Community in London, England. Farm Street is known worldwide for its gracious hospitality to visiting Jesuits—due mostly to the kindness and good humor of Brother Benny, a proud World War II veteran with a fondness for Yanks, chocolate candy, and the opera. I benefited from his generosity one year when I was in England working with the BBC. Benny would greet me on my return every afternoon at four with hot tea, bath buns, and marvelous stories.

One morning after Mass, Benny told me to meet him in the garden so he could introduce me to someone who wanted to meet me. It turned out to be Sir Alec Guinness, who frequently worshiped at Farm Street and who inquired with fervor about my work in the theater with the disabled. Benny's only remark about this (to me) momentous event was, "Yes, he's a nice chap. Remember his wife in your prayers. She's not well."

Hot Cross Buns

We knew that Lent was right around the corner when we could smell the hot cross buns baking. In the Jesuit houses, they were served always on Ash Wednesday morning and again on various other occasions such as Good Friday, Holy Thursday, and Holy Saturday. These are Wernersville hot cross buns.

>   2 packages active dry yeast
>   ¼ cup warm water
>   ½ cup sugar
>   1 cup warm milk
>   1 teaspoon salt
>   ½ teaspoon ground nutmeg
>   4 tablespoons butter, softened
>   6 to 6½ cups unbleached all-purpose flour
>   3 whole eggs plus 1 egg yolk
>   ½ cup currants, soaked in water and drained
>   ⅔ cup chopped dried apricots
>   Cornmeal

FOR THE EGG WASH

>   1 egg white
>   1 teaspoon water

FOR THE ICING

>   1½ cups confectioners' sugar
>   ¼ teaspoon vanilla extract
>   2 to 2½ tablespoons warm milk

Combine the yeast and water in a large bowl. Add 1 tablespoon of the sugar and stir until dissolved. Set aside for 5 minutes.

Stir in the remaining sugar, warm milk, salt, nutmeg, and butter. Beat vigorously for 10 minutes, gradually adding flour until the dough begins to pull away from the sides of the bowl.

Add the whole eggs and the egg yolk to the batter, one at a time, beating until smooth after each addition. Stir in the currants and apricots. Add about 2½ cups more flour to make a soft dough.

Turn out on a lightly floured surface. Knead for 15 to 20 minutes, until dough is smooth and elastic, adding flour as necessary to prevent stickiness.

Lightly oil a large bowl. Place dough in bowl and turn to coat on all sides. Cover with plastic wrap and let rise in a warm, draft-free place until doubled in bulk—1 to 1½ hours.

Punch down the dough. Cover with a tea towel and let rest for about 10 minutes.

Grease a baking sheet and sprinkle with cornmeal or line one with kitchen parchment.

Divide dough into 24 equal portions. Roll each portion into a smooth ball and place on the baking sheet. If you want them separated, place about 3 inches apart. If you want them attached, place them about 1½ inches apart.

Cover with a tea towel and let rise until almost doubled in bulk—about 45 minutes.

Preheat the oven to 375 degrees.

To make the egg wash, beat the egg white slightly with 1 teaspoon water. Lightly brush the wash over the rolls. Make a ½-inch-deep slash in each of the rolls. Bake for 20 to 25 minutes. Transfer to a wire rack to cool. (I actually let them cool for a good 15 minutes before I put the icing on them—otherwise it just runs.)

To make the icing, combine the sugar and vanilla. Gradually beat in the milk until the icing reaches a smooth consistency. Put in a cookie press or icing bag and ice the indentations.

YIELD: *Twenty-four buns*

Olive Bread

Astudent from the Theatre Workshop and I spent five weeks working on a movie in Umbria. She was to play Margaret of Costello, a Dominican nun who was born blind, hunchbacked, and a dwarf, and who had led a great sanctified life in the city of Chiti di Costello where she is the patron Saint. I was given the part of a one-armed sinner who refuses to accept the will of God. This bread was made by a member of the film crew. For him, Umbria was the land of happy olive trees.

> *3 cups unbleached all-purpose flour*
> *1 package active dry yeast*
> *1 tablespoon sugar*
> *1 teaspoon salt*
> *½ cup hot water*
> *2 eggs*
> *¼ pound (1 stick) butter, cut into small pieces*
> *Cornmeal*
> *½ cup pimiento-stuffed olives, chopped*
> *½ cup black olives, chopped*
> *1 egg yolk, beaten*

Combine 2 cups of the flour, yeast, sugar, and salt in a large mixing bowl. Form a well in the dry ingredients and pour in the hot water. Mix thoroughly.

Add the eggs and stir until they are absorbed. Add the butter. Beat for 10 minutes, gradually adding flour until the dough begins to pull away from the sides of the bowl. (Dough will be just a little sticky.)

Turn out on a lightly floured surface. Knead for 8 to 10 minutes, until dough is smooth and elastic, adding flour as necessary to prevent stickiness.

Lightly oil a large bowl. Place dough in bowl and turn to coat on all sides.

Cover with plastic wrap and let rise in a warm, draft-free place until doubled in bulk—about 1½ hours.

Preheat the oven to 350 degrees. Grease a baking sheet and sprinkle with cornmeal or line one with kitchen parchment. Drain and combine the olives.

Punch down the dough. Turn out again and, with a lightly floured rolling pin or with your hands, press the dough out into a 14-inch square. Press the olives into the dough. (They will pop out if you don't force them well enough into the dough.) Roll up the dough like a jelly roll, tucking the ends together. Form the roll into an oval. Cover with a tea towel and let rise until doubled in bulk—about 30 minutes.

Brush the top with the egg yolk. Bake for 45 minutes. Transfer to a wire rack to cool.

YIELD: One loaf

REGARDING PENANCE
THE COMMON RULE 15

—

*I*n regard to the correction and penances, the measure which ought to be observed will be left to the discreet charity of the Superior and of those whom he has delegated in his place, that they may adjust them in accordance with the disposition of the persons and with the edification of each and every one of them for divine glory. Each one ought to accept them in good spirit with a genuine desire of his emendation and spiritual profit, even when the reason for their imposition is not that of some blameworthy defect.

Bagels

Bagels were served to us plain—not even any cream cheese—as part of the austerity menu. It was not until I came to New York that I realized how wonderful they could be. Myer Toby taught me how to make bagels in Atlantic City.

4 to 5 cups all-purpose flour
3 tablespoons sugar
1 tablespoon salt
1 package active dry yeast
1½ cups warm water

FOR THE EGG WASH

1 egg white, beaten
1 tablespoon cold water

Mix 1½ cups of the flour, sugar, salt, and yeast in a large bowl. Gradually add warm water to the flour mixture and beat vigorously for 5 minutes. Beat for another 5 minutes, gradually adding flour until the dough begins to pull away from the sides of the bowl.

Turn out on a lightly floured surface. Knead for 8 to 10 minutes, until dough is smooth and elastic, adding flour as necessary to prevent stickiness.

Place in an ungreased bowl. Cover with plastic wrap and let rise in a warm, draft-free place for 20 minutes. Dough will not double in bulk.

Punch down the dough. Turn out again. Roll into a 10 × 12-inch rectangle and cut into twelve 1 × 12-inch strips. Pinch the ends of strips together to form a circle. Or roll into a ball, put your thumb through the ball, and gradually make a circle.

Place on an ungreased baking sheet. Cover with a tea towel and let rise again for 20 minutes. Dough will not double in bulk.

Preheat the oven to 375 degrees. To make the egg wash, combine the egg and water. Mix thoroughly.

Fill a shallow pan with water 2 inches deep. Bring water to a boil and lower heat. Simmer bagels, a few at a time, for about 3½ minutes. Turn and simmer for another 3½ minutes. Lay on a towel to cool. Place on an ungreased baking sheet. Bake for 10 minutes. Remove from oven and brush with egg wash. Bake for 20 minutes. Transfer to a wire rack to cool.

YIELD: About one dozen

Myer Toby, S.J., was a Jesuit priest who had converted from Judaism. His decision was very painful for his family, but they grew to accept it. He told me this story that revealed much about acceptance.

He went to visit his mother in the hospital wearing his Roman collar. She was in a semiprivate room with another Jewish woman. After the visit he was standing outside his mother's room and overheard this conversation: "Mrs. Toby, very interesting that your son is a priest," declared her roommate. Mrs. Toby replied, "He's making a lot of people very happy. Not his mother, but a lot of people."

Spy Wednesday Biscuits

Dinner on Spy Wednesday begins the Sacred Triduum—three days that also include Holy (or Maundy) Thursday and Good Friday. As we begin the most austere week in Christianity, tasty rich biscuits remind us that Jesus is coming. The Brother baker at Wernersville gave me this recipe.

1 package active dry yeast

1 cup warm water

4 cups flour

½ cup sugar

1 teaspoon baking soda

4 teaspoons baking powder

1 teaspoon salt

1 cup chilled vegetable shortening, cut into bits

½ cup currants, soaked in warm water for 10 minutes and drained

1 cup buttermilk

Cornmeal

10 tablespoons butter, melted and cooled

Combine the yeast and water in a small bowl, stirring until yeast is dissolved. Set aside for 5 minutes.

Sift together the flour, sugar, baking soda, baking powder, and salt in a large bowl. Cut in the shortening until the mixture is the texture of coarse cornmeal. Add the currants. Stir in the yeast mixture and buttermilk, just until all the ingredients are moistened.

Grease a baking sheet and sprinkle with cornmeal or line one with kitchen parchment.

THE SECRETS OF JESUIT BREADMAKING

Turn out on a floured surface and knead gently for 2 minutes. Roll or pat the dough into a rectangle about ½ inch thick. Cut into rounds with a 2½-inch floured biscuit cutter. (Scraps can be gently kneaded together and rolled and cut.) Dip each biscuit into the melted butter and place 1 inch apart on the baking sheet. Cover with a tea towel and let rise in a warm place until doubled in bulk—about 2 hours.

Preheat the oven to 425 degrees. Bake about 15 minutes, until golden brown. Transfer to a wire rack to cool.

YIELD: Forty biscuits

*I*n the kitchen at Wernersville, we had a large loose-leaf binder that contained all our bread recipes. Actually, we had only about twenty recipes. And in typical Novitiate style, this binder was kept *chained* to the shelf over the mixing table. But besides these twenty recipes, the binder contained the rules for the Brother baker and the calendar for the first-, second-, and third-class feast days. Every recipe was filled as well with generations of copious notes from Brothers past regarding the preparation of the recipes and when they had been served. It was really a historical journal of the bakery.

Holy Thursday Apple Bread

The institution of priesthood began with the apostles at the Last Supper. Therefore, Holy Thursday is a special feast for priests and we always had this bread on priest day, as Holy Thursday is called at the novitiate.

> 1 package active dry yeast
> 1¼ cups warm water
> ½ cup light brown sugar
> 1 cup warm skim milk
> 2 teaspoons salt
> 3½ tablespoons vegetable oil
> 5 to 6 cups unbleached all-purpose flour
> 1½ cups whole wheat flour
> ½ cup raisins
> 1 large apple, peeled, cored, and finely chopped

Combine the yeast, 1/2 cup of the water, and a pinch of the brown sugar in a large bowl. Set aside for 5 minutes.

Stir in the remaining water, milk, the remaining brown sugar, salt, raisins, apple, and 2 tablespoons of the oil. Beat vigorously for 10 minutes, until the dough begins to pull away from the sides of the bowl, gradually adding 4 cups of the all-purpose flour.

Turn out on a lightly floured surface. Knead for 8 to 10 minutes, until dough is smooth and elastic, adding the remaining all-purpose flour and whole wheat flour as necessary to prevent stickiness.

Lightly oil a large bowl. Place dough in the bowl and turn to coat on all sides. Cover with plastic wrap and let rise in a warm, draft-free place until doubled in bulk—about 1½ hours.

Grease two 9 × 5-inch loaf pans.

Punch down the dough. Divide into 6 pieces and form into balls. Place 3 balls of dough, side by side, in each pan. Cover with a tea towel and let rise in a warm, draft-free place until doubled in bulk—about 45 minutes.

Preheat the oven to 350 degrees. Bake about 45 minutes, until the loaves are lightly brown. Transfer to a wire rack and let cool at least 45 minutes before cutting.

YIELD: Two loaves

RALPH ASHLEY
—

Brother Ralph Ashley, martyred in 1606, was a baker who worked with Father Henry Garnet. During the Reformation, they were forced into hiding, and took refuge in a "priest hole," a secret small space constructed in many of the great manor houses owned by sympathizers. Unfortunately, it was not supplied well with food or water and eventually they had to emerge and were captured. They were transferred to the Tower of London, and later Ashley and another captured priest, Father Oldcorne, were taken to Red Hill to be executed. After Oldcorne was hung, Ashley kissed the feet of the martyred priest and said, "How happy I am to follow in the steps of my God." The hangmen then pushed him from the ladder. He was beatified December 15, 1929, and his feast day is December 1.

Right before Ignatius entered Rome, he experienced in prayer one of his best known visions or illuminations at a little hamlet outside Rome called La Storta. Versions of the event differ in detail even in Ignatius's words, but in essence it was a vision of Jesus carrying the cross with God the Father at his side and Jesus says to Ignatius, "I wish you to serve us." God the Father added, "I will be propitious to you in Rome." And with that Ignatius was placed by Jesus's side.

Ignatius didn't know or ever fully understand what this meant, but he conjectured that he and his companions might suffer virtual crucifixion in Rome. He certainly took this visitation as a confirmation of the name of Jesus upon which they had earlier decided, even when other people raised great objections to its hubris. But he stuck to it, and the official name became and remains the Society of Jesus.

Loyola Academy Buttermilk Bread

This is soft and chewy and goes great with peanut butter. It comes from Rob Sennott, the publisher of the *Barnstable Patriot*, a weekly newspaper on Cape Cod. He is also chairman of the board of the National Theatre Workshop of the Handicapped. His warm memories of the Jesuit education he received as a high school boy in Chicago motivated him to find a way to repay the Jesuits through his service.

> *1 package active dry yeast*
> *2 cups warm buttermilk*
> *2 teaspoons salt*
> *5⅓ tablespoons butter*
> *¼ cup toasted wheat germ*
> *1 cup whole wheat flour*
> *3½ to 4 cups unbleached all-purpose flour*

Combine the yeast and buttermilk in a large bowl. Stir in the salt and butter. Gradually add the wheat germ, whole wheat flour, and about 2 cups of the all-purpose flour, beating vigorously until the dough pulls away from the sides of the bowl—about 10 minutes.

Turn out on a lightly floured surface. Knead for 8 to 10 minutes, until dough is smooth and elastic, adding flour as necessary to prevent stickiness.

Lightly oil a large bowl. Place dough in bowl and turn to coat on all sides. Cover with plastic wrap and let rise in a warm, draft-free place until doubled in bulk—about 1½ hours.

Grease two 9 × 5-inch loaf pans.

Punch down the dough. Divide in half, shape into loaves, and place in the

(continued)

pans. Cover with a tea towel and let rise again until doubled in bulk—about 45 minutes.

Place in a cold oven set at 375 degrees. Bake for 35 minutes. Transfer to a wire rack to cool.

YIELD: Two loaves

On the most solemn day of the year, Good Friday, we stripped all the tablecloths off the tables in the dining room as a demonstration of austerity. For the same reason, we'd strip the Sanctuary of its linens and the statues and crucifixes. Anything ornamental was hidden.

On Good Friday we traditionally were served fresh apples and ate them while the Junior Scholastic read the solemn readings of Good Friday from the pulpit in the dining room. The collective crunching of 130 men eating apples without the tablecloths, which were the main sound absorbers, was a cacophomaniac's dream. We were so hysterical that we were released from the dining room before the reading was completed—a most unusual occurrence.

Bran Bread

Brother Fitzgerald insists that this is the best bran bread ever made.

 1 tablespoon active dry yeast
 2 cups warm buttermilk
 2 tablespoons honey
 3 tablespoons oil
 2 teaspoon salt
 1¼ cups whole wheat flour
 1½ cups bran (see note)
 2½ to 3 cups unbleached all-purpose flour

Combine the yeast and buttermilk in a large bowl and stir until dissolved. Stir in the honey, oil, and salt. Gradually add the whole wheat flour, bran, and about 1½ cups of the all-purpose flour, beating vigorously until the dough pulls away from the sides of the bowl—about 10 minutes.

Turn out onto a lightly floured surface. Knead for 8 to 10 minutes, until dough is smooth and elastic, adding all-purpose flour as necessary to prevent stickiness.

Lightly oil a large bowl. Place dough in bowl and turn to coat on all sides. Cover with plastic wrap and let rise in a warm, draft-free place until doubled in bulk—about 1½ hours.

Punch down the dough. Divide in half, shape into loaves, and place in the pans. Cover with a tea towel and let rise until doubled in bulk—about 45 minutes.

Bake in a cold oven set at 350 degrees for 40 minutes. Transfer to a wire rack to cool.

NOTE: Brother suggests that you use bran flakes, which add better texture.

YIELD: *Two loaves*

The rivalry between Boston College and College of the Holy Cross, which manifests itself at football games and debating matches, is legendary. There are some Jesuits at Boston College who have never been to Worcester, the home of Holy Cross, and some at Holy Cross who claim never to have been to Boston and are proud of it. Over the years I've been warmly received at both places and at both places was able to gather recipes from their chefs. So in the tradition of this rivalry, I give you what can only be considered dueling recipes.

100% Whole Wheat Bread

This bread, which is from the kitchen of the College of the Holy Cross in Worcester, Massachusetts, will take a little longer to rise because it takes whole grain time to soften and time to mature, but it has richer flavor.

1 tablespoon active dry yeast
2½ cups warm water
3 tablespoons oil
2 tablespoons honey
1 tablespoon molasses
2 teaspoons salt
5 to 6 cups whole wheat flour

To make the sponge, combine the yeast and water in a large bowl and stir until dissolved. Stir in the oil, honey, molasses, and salt. Gradually add about 2½ cups of whole wheat flour. Cover and let ferment for about 1 hour.

Stir down the sponge. Beat for 10 minutes, gradually adding about 2 more cups of the flour, until the dough begins to pull away from the sides of the bowl.

Turn out on a lightly floured surface. Knead for 8 to 10 minutes, until dough is smooth and elastic, adding flour as necessary to prevent stickiness. (This bread will feel heavier and more dense than breads with white flour in them.)

Lightly oil a large bowl. Place dough in bowl and turn to coat on all sides. Cover with plastic wrap and let rise in a warm, draft-free place until doubled in bulk—a good 1½ hours.

Preheat the oven to 350 degrees. Grease two 9 × 5-inch loaf pans.

Punch down the dough. Divide in half and shape into loaves. Place in the pans. Cover with a tea towel and let rise until doubled in bulk—about 45 minutes. Bake for 40 minutes. Transfer to a wire rack to cool.

YIELD: Two loaves

Whole Wheat and Oatmeal Bread

And this is Boston College's recipe, for when time is of the essence.

> 3 cups whole wheat flour
> 2 tablespoons active dry yeast
> 1 tablespoon salt
> 5⅓ tablespoons butter
> 2½ cups milk
> ½ cup water
> ½ cup molasses
> 2 tablespoons honey
> 1½ cups quick rolled oats
> 2 eggs
> 4 to 5 cups unbleached all-purpose flour
> Cornmeal

Combine the whole wheat flour, yeast, and salt in a large bowl.

Heat the butter, milk, water, molasses, and honey until warm and the butter is partially melted. Pour into the whole wheat mixture and stir well. Stir in the oats and eggs. Beat for 10 minutes, gradually adding all-purpose flour until the dough begins to pull away from the sides of the bowl.

Turn out on a lightly floured surface. Knead for 8 to 10 minutes, until dough is smooth and elastic, adding flour as necessary to prevent stickiness.

Lightly oil a large bowl. Place dough in bowl and turn to coat on all sides. Cover with plastic wrap and let rise in a warm, draft-free place until doubled in bulk—a good 1½ hours.

THE SECRETS OF JESUIT BREADMAKING

Preheat the oven to 375 degrees. Grease three 9 × 5-inch loaf pans, or grease two baking sheets and sprinkle with cornmeal or line with kitchen parchment.

Punch down the dough. Divide into thirds, shape into the desired form, and place in pans or on baking sheets. Cover with a tea towel and let rise again until doubled in bulk—about 45 minutes. Bake for 30 to 35 minutes. Transfer to a wire rack to cool.

YIELD: Three loaves

One of our Eastern European Brothers, Brother William Sudzina, kept a black fast, meaning he ate only bread and water during the forty days. But the bread that he ate was a black pumpernickel that the Brother baker fortified with nuts, egg, ascorbic powder, lots of butter, and who knows what else. I bumped into him years later and kidded him about his bread being so rich and so nutritionally complete that he probably ate better than the rest of us during Lent.

O'Brien's Oatmeal Bread

Brother John O'Brien, a vigorous teacher of Latin at Gonzaga Prep in Spokane, Washington, was sixty-eight years old when I met him. He told me about making retreats at the Sacred Heart Mission in DeSnet, Idaho, and introducing the Native Americans to this oatmeal bread.

> 1½ cups warm water
> 1 package active dry yeast
> 2 tablespoons vegetable shortening or vegetable oil
> 1½ cups oats
> ½ cup molasses
> 2 tablespoons sugar
> 1½ teaspoons salt
> 3 cups unbleached all-purpose flour
> 1 egg

Combine the yeast and the water in a medium bowl, stirring until dissolved. Set aside for 5 minutes.

In a large bowl, combine the vegetable shortening, oats, molasses, sugar, salt, 2 cups of the flour, and the egg. Mix well. Add the yeast and mix again. Beat vigorously, gradually adding more flour until the dough begins to pull away from the sides of the bowl.

Turn out on a lightly floured surface. Knead for 8 to 10 minutes, until dough is smooth and elastic, adding flour as necessary to prevent stickiness.

Lightly oil a large bowl. Place dough in the bowl and turn to coat on all sides. Cover with plastic wrap and let rise in a warm, draft-free place until doubled in bulk—about 1½ hours.

Divide dough in half. Turn out on a lightly floured surface, cover with a tea towel, and let rest for about 10 minutes.

Grease two 9 × 5-inch loaf pans. Shape dough into loaves and place in pans. Cover with a tea towel and let rise until doubled in bulk—about 45 minutes.

Preheat the oven to 400 degrees. Bake about 30 minutes. Transfer to a wire rack to cool.

YIELD: *Two loaves*

THE FEAST OF ST. JOSEPH
—

St. Joseph is really the first Brother. He was never ordained but was in total service to the Lord and certainly was committed to a life of service and purity. He was known as the protector of the Church because he was the sole protector of Mary and Jesus. He's claimed by every country as their own, but the Italians have loved him very much and actually have a bread in his honor called *pane di San Giuseppe*. There are many traditions around the feast of St. Joseph in the Italian community, but one is always that of hospitality. The tradition in New Orleans is that on this day you put out food on a table and everyone can come into your house and eat it. The Feast of St. Joseph, which is March 19, is a very favorite feast of mine.

Pane di San Giuseppe

ST. JOSEPH'S BREAD

The Feast of St. Joseph was also the day that I made my vows as a Jesuit Brother. As a surprise for me, my friends in the bakery made St. Joseph's bread and served it at dinner. It's a very simple, straightforward recipe, but the bread can be shaped like a man's beard, like the one St. Joseph wore as an older man.

> 2 to 3 cups unbleached all-purpose flour
> ½ tablespoon active dry yeast
> 1 tablespoon honey
> ⅔ cup hot water
> ½ teaspoon salt
> 2 tablespoons butter
> 3 tablespoons aniseed
> ⅓ cup golden raisins
> Cornmeal

Combine 1½ cups of the flour, the yeast, honey, water, salt, butter, and aniseed in a large bowl. Mix thoroughly. Add the raisins. Beat for another 10 minutes, adding flour until the dough begins to pull away from the sides of the bowl.

Turn out on a lightly floured surface. Knead for 8 to 10 minutes, until dough is smooth and elastic, adding flour as necessary to prevent stickiness.

Lightly oil a large bowl. Place dough in bowl and turn to coat on all sides. Cover with plastic wrap and place in a warm, draft-free place until doubled in bulk—about 1 hour.

Grease a baking sheet and sprinkle with cornmeal or line one with kitchen parchment.

(continued)

Punch down the dough. Shape into a long loaf (see note). Place the loaf on the baking sheet and make three or four ½-inch diagonal slashes on the top. Cover with a tea towel and let rise until doubled in bulk—about 30 minutes.

Preheat the oven to 350 degrees. Mist loaves with water or vinegar before baking and twice during baking. Bake about 40 minutes. Transfer to a wire rack to cool.

NOTE: Traditionally, you shape the bread to look like a patriarch's beard by making five torpedo loaves of graduated lengths, 1 long, 2 medium, and 2 short. Place them close together on a baking sheet in the following order: 1 short, 1 medium, 1 long, 1 medium, 1 short. They will rise together and you'll have *pane di San Giuseppe.*

YIELD: *One loaf or beard shape*

VOW DAY

What novices look forward to the most is when they are officially incorporated into the Society of Jesus. After making their vows of poverty, chastity, and obedience, they can in fact officially become full-fledged Jesuits and put S.J. after their names.

Vows were celebrated on four days of the year and marked various individual anniversaries throughout the novitiate.

I left home September 17 and so two and a half years later I was able to make my vows on March 19, the feast of St. Joseph. It was a very special day for me not just because of my vows but because on the eighteenth of March I had turned twenty-one.

Vow Cake

his is the only cake recipe in this book, but it was served on vow days and my vow day was during Lent. We all loved this cake and I arm-wrestled this recipe from Brother Dragansky, thinking it was an ancient formula, steeped in Jesuit history. You can imagine how "bathed in truth" I was when I discovered that it was a basic *genoise*, or French sponge cake. Brother Dragansky always topped it with a lemon butter cream icing.

FOR THE CAKE

> ½ cup sugar
>
> 3 eggs
>
> ½ teaspoon vanilla extract
>
> ½ cup unbleached all-purpose flour, sifted three times with a pinch of salt
>
> 3 tablespoons butter, melted (I clarify mine but it's optional)

FOR THE ICING

> ¼ pound (1 stick) butter, softened
>
> 1 pound confectioners' sugar
>
> Juice of 1 lemon

Preheat the oven to 350 degrees. Butter and flour one 9-inch cake pan and line it with buttered kitchen parchment.

Gradually beat the sugar into the eggs in a large bowl (preferably copper). Set the bowl over a pan of hot (not boiling) water and beat for 10 minutes. Remove the bowl from the heat and add the vanilla. Continue to beat until the mixture is cool.

Gently fold in the flour, one third of it at a time. Fold in the butter. The batter quickly loses volume after the butter is added, so immediately pour the batter into the cake pan. Bake for 35 to 40 minutes, or until the cake pulls away from the sides of the pan and the top springs back when lightly pressed. Let cool on a wire rack. Run a knife around the sides of the cake to loosen it and place upside down on a wire rack to cool completely.

To make the icing, melt the butter. Add the sugar and lemon juice and beat until smooth. Spread on the cooled cake.

YIELD: One cake

Let whatever ready money is at hand be spent in caring for the sick. We who are well can easily live on hard bread, if nothing else is available.

—*Maxim of St. Ignatius on Religious Life*

Sister Courtney's
Buttermilk Bread

Sister Courtney, once a Poor Clare nun, now runs a goat farm in New Hampshire with her mother. They make and sell goat cheese—the brand name of which is Nunsuch! She also with affection names all the goats after the nuns she lived with.

1 cup buttermilk, scalded
3 tablespoons sugar
2½ teaspoons salt
⅓ cup vegetable shortening
1 tablespoon active dry yeast
1 cup warm water
½ teaspoon baking soda
5½ to 6 cups unbleached all-purpose flour

Combine the buttermilk, sugar, salt, and vegetable shortening. Cool to lukewarm.

Combine the yeast and water in a large bowl, stirring until yeast is dissolved. Stir in the buttermilk mixture and baking soda. Beat vigorously for 10 minutes, gradually adding about 3 cups of the flour until the dough begins to pull away from the sides of the bowl.

Turn out on a lightly floured surface. Knead for 8 to 10 minutes, until dough is smooth and elastic, adding flour as necessary to prevent stickiness.

Lightly oil a large bowl. Place dough in the bowl and turn to coat on all sides. Cover with plastic wrap and let rise in a warm, draft-free place until doubled in bulk—about 1 hour.

Punch down the dough. Turn out again. Cover with a tea towel and let rest for 15 minutes.

Grease two 9 × 5-inch loaf pans.

Divide dough in half, shape into loaves, and place in the pans. Cover again and let rise until doubled in bulk—about 1 hour.

Preheat the oven to 400 degrees.

Bake for 45 minutes. Transfer to a wire rack to cool.

YIELD: Two loaves

THE GREAT CARAWAY SCHISM

—

*T*he great controversy in Irish soda bread is caraway seeds versus no caraway seeds. It seems that whole schisms have been created in Irish families over this issue. Father Tom O'Malley, who is president of Loyola Marymount in Los Angeles, said that his family had a caraway rift and his aunts couldn't discuss the subject. I also heard that using caraway seeds is very Catholic and not using them is very Protestant, but there doesn't seem to be any truth to that rumor.

Irish Soda Bread

The Irish Brothers looked at me sideways when I asked them for their soda bread recipe. "It's like boiling water," said one Brother, "you don't need a recipe." I had to wait until I returned to the States to get an Irish soda bread recipe from Brother Fitzgerald.

5 cups sifted all-purpose unbleached flour

¾ cup sugar

1½ teaspoons salt

1 teaspoon baking soda

2 teaspoons baking powder

¼ pound (1 stick) butter

2½ cups light and dark raisins, soaked for 15 to 20
    minutes and drained (I love the mixture of raisins)

3 tablespoons caraway seeds

2½ cups buttermilk

1 egg, slightly beaten

Preheat the oven to 350 degrees. Generously butter two 9 × 5-inch bread pans.

Stir together the sifted flour, sugar, salt, baking soda, and baking powder. Cut in the butter and mix very thoroughly with your hands until it gets grainy. Stir in raisins and caraway seeds.

Add the buttermilk and egg to the flour mixture. Stir until well moistened. Shape dough into two loaves and place in the pans.

Bake for 1 hour. Test with a toothpick for doneness. Cool in the pans for 3 to 5 minutes. Transfer to a wire rack to cool.

YIELD: Two loaves

I lived for ten years at America House, where the Jesuit weekly magazine is published. One St. Patrick's Day, the editor, Reverend Joseph A. O'Hare, S.J., threw an open house for family and friends of the magazine who'd come to watch the huge parade down Fifth Avenue (a block away). We all took turns at the front door, greeting guests but ever mindful that their first need was to find the bathroom after standing on the street for hours. Their next stop would be a beautiful conference room that had been turned into a hospitality center, complete with Irish coffee, cold cuts, and Irish soda breads—not just any old Irish soda bread. Father O'Hare had retrieved it in the early morning hours from his old neighborhood bakery in the Bronx. This was his idea of "roots," with delicious results. Father O'Hare is now president of Fordham University, the main campus of which is right down the street from the bakery in the Bronx.

Irish Brown Bread

Brother Gerald Marks of Belvedere College in Dublin was eager to give me an Irish brown bread recipe. British recipes use pound measurements and I have given you Brother Marks's recipe the way he gave it to me, but I've also given you our equivalents.

1 pound (3½ cups) whole wheat flour
1 pound (3½ cups) unbleached all-purpose flour
½ ounce (3 teaspoons) baking soda
4 ounces (¼ pound, 1 stick) butter
1½ pints (3 cups) buttermilk

Preheat the oven to 350 degrees. Butter two 9 × 5-inch loaf pans.

Combine the whole wheat flour, all-purpose flour, and baking soda. Add the butter and buttermilk to the flour mixture. Divide the dough in half and put it in the pans. Bake for 45 to 60 minutes. Transfer to a wire rack to cool.

YIELD: Two loaves

DAILY BREADS

May the Lord
accept this, our offering,
and bless our food that
it may bring us strength
in our body, vigor in our
mind, and selfless
devotion in our
heart for his
service

—SWAMI PARAMANANDA,
*BOOK OF DAILY THOUGHTS
AND PRAYER*

One of the most famous Gospel passages is the prayer that Jesus taught us to pray in Luke 11:3, "Give us each day our daily bread." Jesus knew that bread was the perfect food to feed the world forever. Every day we celebrate not only the daily gift of bread of life but we celebrate the daily gift of life—we're not alone. Every single day can be made special by having fresh baked bread.

The older Brothers told us that when they began to work in the kitchen or in the bakery, they would make the humble gesture—they would get down on their knees and kiss the floor and dedicate their day to the work at hand. We were considered somewhat more modern and began our day in the bakery by kissing the ties of our aprons as we put them over our necks, and dedicating our work to the Lord while we labored putting out the meal or in the bakery with this prayer: Lord, make me a new man as I clothe myself with the apron of your love. It was a small ritual that led us to believe that the work we were doing was sacred and that the space that we were working in was a sacred space.

These daily breads are adaptable to most menus and will complement most meals rather than overwhelm them.

Brother's Bread

This was the first recipe in our loose-leaf binder at Wernersville and this bread was probably made more than any other. I've also seen it referred to as peasant bread.

1 tablespoon active dry yeast
2¼ cups warm water
1 tablespoon sugar
1½ tablespoons salt
6 to 7 cups unbleached all-purpose flour
Cornmeal
Vinegar

Combine the yeast and water in a large bowl, stirring until yeast is dissolved. Stir in sugar and salt. Mix well. Set aside for 5 minutes.

Beat for 10 minutes, gradually adding flour until the dough begins to pull away from the sides of the bowl.

Turn out on a lightly floured surface. Knead for 8 to 10 minutes, until dough is smooth and elastic, adding flour as necessary to prevent stickiness.

Lightly oil a large bowl. Place dough in bowl and turn to coat on all sides. Cover with plastic wrap and let rise in a warm, draft-free place until doubled in bulk—about 1½ hours.

Grease a baking sheet and sprinkle with cornmeal or line one with kitchen parchment.

Punch down the dough. Divide in half, shape into two round loaves, and place on the baking sheet. Carve an X in the top of the loaf and spray with vinegar. Place in a cold oven and bake at 400 degrees for 45 minutes. Transfer to a wire rack to cool.

YIELD: Two loaves

Bread is the warmest and kindest word in any language. It is a word that Jesus chose to represent himself. It is a word that means life, hope, and comfort. It's a miracle.

Italian	pane
Latin	panis
Spanish	pan
French	pain
German	Brot
Portuguese	pane
Irish	arán
Polish	chleb
Zulu	isinkwa
Greek	ψωμί
Hindi	रोटी
Arabic	خبز
Hebrew	לחם
Chinese	麵飽
Armenian	հաg
Japanese	パン
Russian	хлеб
American sign language	

Brother Fitzgerald's
Basic White Bread

Brother Bob Fitzgerald, S.J., from St. Joseph's University in Philadelphia, is a very quiet, mild-mannered great Irishman, great wit, and great man of prayer. He also learned how to bake bread as a novice and never stopped baking bread his whole life. He said to me one day as sort of an admonishment that anybody can bake fancy bread, but the test of a great baker is to bake a delicious basic white bread.

> *4 packages (9 teaspoons) active dry yeast*
> *2½ cups warm milk (may also substitute potato water)*
> *2 tablespoons salt*
> *3 tablespoons sugar*
> *6 to 8 cups flour*
> *3 tablespoons butter, softened*

Combine the yeast and ½ cup of the lukewarm milk in a small bowl, stirring until yeast is dissolved. Set aside for 5 minutes.

Mix the salt, sugar, 3 cups of the flour, and the remaining milk. Stir in the yeast mixture. Add the butter. Beat for 10 minutes, continuing to add flour until the dough begins to pull away from the sides of the bowl.

Turn dough out on a lightly floured surface. Knead for 8 to 10 minutes, until dough is smooth and elastic. Add more flour as necessary to prevent stickiness.

Lightly oil a large bowl. Place dough in bowl and turn to coat on all sides. Cover with plastic wrap and let rise in a warm, draft-free place until doubled in bulk—about 45 minutes.

Punch down the dough. Turn out again and gently knead for about 2 minutes. Cover with a tea towel and let rise again until doubled in bulk—about 1 hour.

Grease two 9 × 5-inch loaf pans.

Turn out again. Divide in half, shape into loaves, and place in the pans. Cover with a tea towel and let rise until doubled in bulk—about 30 minutes.

Place oven rack in the middle of the oven. Preheat the oven to 425 degrees.

Bake for 40 minutes, until loaves are golden brown (see note). Transfer to a wire rack to cool.

NOTE: Brother Fitzgerald prefers to brush his loaves with an egg wash before he bakes them. He uses 1 egg and ¼ cup of water mixed together. You can also brush with butter after they have baked.

YIELD: Two loaves

The early history of the Society of Jesus is grounded in Italy. Ignatius, at the University of Paris, gathered nine followers who were very excited about sticking with each other and trying to serve God in some way, although how they were to accomplish this was not clear. Eventually they found their way to Venice, where they begged alms for the poor, scrubbed floors, cleaned hospitals, and begged bread to distribute to the poor. It was in Venice that St. Ignatius and his followers became ordained priests.

Rosemont's Bread

Brother Robert Comber, a retired Brother at Wernersville, gave me this recipe, which came from his sister, Mother Thecla, Sister of the Holy Child Jesus, and head of the biology department at Rosemont College in Philadelphia. She got the recipe from the cook at Rosemont.

> 2 cups milk
> 2 tablespoons sugar
> 2 teaspoons salt
> 1 tablespoon lard or vegetable shortening
> 1 tablespoon active dry yeast
> ¼ cup warm water
> 6 to 7 cups sifted unbleached all-purpose flour

Scald the milk and stir in sugar, salt, and lard. Cool to lukewarm.

Combine the yeast and water in a large bowl, stirring until yeast is dissolved. Set aside for 5 minutes.

And the milk mixture and 3 cups of the flour to the yeast mixture. Beat for 10 minutes, gradually adding flour until the dough begins to pull away from the sides of the bowl.

Turn out on a lightly floured surface. Knead for 8 to 10 minutes, until dough is smooth and elastic, adding flour as necessary to prevent stickiness. Cover with a tea towel and let rest for 10 minutes.

Lightly oil a large bowl. Place dough in bowl and turn to coat on all sides. Cover with plastic wrap and let rise in a warm, draft-free place until doubled in bulk—about 1½ hours.

Grease two 9 × 5-inch loaf pans.

Turn out again. Divide in half, shape into loaves, and place in the pans. Cover and let rise until doubled in bulk—about 1 hour.

Preheat the oven to 400 degrees. Bake for 35 minutes. Transfer to a wire rack to cool.

YIELD: Two loaves

In the Wernersville kitchen, there was a delightful chain of command for baking bread. The senior Brother was the baker in charge—he was the one who selected the recipes for the day. Novice Brothers would come in for four to five hours a day to learn the craft of baking, but they were not responsible for the choosing of the recipes or for the distribution of breads. A portion of the breads was always given to the poor in the neighborhood. There was a large wicker basket where we put the breads of the day. Someone from the village would come up and take the breads, and they would return the empty basket with a personal note—a thank-you note. That was one of our little contacts with the outside world—there was someone out there very grateful for the breads that we baked.

Overnight Basic Italian

I make a basic Italian dough and let it rise slowly overnight. I mix it together before I go to bed at night and put it in the refrigerator. The next morning I take it out of the refrigerator and punch it down and form it into loaves and bake it.

1 tablespoon active dry yeast
1¾ cups warm water (approximately)
1 teaspoon salt
4 to 5 cups unbleached all-purpose flour
Cornmeal
Vinegar

Combine the yeast and ¼ cup water in a large bowl, stirring until yeast is dissolved. Set aside for 5 minutes.

Add the remaining 1½ cups of water and salt. Beat for 10 minutes, gradually adding flour until the dough begins to pull away from the sides of the bowl.

Turn out on a lightly floured surface. Knead for 8 to 10 minutes, until dough is smooth and elastic, adding flour as necessary to prevent stickiness.

Lightly oil a large bowl with olive oil (see note). Place dough in bowl and turn to coat on all sides. Cover with plastic wrap and let rise slowly in the refrigerator for 10 to 12 hours or overnight.

Grease a baking sheet and sprinkle with cornmeal or line one with kitchen parchment.

Punch down the dough. Turn out again. Divide in half, shape into torpedo-like loaves, and place on the baking sheet. (I like to bake these loaves on a baking stone to get an Old World rustic effect.) Cover with a tea towel and let loaves come to room temperature—about 45 minutes.

Make diagonal slashes in the loaves. Cover and let rise until doubled in bulk—about 40 minutes.

Preheat the oven to 400 degrees. Spray the loaves with vinegar and gently slide into oven. Bake for 35 to 40 minutes. Spray the loaves again after 20 minutes of baking. Transfer to a wire rack to cool.

NOTE: I always use olive oil with Italian bread.

VARIATION

This recipe is also good for breadsticks. I like them plain, but you can add cheese or herbs to the dough or simply sprinkle them on sticks before you bake. To form the sticks, pinch off 1-inch pieces of the dough after you punch down the dough the first time. On a lightly floured surface. roll each piece into a breadstick—10 to 12 inches long. Place the sticks on a baking sheet about 1 inch apart, or place in pans especially designed to bake bread sticks. Cover with a tea towel and let rise until doubled in bulk.

Brush with an egg wash. Bake for 10 minutes, until crisp and lightly brown. Transfer to a wire rack. They are good to serve with soup or just for munching.

YIELD: Two loaves

When Ignatius and his men banded together, Catholic Europe was in turmoil. Henry VIII had divorced Catherine of Aragon, married and executed Anne Boleyn, passed the Act of Supremacy, and removed Thomas More's head. Spain and France were at war and the Inquisition was established in Portugal. St. Peter's was not yet completed and wouldn't be for another 50 years. Michelangelo was still at work in the Sistine Chapel.

Tipton's Bread

Thomas Tipton is the chef at the Farm Street Community in London. This recipe has been baked at Farm Street for over sixty years. The flour he used to make this bread was so coarse it looked like shredded cardboard and never could have made it through a sifter. Seeing it was an instant lesson in the difference in the way European and American grains are refined. However, his flour made a lovely heavy grain bread that I've tried to replicate. Although the flour I use is different, I use his measurements, but I have included our equivalents for you.

FOR THE BREAD

2 pounds (10 cups) bread flour
1 ounce fresh yeast (1 tablespoon active dry yeast)
1 ounce sugar (⅛ cup)
2 pints (4 cups) lukewarm water
1 pound (3½ cups) whole wheat flour
1 ounce (⅛ cup) salt
Cornmeal

FOR THE EGG WASH

1 egg
¼ pint (½ cup) water

Combine 3 cups of the white flour, yeast, 1½ tablespoons of the sugar, and ½ pint of the water. Cover with plastic wrap and let ferment for about 20 minutes. (You're making a bit of a starter.)

Stir in the remaining sugar and the salt and water. Beat for another 10 minutes, gradually adding the remaining flours until the dough begins to pull away from the sides of the bowl. The dough will be very sticky.

Lightly oil a large bowl. Place dough in bowl and turn to coat on all sides.

Cover with plastic wrap and let rise in a warm, draft-free place until doubled in bulk—about 1 hour.

Preheat the oven to 450 degrees. Grease two baking sheets and sprinkle with cornmeal or line them with kitchen parchment.

Punch down the dough. Divide into 4 pieces, shape each into a tight ball, and place on the baking sheets. Cover with a tea towel and let rise until doubled in bulk—about 30 minutes.

To make the egg wash, combine the egg and water and mix thoroughly. Brush the loaves with the egg wash. Make a slash down the center of each loaf. Bake for 45 minutes. Transfer to wire racks to cool.

YIELD: Four loaves

SOURDOUGH BREAD

—

We always identify sourdough breads with San Francisco and the Gold Rush and the Yukon Gold Rush, but the Egyptians really invented it several centuries before Christ. The ancient Greeks and Romans used sourdough starters, too. The Jesuit missionary Francis Xavier, aboard ship going to India, kept a sourdough starter alive in his cassock and baked bread with it every day on the high seas.

Sourdough breads depend on a starter, which is easily made and not as complicated as some people claim. A starter is made from flour, milk or water, some yeast, and maybe some sweetener that is allowed to ferment. If you've ever kept leftover mashed potatoes or canned fruit and seen them ferment, you have an idea of how sourdough works.

Once you get a starter under way, you have to replenish it with equal parts of flour and warm milk or water. For instance, if you have used one cup of the starter in a recipe, then you blend in one cup of flour and one cup warm milk or water. Stir it, cover it, and let it stand in a warm place for several hours or overnight, until it gets bubbly. Between uses, refrigerate the starter.

If you use the starter regularly, at least every week or so, it should last indefinitely. When I was finishing my master's thesis in Paris, Father Frank Burch, S.J., took me down to the basement of a very famous bakery, named Poilâne, where the mother, as a starter is sometimes called, is thought to have been in existence for one hundred years.

One of the great advantages of living in community and having a lineage of Brother bakers is that you can scrounge a tablespoon or so of starter from a flourishing pot and start your own with it. But if you have to make your own, here are two recipes, one that uses commercial yeast and one that catches wild yeast that's in the air.

Commercial Yeast Starter

1 tablespoon active dry yeast
1 cup warm water
1 cup warm nonfat milk
2 cups flour

Combine the yeast and water in a medium bowl, stirring until dissolved. Mix in the milk. Add the flour and beat until smooth. Transfer the mixture to a 2-quart container, preferably pottery or enamel. Cover tightly and let stand at room temperature until the mixture begins to sour—24 to 48 hours. Stir it every couple of hours. If you're not going to use it immediately, stir it down and refrigerate.

YIELD: Three cups

Wild Yeast Starter

4 cups unbleached all-purpose flour

2 teaspoons salt

2 tablespoons honey

4 cups potato water (sometimes I put potato peels in the
water because they ferment very quickly)

Mix the flour, salt, honey, and potato water in a large nonmetal container. Let the mixture stand, loosely covered (it needs air) in a warm place. In two or three days, if you have captured some wild yeast, the mixture will begin to froth and expand. Drape some plastic wrap over it. And after a couple of days you might want to add some yeast as a booster.

YIELD: Three cups

Basic Sourdough Bread

I had never baked sourdough bread until I studied at the Culinary Institute. This is a basic recipe I picked up there.

> 1 cup sourdough starter
> 1 tablespoon active dry yeast
> 2 cups warm water
> 2 teaspoons sugar
> 2 teaspoons salt
> 5 to 6 cups unbleached all-purpose flour
> 2 cups bread flour
> Cornmeal
> 1 teaspoon cornstarch, blended with ⅓ cup water, for a
>   wash

Let the starter come to room temperature. Combine the yeast and ¼ cup of the water in a large bowl. Add the sugar and stir until dissolved. Set aside for 5 minutes.

Stir in the remaining 1¾ cups water, salt, and the starter. Add 4 cups of the all-purpose flour, 1 cup at a time. Beat vigorously for 5 minutes, gradually adding the bread flour. Beat for another 5 minutes, continuing to add flour until the dough begins to pull away from the sides of the bowl.

Turn out on a lightly floured surface. Knead for 20 minutes, until dough is smooth and elastic, adding flour as necessary to prevent stickiness.

Dust a large bowl with flour. Place dough in bowl and turn to coat on all sides. Cover with plastic wrap and let rise in a warm, draft-free place until doubled in bulk—about 1 hour.

Grease a baking sheet and sprinkle with cornmeal or line one with kitchen parchment.

Punch down the dough. Cover with a tea towel and let rest for 10 minutes. Divide in half, shape into tight balls, and place on the baking sheet. Cover with a tea towel and let rise until doubled in bulk—45 minutes to 1 hour.

Preheat the oven to 400 degrees.

To make the wash, bring the cornstarch and water to a boil in a small pan over low heat. Stir until it becomes thick and clear. Brush each loaf with it. Slit the tops of the loaves in the traditional tic-tac-toe sign. Bake about 35 minutes, until golden brown. Transfer to a wire rack to cool.

YIELD: Two loaves

Brother Buchman's Cracked Wheat

Brother Buchman has been a cook and baker his entire life as a Jesuit. When I was a student at Xavier University in Cincinnati and living at Melford Novitiate, he was in charge of the kitchen. Brother Buchman was in a constant cheerful state because he felt that if he got into a bad mood he'd eventually have to get into a good mood again. So he just decided to cut out the middleman. Needless to say his patience with us in his kitchen was infinite.

FOR THE STARTER

> *1 package active dry yeast*
> *2 cups warm water*
> *¾ cup cracked wheat*
> *2 cups bread flour*

FOR THE BREAD

> *1 package active dry yeast*
> *½ cup warm water*
> *2 tablespoons honey (more if you prefer a sweeter bread)*
> *2 tablespoons vegetable oil*
> *2 teaspoons salt*
> *1 cup whole wheat flour*
> *2 to 3 cups bread flour*

To make the starter, combine the yeast, water, cracked wheat, and bread flour in a large bowl. Beat vigorously for 3 minutes. Cover tightly with plastic wrap and let rise in a warm, draft-free place for 12 to 24 hours.

To make the bread dough, combine the yeast and warm water in a large bowl, stirring until yeast is dissolved. Mix in all the starter, honey, oil, salt, and whole wheat flour. Beat for 10 minutes, gradually adding bread flour until the dough begins to pull away from the sides of the bowl.

Turn out on a lightly floured surface. Knead for 8 to 10 minutes, until dough is smooth and elastic, adding flour as necessary to prevent stickiness.

Lightly oil a large bowl. Place dough in bowl and turn to coat on all sides. Cover with plastic wrap and let rise in a warm, draft-free place until doubled in bulk—about 1 hour.

Grease two 9 × 5-inch loaf pans.

Punch down the dough. Divide in half, shape into loaves, and place in the pans. Cover with a tea towel and let rise again until doubled in bulk—20 to 30 minutes.

Preheat the oven to 375 degrees. Bake for 35 to 45 minutes. Transfer to a wire rack to cool.

YIELD: Two loaves

COMMON BOOK

10

—

*I*f there are Brothers working at some distance from the house, e.g., in the fields, a bell is sounded a quarter hour before the noon examination of conscience to call them home.

Cracked Wheat Bread

Brother Fred Barth was stationed for years at Georgetown, and although middle-aged when I met him, he had the energy and enthusiasm of a teenager. He was generous to a fault. He told me he "stole" this recipe from the cook at Georgetown University.

> 2 tablespoons active dry yeast
> ¾ cup warm water
> 3 cups cooked cracked wheat (see note)
> 3 tablespoons butter, melted
> 3 tablespoons brown sugar
> 1 tablespoon salt
> 5½ to 6 cups unbleached all-purpose flour

Combine the yeast and water in a small bowl, stirring until yeast is dissolved. Set aside for 5 minutes.

Mix the cracked wheat, butter, brown sugar, and salt. (Let cool if using cooked cracked wheat.) Add the yeast mixture. Beat for 10 minutes, gradually adding flour until the dough begins to pull away from the sides of the bowl.

Turn out on a lightly floured surface. Knead for 8 to 10 minutes, until dough is smooth and elastic, adding flour as necessary to prevent stickiness.

Lightly oil a large bowl. Place dough in bowl and turn to coat on all sides. Cover with plastic wrap and let rise in a warm, draft-free place until doubled in bulk—about 1½ hours.

Grease two 9 × 5-inch loaf pans. Punch down the dough. Divide in half, shape into loaves, and place into pans. Cover with a tea towel and let rise again until doubled in bulk—a little less than an hour.

Preheat the oven to 400 degrees.

Bake for 30 minutes. Transfer to a wire rack to cool.

There are two ways to prepare the cracked wheat for this bread. You can either take 1 cup of cracked wheat and 3 cups of water and cook for 30 to 40 minutes, or take 1 cup of cracked wheat and 3 cups of water and soak it overnight.

YIELD: Two loaves

All the areas of the kitchen were divided into jobs. They were given Latin names because the scholastics were chatting in Latin while they were cleaning up. The job of cleaning up the kitchen afterward was called *lavetrina,* and the *praepos,* the person in charge of *lavetrina,* was responsible for a crew of ten men who worked at the *machina,* the Latin word for the dishwashing machine where they poured hundreds of dishes through in a very short time, all in silence. Any time instructions were to be given they were in Latin. There were those who manned the buckets cleaning the floor, those swabbing down the tables, then there were the people who were on pots and pans. Pots and pans were, of course, huge. A note on the pots and pans: The novice Brothers were trained to clean their pots and pans immediately as they cooked. A sign of a very good cook was that at the end of the meal, most of the pots and pans were clean.

Whole Wheat–Wheat Germ Bread

Like many other Americans, Jesuits have become much more health conscious about the food we eat and this is one of P. J. Maurer's healthy breads.

> 1 tablespoon active dry yeast
>
> 2 cups warm water
>
> 2 teaspoons salt
>
> 2 tablespoons oil
>
> ¼ cup honey
>
> 1 cup toasted wheat germ
>
> ½ cup whole wheat flour
>
> 3½ to 4 cups unbleached all-purpose flour

Combine the yeast and water in a large bowl, stirring until yeast is dissolved. Set aside for 5 minutes.

Stir in the salt, oil, and honey. Beat vigorously for 10 minutes, gradually adding the wheat germ, whole wheat flour, and about 2½ cups of the all-purpose flour, until the dough pulls away from the sides of the bowl.

Turn out on a lightly floured surface. Knead for 8 to 10 minutes, until dough is smooth and elastic, adding flour as necessary to prevent stickiness.

Lightly oil a large bowl. Place dough in bowl and turn to coat on all sides. Cover with plastic wrap and let rise in a warm, draft-free place until doubled in bulk—a good 1½ hours.

Grease two 9 × 5-inch loaf pans.

Punch down the dough. Divide in half, shape into loaves, and place in the pans. Cover with a tea towel and let rise until doubled in bulk—about 45 minutes.

Place in a cold oven and bake at 375 degrees for 35 minutes. Transfer from pans to a wire rack to cool.

YIELD: Two loaves

COMMON RULE

20

—

*L*et each be careful to observe in his own person, in his room, place of work, and generally throughout the house, that cleanliness which is recommended to all of Ours.

Honey Whole Wheat

Marquette University's Jesuit community makes a honey whole wheat bread. They don't know where they got it, but for as long as anyone can remember the recipe has been taped on the kitchen door.

> 2 tablespoons active dry yeast
> 5 cups warm water
> 5 tablespoons vegetable shortening or lard
> ¼ cup honey
> 4 cups whole wheat flour
> ½ cup instant potatoes, not reconstituted (see note)
> ½ cup nonfat dry milk
> 1 tablespoon salt
> 6½ to 8 cups sifted unbleached all-purpose flour

Combine the yeast and ½ cup of the water in a small bowl, stirring until yeast is dissolved. Set aside for 5 minutes.

Melt the vegetable shortening in a 6-quart saucepan. Remove from the heat and add the honey and remaining 4½ cups of water.

Mix the whole wheat flour, instant potatoes, dry milk, and salt. Add to the shortening and beat until smooth. Add the yeast. Beat for 10 minutes, gradually adding flour until the dough begins to pull away from the sides of the bowl.

Turn out on a lightly floured surface. Knead for 8 to 10 minutes, until dough is smooth and elastic, adding flour as necessary to prevent stickiness.

Lightly oil a large bowl. Place dough in bowl and turn to coat on all sides. Cover with plastic wrap and let rise in a warm, draft-free place until doubled in bulk—about 30 minutes.

Grease two 9 × 5-inch loaf pans.

Punch down the dough. Turn out on a lightly floured surface. Divide in half, shape into loaves, and place in the pans. Cover with a tea towel and let rise until doubled in bulk—about 1 hour.

Preheat the oven to 400 degrees. Bake for about 50 minutes. Transfer to a wire rack to cool.

NOTE: Instead of the instant potatoes, you can use 1 cup unsalted mashed potatoes. In this case, add them earlier, mixing them in with the honey mixture.

YIELD: Two loaves

The first winter that Francis Xavier spent in Rome was very bitter and the great zealous missionary did not enjoy good health. While the fathers were out preaching, trying to rescue prostitutes, begging for food for the poor, and distributing the food to the poor, he stayed home. When the companions returned home after a hard day's work, he had toasted pieces of bread waiting for them so they would have some nourishment.

Shredded Wheat Bread

My father was a dentist and a very sophisticated man of medicine, but he had many simple home remedies. He thought that most things on the exterior of the body could be cured with bicarbonate of soda; internally, shredded wheat could do it all. One of his patients gave this recipe to him and he passed it on to me. I would often bake it for him. It makes wonderful toast, but I'm not sure it cures anything.

2¾ cups boiling water
3 large shredded wheat biscuits
1 tablespoon salt
3 tablespoons butter
½ cup molasses
¼ cup honey
1 tablespoon active dry yeast
¼ cup warm water
8 cups unbleached all-purpose flour

Pour the boiling water over the shredded wheat in a large bowl. Add the salt, butter, molasses, and honey. Cool to lukewarm.

Combine the yeast and warm water in a small bowl, stirring until yeast is dissolved. Set aside for 5 minutes.

Add the yeast to the shredded wheat mixture. Beat for 10 minutes, gradually adding flour until the dough begins to pull away from the sides of the bowl.

Turn out on a lightly floured surface. Knead for 8 to 10 minutes, until dough is smooth and elastic, adding flour as necessary to prevent stickiness.

Lightly oil a large bowl. Place dough in bowl and turn to coat on all sides.

Cover with plastic wrap and let rise in a warm, draft-free place until doubled in bulk—about 1½ hours.

Grease three 9 × 5-inch loaf pans.

Punch down the dough. Cover and let rise until doubled in bulk—about 45 minutes. Turn out again and knead gently for about 2 minutes. Divide into three equal portions, shape into loaves, and place in the pans. Cover with a tea towel and let rise until doubled in bulk—about 30 minutes.

Preheat the oven to 400 degrees. Bake for 35 to 40 minutes, until brown. Transfer to a wire rack to cool.

YIELD: Three loaves

COMMON RULE

2

*T*here should be a proper order, as far as may be possible, for the time of eating, sleeping, and rising, and ordinarily all should observe it.

ST. NICHOLAS OWEN

—

$\mathcal{A}$mong the English martyrs of the sixteenth and seventeenth centuries, St. Nicholas Owen is unique. He was a mason and carpenter by trade and used his talents in the service of the persecuted church. He devised and constructed hiding places, called priest holes, in various mansions used as priest centers throughout England. He always worked alone in total secrecy with only the owner of the house aware of his presence. Some of these priests holes were big enough to accommodate six to ten people.

Eventually, Brother Owen was forced to hide in one of his own concealed rooms. But he was captured with three other Jesuits on January 20, 1606. They were taken to the Tower of London and gruesomely tortured. Nicholas Owen was beatified by Pius XI on December 15, 1929, and was canonized by Paul VI on October 25, 1970. We celebrate his feast on December 1, the same day that we commemorate twenty-five other Jesuits who died in martyrdom in England and Wales.

Swedish Rye Bread

Brother Stanley Leikus was plant manager at my high school, St. Joseph's Prep School, in Philadelphia. Nothing would have worked in our hundred-year-old building without his supervision. He knew automobiles, electricity, heating—he ran the whole show. He often baked this Swedish rye bread.

1 tablespoon active dry yeast
2 cups warm water
1 cup scalded milk, cooled to lukewarm
½ cup molasses
5 cups rye flour
1 tablespoon butter, melted
1 tablespoon caraway seeds
1 teaspoon flaxseed
1 tablespoon salt
1 to 1½ cups unbleached all-purpose flour
Cornmeal

To make the sponge, combine the yeast and ¼ cup of the warm water in a large bowl. Stir until yeast is dissolved. Stir in the milk, molasses, and the remaining 1¾ cups of the water. Gradually add 2½ cups of the rye flour and beat for 3 minutes. Cover with plastic wrap and let rise in a warm, draft-free place until doubled in bulk—about 3 hours.

Add the butter, caraway seeds, flaxseed, and salt. Beat vigorously, gradually adding all the all-purpose flour and enough of the rye flour until the dough pulls away from the sides of the bowl—about 10 minutes.

Turn out on a lightly floured surface. Knead for 8 to 10 minutes, until dough is smooth and elastic, adding flour as necessary to prevent stickiness.

(continued)

Lightly oil a large bowl. Place dough in bowl and turn to coat on all sides. Cover with plastic wrap and let rise in a warm, draft-free place until doubled in bulk—a good 1½ hours.

Preheat the oven to 375 degrees. Grease a baking sheet and sprinkle with cornmeal or line one with kitchen parchment.

Punch down the dough. Divide in half, shape into torpedolike loaves, and place on the baking sheet. Make slashes every 2 inches on the tops of the loaves. Cover with a tea towel and let rise until doubled in bulk—about 45 minutes.

Bake for 45 to 50 minutes. Transfer to a wire rack to cool.

YIELD: Two loaves

Pumpernickel bread actually grew out of necessity when there was a shortage of wheat flour during the nineteenth century. A Swiss baker named Pumper Nickel stretched his limited amount of wheat flour available for his bread by combining it with pumpernickel flour, which is milled from rye grain.

I'm always rather touched by the invention of pumpernickel bread. The purpose of religious poverty in the Jesuits is that we should try hard to limit rather than expand consumption. Curiously in proceedings of our Jesuit life, the last general congregation said that we should be animated by the spirit of poverty and that this poverty should be filled with activity by which we resemble men who must earn their daily bread. It should be equitable and just, ordered in the first place to give each one his due. Finally, it should be generous so that by our labor we may help our poor houses, our works, and the poor. Actually, the spirit of poverty should animate us in our prayer to be happy to share with each other and with all. I certainly think Mr. Pumper Nickel had this spirit in his invention.

Brother Andrews's Pumpernickel Bread

When I first arrived in New York City, Brother Steve Andrews was the minister at St. Francis Xavier High School on Sixteenth Street. He informed me there was only one kind of bread and it was the New York pumpernickel with raisins.

1 cup dark raisins

1 cup boiling water

1½ tablespoons unsweetened cocoa powder

2 tablespoons instant coffee granules

1 tablespoon active dry yeast

1½ cups warm water

1 tablespoon sugar

3 cups bread flour

2 cups rye flour

2 cups whole wheat flour

½ cup molasses

2 teaspoons salt

1 tablespoon yellow cornmeal

FOR THE GLAZE

1 large egg white

1 tablespoon water

Soak the raisins in ½ cup of the boiling water for 30 minutes. Drain well.

Dissolve the cocoa powder and coffee granules in the remaining ½ cup of boiling water. Set aside.

Combine the yeast and the 1½ cups warm water in a large bowl. Add the sugar and stir until dissolved. Set aside for 5 minutes.

Mix 2 cups of the bread flour, the rye flour, and the whole wheat flour, 1 cup at a time. Add the molasses.

Combine the flour and yeast mixtures. Beat for 10 minutes, gradually adding flour until the dough begins to pull away from the sides of the bowl. Cover with a tea towel and let rest for 20 minutes.

Add the raisins, cocoa mixture, and salt to the dough. Turn out on a lightly floured surface and knead for 5 to 10 minutes, until smooth and elastic, adding more bread flour as needed to prevent stickiness.

Lightly oil a large bowl. Place dough in bowl and turn to coat on all sides. Cover with plastic wrap and let rise in a warm, draft-free place until doubled in bulk—about 2 hours.

Grease a baking sheet and sprinkle with cornmeal or line one with kitchen parchment.

Punch down the dough. Divide in half, shape into round loaves, and place on the baking sheet. Cover with a tea towel and let rise again until doubled in bulk—about 1 hour.

Place the oven rack in the lower third of the oven. Preheat the oven to 435 degrees.

Prepare the glaze by combining the egg white and water. Slash the tops of the loaves and brush loaves with the glaze. Bake 35 to 40 minutes, until the loaves are dark brown. Transfer to a wire rack to cool.

YIELD: Two loaves

Oatmeal Bannocks

The Sister in the kitchen at Poor Clare Monastery gave me this recipe for oatmeal bannocks. They are sconelike and great with lots of butter and jam.

2½ to 3 cups unbleached all-purpose flour
⅓ cup sugar
¾ teaspoon salt
1 cup old-fashioned rolled oats
2 tablespoons active dry yeast
½ cup milk
½ cup water
4 tablespoons butter
1 egg
½ cup currants

Combine ¾ cup of the flour, the sugar, salt, oats, and yeast in a large bowl. Mix thoroughly.

Combine the milk, water, and butter in a saucepan. Cook over low heat until liquids are warm. Butter does not need to melt completely. Add milk mixture to the flour mixture and beat for 5 minutes. Add the egg and ½ cup flour. Beat for another 5 minutes, gradually adding flour until the dough begins to pull away from the sides of the bowl.

Turn out on a lightly floured surface. Knead for 8 to 10 minutes, until dough is smooth and elastic, adding flour as necessary to prevent stickiness.

Lightly oil a large bowl. Place dough in bowl and turn to coat on all sides. Cover with plastic wrap and let rise in a warm, draft-free place until doubled in bulk—about 45 minutes.

Grease two 8-inch round cake pans.

Punch down the dough. Gently knead in the currants. Divide the dough in half and roll each half into an 8-inch circle. Put in the pans. Make 8 wedges, cutting like a pie, but not completely through to the bottom.

Cover with a tea towel and let rise again until doubled in bulk—about 30 minutes. Preheat the oven to 375 degrees.

Bake for 20 minutes. Remove from the pans and cool on wire racks.

YIELD: *Sixteen wedges*

The relationship between religious Brothers and religious Sisters has always been strong, particularly among cloistered communities. When I was a guest of Loyola University in New Orleans, I was invited to spend some time with a friend of mine, Sister Courtney, who was a very accomplished potter, and a member of the cloistered Poor Clare Monastery on Magazine Street. I was invited for early morning Mass and breakfast. They had only cold cereal for themselves, but went out of their way to put on a splendid meal of bacon, eggs, and toasted bannocks for me.

number of years ago I took a four-month sabbatical in Maine, where I actually built a little sailboat that was designed by E. B. White's son, Joel. Once I built it and painted it, I had to learn how to sail it. This was really quite a magnificent experience for me.

I found the ecumenical flavor of Maine particularly exciting. Maine has a population of just about a million people and only about 150 priests. You have to be very attentive to where you are going to find your liturgy. On the beautiful Deer Isle there's a church called St. Mary's Star of the Sea, and at nine in the morning it had a Roman Catholic Liturgy performed by a Roman Catholic priest who has a wife. (He had been a member of the Church of England, had converted to Roman Catholicism, and came to Roman Catholicism as a priest and also brought his wife.) At eleven in the morning this same church becomes an Episcopalian Church, St. Brendan the Navigator, and its priest is a woman. The only thing that they change for the different services are the candlesticks. And on Holy Thursday, they share a liturgy with a Methodist minister.

The congregations from all three churches decided to have a workshop on centering prayer, which I was invited to attend. Part of the program included viewing the video tapes of Basil Pennington, the Cistercian, on centering prayer, which I was delighted to see. At the end of the workshop, I turned to the woman who invited me and thanked her for inviting me but felt compelled to ask her if she knew I was Jesuit. She said, "Oh it wouldn't matter. We take all kinds here."

Blueberry Muffins

At one of the occasions at St. Brendan the Navigator Church in Maine, the warden of the parish, Barbara Bennett, served the most delicious wild blueberry muffins that I ever tasted. This recipe is also excellent with other berries as well.

> ½ cup vegetable shortening
> ¾ cup sugar
> 2 eggs
> 2 cups unbleached all-purpose flour
> ½ teaspoon salt
> 2 teaspoons baking powder
> 2½ cups fresh blueberries (preferably wild)
> ½ cup whole milk

Preheat the oven to 375 degrees. Grease a 12-tin muffin pan.

Cream the vegetable shortening and the sugar. Add the eggs, one at a time, and mix thoroughly.

Mix the flour, salt, and baking powder in a large bowl. Add ½ cup of the blueberries. Alternately add the milk and egg mixture to the flour mixture. Stir in the remaining berries.

Pile the batter high in the muffin tins. Bake for 25 to 30 minutes. Let muffins cool for about 5 minutes in the tin and then carefully turn over on a wire rack and let cool.

YIELD: Twelve muffins

Altar Bread

On a recent trip to Deer Isle, Maine, my friend Carolyn Mor baked altar bread for a communion service the next morning at her Anglican Church, St. Brendan the Navigator. Her recipe was from the Episcopal Sisters of St. Helena from Vails Gate, New York.

1 tablespoon active dry yeast
⅞ cup lukewarm water (or a little more)
5 tablespoons honey
2½ tablespoons vegetable oil
½ teaspoon salt
2⅔ cups whole wheat flour
½ cup unbleached all-purpose flour
Cornmeal

Combine the yeast and water in a large bowl, stirring until yeast is dissolved. Add the honey, oil, and salt and set aside for 5 minutes.

Add the whole wheat flour and beat for about 5 minutes. Beat for another 5 minutes, gradually adding all-purpose flour until the dough begins to pull away from the sides of the bowl. Turn out on a lightly floured surface. Knead for 5 minutes, until dough is smooth and elastic; add flour as necessary to prevent stickiness.

Lightly butter a large bowl. Place dough in bowl and turn to coat on all sides. Cover with a damp cloth and let rise in a warm, draft-free place until doubled in bulk—about 2 hours. Divide dough into 9 rolls. Cut crosses on the tops. Cover and let rise for 20 minutes.

Preheat the oven to 375 degrees. Grease a baking sheet and sprinkle with cornmeal or line one with kitchen parchment.

Bake for 8 to 10 minutes. Transfer to a wire rack to cool.

YIELD: Nine rolls

Onion Bread

This onion bread was served at a feast at our Brothers' Spring Hill Conference in Mobile, Alabama.

1 cup milk, scalded
3 tablespoons sugar
1 tablespoon salt
1½ tablespoons oil
2 tablespoons active dry yeast
¾ cup warm water
½ cup chopped onion
6 cups unbleached all-purpose flour

Combine the milk, sugar, salt, and oil in a large bowl and cool until lukewarm.

Dissolve the yeast in warm water and stir into the milk mixture. Add the onion. Beat vigorously for 10 minutes, gradually adding about 4 cups of the flour, until the dough begins to pull away from the sides of the bowl.

Turn out on a lightly floured surface. Knead for 8 to 10 minutes, until dough is smooth and elastic, adding flour as necessary to prevent stickiness.

Lightly oil a large bowl. Place dough in bowl and turn to coat on all sides. Cover with plastic wrap and let rise in a warm, draft-free place until doubled in bulk—about 45 minutes.

Grease two 9 × 5-inch loaf pans.

Punch down the dough. Divide in half, shape into loaves, and place in the pans. Cover with a tea towel and let rise until doubled in bulk—about 20 minutes.

Preheat the oven to 350 degrees. Bake for 1 hour. Transfer to a wire rack to cool.

YIELD: Two loaves

esuits have been involved in the study of earthquakes for years and we have many seismologists and seismology centers throughout the world. One day there was a great furor at the center on the outskirts of Cincinnati in Milford, Ohio. All the scientists were hovering over the seismograph, which was recording unusual activity that they couldn't account for. Eventually, they discovered that a cow had broken through the cyclone fence that surrounded the building that housed the seismograph. The cow was rubbing up against the building and causing the seismograph to go berserk.

Zucchini Bread

In Maine I saw roadside signs that said "cukes and zukes" and had no idea what they meant, but knew I was going to have to be brave and ask someone. (A number of years before when I was in Vermont, I was mystified by the "frost heave" announcements and with a certain amount of humility had to ask the locals for an explanation. I was sure the cukes and zukes were going to be one of those things.) I asked my friend Carolyn Mor and she said cucumbers and zucchini! She also gave me this recipe.

> 3 eggs, beaten
> 1 cup vegetable oil
> 2 cups sugar
> 2 teaspoons vanilla extract
> 2 to 3 medium zucchini, unpeeled and coarsely shredded
>   (about 3 cups)
> 3 cups unbleached all-purpose flour
> 2 teaspoons baking soda
> 1 teaspoon salt
> ½ teaspoon baking powder
> ¾ teaspoon grated nutmeg
> 1 cup chopped nuts (I use walnuts)
> ½ cup currants, soaked in water for at least 10 minutes
>   and drained
> 1 can (8 ounces) crushed pineapple, drained

Preheat the oven to 350 degrees. Grease and flour two 9 × 5-inch loaf pans. Mix the eggs, vegetable oil, sugar, and vanilla for about 5 minutes, until thick and foamy. Stir in the zucchini, flour, baking soda, salt, baking powder, nutmeg, nuts, currants, and pineapple.

Pour the batter into the pans. Bake for 45 to 60 minutes. Test with a toothpick for doneness. Cool in the pans on a wire rack about 10 minutes. Remove from the pans and finish cooling.

YIELD: Two loaves

A Jesuit superior was once asked why his community seemed so happy and this superior said, "We have good food and we keep a clean house."

ather Robert Parsons wrote this letter to Father
Gonzales Del Rio, rector of the seminary at
Valladolid on May 12, 1595. Parsons, who established
many schools in Spain, was at that time the local
superior. He had much advice for the Brother baker.

Concerning the bread and the bakery—and I have
already written your reverence my views. It cost us more
than 200 ducats to install the bakery and it saved us as
much in the first year; and so I do not see why we need
throw stones at it when it is a good piece of work, and do
away with it; in fact, other Colleges in the neighborhood,
and the Seminary at Seville in particular, are thinking of
installing one very shortly, in spite of its being a rather
expensive matter. With regard to the bread, I wrote to your
Reverence that I was agreeable to its being improved,
provided that economy suitable to the poverty of the house
were observed; though former students have found no fault
with it in the past. I hear that is already improved by one
fifth, that is to say that five measures are now used for the
quantity of bread formerly made with four measures. In the
case of fifty mouths, this means bread for ten or a dozen
persons, that is more than 100 measures of bread in the
year; for 500 measures just sufficed for your house before,

and now 600 will not be enough. However, everything must be conceded so as to give satisfaction, and so I will let it pass with good favor provided nothing further is done by way of refining the flour, for it would be too great an expense. The present increase over what we spent before will cost us what would be the upkeep of two or three students; and those whose task it is to seek the means to find food for these colleges know what that means, and the great efforts it costs us to find the support of even one student. And so I beg your Reverence in all charity, as I did before, to have great care for the patrimony of your college.

Bath Buns

Brother Hodkinson of Hethrop College in England gave me his recipe for bath buns. His recipe, however, made 120 buns, enough to feed his house of Jesuits. Brother kindly broke the recipe down for me so that it makes 6 buns, enough to feed a table of Jesuits.

This is a great breakfast treat, tasty and traditional as well. The English Jesuits, of course, would save these leftovers from breakfast and have them for their 4 o'clock high tea. In America, we would put them in the coffee room for our afternoon *haustus*.

> 1 package active dry yeast
> ⅔ cup warm milk
> 1½ tablespoons sugar
> 3 cups unbleached all-purpose flour
> ½ teaspoon salt
> ¼ pound (1 stick) butter
> 2 eggs, beaten
> Cornmeal
> 3 tablespoons currants, soaked in warm water for 10
>   minutes, until plump (see note)
> 3 tablespoons candied lemon peel or grated lemon zest
> 6 sugar cubes, crushed

Combine the yeast, milk, and sugar in a small bowl, stirring until dissolved. Set aside for 5 minutes.

Sift together in a large bowl the 3 cups flour with the salt. Cut in the butter. Add the beaten egg (reserve 2 tablespoons for glazing) and the yeast mixture.

Turn out on a lightly floured surface. Knead for 8 to 10 minutes, until dough is smooth and elastic, adding flour as necessary to prevent stickiness.

Lightly oil a large bowl. Place dough in bowl and turn to coat on all sides. Cover with plastic wrap and let rise in a warm, draft-free place until doubled in bulk—about 1 hour.

Grease a baking sheet and sprinkle with cornmeal or line one with kitchen parchment.

Punch down the dough. Divide into 6 pieces, shape into buns, and place on the baking sheet. Brush the tops of each with the reserved egg and sprinkle with the currants, the lemon peel, and the crushed sugar. Cover and let rise until doubled in bulk—about 20 minutes.

Preheat the oven to 400 degrees.

Bake for 15 to 20 minutes. Transfer to a wire rack to cool.

NOTE: Soaking the currants keeps them from burning during baking.

YIELD: *Six buns*

*T*he Center for the Working Child in Tacna, Peru, which includes a bakery *(panaderia)*, is now in its seventh year. The center was started by a lay teacher, Jeff Thielman, and his students from the local Jesuit school, Cristo Rey. The original purpose was to offer the shoeshine boys a morning of organized sporting activities on the school grounds. But Jeff quickly saw that the boys needed and deserved so much more than a simple morning of sports. In 1992, the center was recognized and officially commissioned as a Jesuit mission site, offering religious formation, sacramental preparation, health care awareness, recreation, job training, nutritional assistance, and much more. With the intention of providing job training and generating money, the center includes a laundry service, mini-clothing factory, and carpentry shop, as well as the bakery.

The bakery, built by fathers and mothers of the working children, was inaugurated in 1991. It initially baked bread only for the center and for the Jesuit school. However, the bakery has risen to never imagined levels, running two separate shifts and producing more than six types of traditional breads. Rechristened *pan centro* in 1993, the bakery delivers bread twice daily to more than eight stores, which in turn sell it to the public.

Pan Maraqueta

Craig Pelcin, who works with the International Jesuit Volunteer Corps at the Center for the Working Child, sent me this recipe. It's a delicious bread, typical of Tacna, crispy on the outside and soft on the inside. It makes 1,500 rolls so you might want to break it down.

> 50 kilograms unbleached all-purpose flour
> Enough water to make a soft dough
> 480 grams active dry yeast
> 500 grams sugar
> 600 grams salt
> Baked flour

Mix the flour, water, yeast, sugar, and salt into a dough. Let the dough rise on a wood table for 2 hours.

Form small balls from the dough (35 to 40 grams). Put the balls in rows on top of a cotton cloth with folds of cloth separating the rows. The cloth rests on the wood table.

Sprinkle the rolls with flour that has been baked on a tray until it is a golden brown color.

As soon as the rolls have been separated and sprinkled with flour, put them directly in the oven. The rolls go directly onto the oven bricks—no sheet or pan needed. Bake at 400 degrees for 15 to 20 minutes.

YIELD: Fifteen hundred rolls

*F*ather Vincent J. O'Keefe, former vicar general of the Society of Jesus and former president of Fordham University, reminded me of the connection between the Italian word for bread—*compania*—and the Company of Jesus. Ignatius originally chose the name *compagnia di Gesu*, the company of Jesus. *Compania* means with bread, people coming together around bread, so in fact the roots of the original name of the Society of Jesus mean men coming around bread. The word *societas* came into use later.

Brother Brennan's Three-Seed Bread

I first met Brother Paul Brennan at an art show in Philadelphia. He was the man most responsible for my joining the Brothers.

1 tablespoon active dry yeast
2¼ cups potato water (see note)
3 cups whole wheat flour
½ cup safflower oil
¼ cup honey
½ cup poppy seeds
½ cup sesame seeds
½ cup sunflower seeds
1 teaspoon salt
1½ cups rolled oats, moistened with ¾ cup boiling water
2 cups unbleached all-purpose flour

Combine the yeast and the potato water in a large bowl, stirring until yeast is dissolved. Gradually stir in the whole wheat flour. Cover with plastic wrap and let ferment for about 20 minutes. (You're making a bit of a starter.)

Add the safflower oil, honey, poppy seeds, sesame seeds, sunflower seeds, salt, and rolled oats. Beat vigorously for 10 minutes, gradually adding 1½ to 2 cups of the all-purpose flour until dough begins to pull away from the sides of the bowl.

Turn out on a lightly floured surface. Knead for 10 to 15 minutes, until dough is smooth and elastic, adding flour as necessary to prevent stickiness.

Lightly oil a large bowl. Place dough in bowl and turn to coat on all sides.

(continued)

Cover with plastic wrap and let rise in a warm, draft-free place until doubled in bulk—about 1 hour.

Preheat the oven to 350 degrees. Grease two 9 × 5-inch pans.

Punch down the dough. Divide dough in half, shape into loaves, and place in the pans. Cover with a tea towel and let rise until doubled in bulk—about 30 minutes. Bake for 45 to 50 minutes. Transfer loaves to a wire rack to cool.

NOTE: A simple way of making potato water is to peel a potato, cover with water, and boil for 15 to 20 minutes. Reserve the water from the boiled potato.

VARIATION

For a more festive, fruity bread, Brother Brennan would substitute 1½ cups raisins and 1½ tablespoons of cinnamon for the poppy, sesame, and sunflower seeds. He would also reduce the oil to ¼ cup.

YIELD: Two loaves

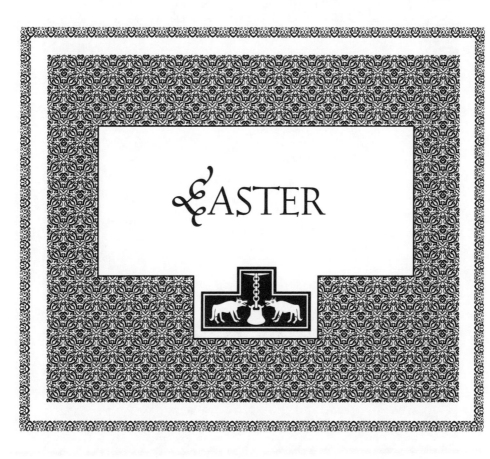

EASTER

*Eat your bread with joy and
drink with merry heart,
because it is now that
God favors your works.*

—MOUNT ST. MARY'S ABBEY,
WRENTHAM, MASSACHUSETTS

oly Week is the most solemn time of the year, but it culminates in the greatest celebration, too. Christ is risen! This is a happy moment. It's the core of our belief—either you believe in the resurrection of Christ or you don't. Holy Week passes very quickly as the momentous events in the life of Jesus happened very quickly. He was fingered, arrested, tried, and crucified in a very short period of time.

At the novitiate, it was a week of extra work, chapel all the time, and total silence from Spy Wednesday until we broke the fast at 12:30 Easter morning. By Easter day, we were churched out and absolutely exhausted.

Kitchen for me has always been a sacred place, where confidences were exchanged, our family life took place, where all the great decisions that my parents had talked about somewhere at some time were finally announced. Scenes of conflict, sorrow, and great joy, and most of all comfort, fill my memory. I try to extend this into my Jesuit life and make my kitchen a place of great warmth for family and friends, who inevitably end up there when they visit. Sharing food and drink is one of the oldest rituals in the world, and one that Jesus blessed in the Last Supper. And, over the years, I've discovered how important bread is in cultures that celebrate Easter much more than we do. In fact, in many of those cultures, bread is synonymous with Easter.

Brioche

Father Frank Burch took me on a gastronomic tour of Paris and introduced me to my first brioche. The Jesuit Community at Rue de Grenelle provided me with this recipe.

FOR THE BRIOCHE

> 1 tablespoon active dry yeast
> ¼ cup warm water
> ¼ pound (1 stick) butter
> 2 tablespoons sugar
> ½ teaspoon salt
> 3 eggs plus 1 egg yolk
> ½ cup warm milk
> 3¼ to 3½ cups unbleached all-purpose flour

FOR THE EGG GLAZE

> 1 egg yolk
> 1 tablespoon milk

Combine the yeast and water in a small bowl, stirring until dissolved. Set aside for 5 minutes.

Cream the butter in a large bowl. Add the sugar, salt, eggs, and egg yolk and mix thoroughly. Add the milk and the yeast mixture. Beat for 10 minutes, gradually adding flour until the dough begins to pull away from the sides of the bowl.

Turn out on a lightly floured surface. Knead for 8 to 10 minutes, until dough is smooth and elastic, adding flour as necessary to prevent stickiness.

Lightly oil a large bowl. Place dough in bowl and turn to coat on all sides. Cover with plastic wrap and let rise in a warm, draft-free place until doubled in bulk—about 1 hour.

THE SECRETS OF JESUIT BREADMAKING

Grease a 2-quart brioche pan.

Punch down the dough. Turn out again and gently knead for 2 minutes. Cut off one fifth of the dough and set aside. Shape the remaining dough into a ball and place in the pan. Cut an X in the top of the dough with scissors. Shape the reserved dough into a tear drop and place the pointed end into the X. Cover with a tea towel and let rise until doubled in bulk—about 30 minutes.

Preheat the oven to 375 degrees.

To make the egg glaze, mix the egg yolk with the milk. Brush loaf with the glaze. Bake for 30 to 35 minutes. Transfer to a wire rack to cool.

VARIATION

Divide the dough into 3 ropes and braid. Sprinkle poppy seeds or sesame seeds on the top of the braid. Bake for 30 to 35 minutes on a greased baking sheet.

YIELD: One large loaf

RAPHAEL BANDERA

—

Brother Raphael Bandera is a very famous Jesuit from Malaga, Spain, who has been stationed at the Curia, the Jesuit headquarters in Rome, for many years. As infirmarian, he would find out from which native land the Jesuits under his care came and try to create a native dish or bread for them. As a result, the Jesuit Curia served breads from all over the world.

Brother Bandera gave me many recipes, but none called for whole wheat flour. When I asked him if he ever used it he looked very offended and hurt. I was sure I had said something wrong. But he explained that in Italy, whole wheat is traditionally bread for the poor and he would never serve whole wheat bread nor give it to the poor. It would remind them of their poverty and he would feel he was giving them inferior bread.

Focaccia

Τhis is a basic but terrific focaccia recipe that Brother Bandera introduced me to. I wrote this recipe down while watching him make this bread, but it wasn't easy. Brother worked very quickly and wasn't about to slow down for me. He speaks six languages all very quickly and equally terribly and I'm sure he was mixing up languages that day as well as ingredients.

2 tablespoons active dry yeast
½ cup warm water
4 cups unbleached all-purpose flour
¼ cup olive oil
1 teaspoon salt
Pinch of coarse ground pepper
Pinch of dried oregano
Pinch of sage
Pinch of dried marjoram
Cornmeal

Combine the yeast and water in a small bowl, stirring until yeast is dissolved. Set aside for 5 minutes.

Sift the flour into a slightly warm bowl and make a well in the middle of the flour. Gently fold in the yeast. Cover with plastic wrap and let rest in a warm, draft-free place for 20 minutes.

Turn out on a lightly floured surface. Knead for 8 to 10 minutes, until dough is smooth and elastic, adding flour as necessary to prevent stickiness.

Lightly oil a large bowl. Place dough in bowl and turn to coat on all sides. Cover with plastic wrap and let rise in a warm, draft-free place until doubled in bulk—1 to 2 hours.

(continued)

Punch down the dough. Turn out again and gently knead in the olive oil, salt, pepper, and herbs.

Grease a baking sheet and sprinkle with cornmeal or line one with kitchen parchment.

Roll out on a floured surface into a ½-inch-thick rectangle. Place on the baking sheet, cover with a tea towel, and let rise until doubled in bulk—for 20 minutes.

Preheat the oven to 425 degrees. Prick the surface with a fork and sprinkle lightly with salt and pepper and more herbs. Bake for 10 minutes and reduce the oven temperature to 375 degrees. Bake another 20 minutes. Transfer to a wire rack to cool.

YIELD: One loaf; serves six

Brother Bandera's Italian Bread

Brother Bandera let me know that Italian bread first of all is work. He said it's really the most difficult to knead of almost any bread. This recipe makes a dry dough, but it bakes into a deliciously moist bread.

> 2 tablespoons active dry yeast
> 1 tablespoon honey
> 2 cups hot water
> 4 teaspoons salt
> ¼ cup plus 1 tablespoon extra virgin olive oil
> 8 to 9 cups unbleached all-purpose flour
> ¼ cup yellow cornmeal

Combine the yeast, honey, water, and salt in a large mixing bowl and stir until the yeast and salt are dissolved. Stir in ¼ cup olive oil. Beat 10 minutes, gradually adding about 6 cups of the flour until the dough begins to pull away from the sides of the bowl.

Turn out on a lightly floured surface. Knead for 8 to 10 minutes, until dough is smooth and elastic, adding flour as necessary to prevent stickiness.

Lightly grease a large bowl with the 1 remaining tablespoon olive oil. Place dough in bowl and turn to coat on all sides. Cover with plastic wrap and let rise in a warm, draft-free place until doubled in bulk—about 1½ hours.

Punch down the dough. Turn out again and knead gently for 2 minutes. Divide into three balls and flatten each ball with a rolling pin into a rectangle approximately 10 × 12 inches. Roll each rectangle into a torpedo shape. Start from the longer side of the rectangle and roll tightly, pinching each time you turn the dough into itself to make certain that there are no air spaces. Pinch the seams closed, rolling them back and forth a little bit to be certain. Pinch the ends closed and tuck them under.

(continued)

Grease two baking sheets and sprinkle with cornmeal or line them with kitchen parchment.

Place the loaves on the baking sheets, seams and tuck sides down. Make three 1-inch-deep diagonal slashes evenly spaced across the loaf. Mist with water until they are really wet. Cover with tea towels and let rise until doubled in bulk—about 45 minutes. When risen, the slashes will gape wide.

Mist the bread again. Place in a cold oven set at 375 degrees. Bake for 30 to 40 minutes. During the baking, spray the loaves a couple more times—at the 10-minute mark and the 15-minute mark. Transfer to a wire rack to cool. If you want the crust to crackle, let the bread cool in front of a window or cool fan.

VARIATION

Brother Bandera would also serve this bread for breakfast and would let it have its first rise in the refrigerator overnight. (It can stay in there longer, but it shouldn't stay more than 24 hours.) He would take it from the refrigerator, punch it down, shape it into loaves, and bake it.

YIELD: Three loaves

MADAME DUCHESNE

Madame Duchesne (she is now a Saint) was a Sister of the order of the Religious Sacred Heart, stationed in Florissant, Missouri, in the late 1700s—a real pioneer woman, establishing schools for girls. During that same period, a Jesuit priest named Father Van Quickenborn came to Florissant with some novices to establish a novitiate. The first winter he and his men spent there was bitter cold and they were ill-prepared for their harsh circumstances. They were short of food and clothing and most of them had fallen ill. Madame Duchesne and her companions were much better prepared and in fact had food to spare. Out of compassion for the Jesuit novices, she baked a cherry pie for Van Quickenborn and his men. But when offered the pie, in a show of total male arrogance and stupidity, he banished her from the novitiate, saying he would have no female interference.

Sister's Herb Bread

When we were making the movie in Umbria, we stayed in a convent with the sisters at Citti di Costello. Sister made this tasty bread, and when I asked her what kind it was, I thought she was saying garden bread because she simply pointed to the garden. But in fact she was pointing to the fresh herbs in the garden.

> *1 package active dry yeast*
> *2 cups warm water*
> *3 to 4 cups unbleached all-purpose flour*
> *1 cup cornmeal, plus additional for dusting*
> *1 cup rye flour*
> *Chopped handfuls of oregano, basil, and sage—less than*
> *   ½ cup total*
> *2 tablespoons olive oil*
> *1 teaspoon salt*
> *1 cup whole wheat flour*

Combine the yeast and water in a large bowl, stirring until yeast is dissolved. Set aside for 5 minutes.

Stir in about 2 cups of the unbleached all-purpose flour, all of the cornmeal, and all of the rye flour. Beat vigorously for about 2 minutes. Add the herbs. Cover with plastic wrap and set aside for about an hour.

Beat the oil, salt, and whole wheat flour into the flour mixture. Continue to beat for 10 minutes, gradually adding all-purpose flour until the dough begins to pull away from the sides of the bowl.

Turn out on a lightly floured surface. Knead for 8 to 10 minutes, until dough is smooth and elastic, adding all-purpose flour as necessary to prevent stickiness.

Lightly oil a large bowl. Place dough in bowl and turn to coat on all sides. Cover with plastic wrap and let rise in a warm, draft-free place until doubled in bulk—about 30 minutes.

Preheat the oven to 400 degrees. Grease a baking sheet and sprinkle with cornmeal or line one with kitchen parchment.

Punch down the dough. Turn out again and knead gently for 2 minutes. Divide in half, shape into torpedolike loaves, and put on the baking sheets. Dust the tops with cornmeal. Cover with a tea towel and let rise until doubled in bulk—another 40 minutes. Make three diagonal slashes on the tops. Brush with water and bake for 30 to 35 minutes. Sister tested them regularly because she wanted them to have a certain crust. She put them on a wire rack but served them almost immediately.

YIELD: Two loaves

George Coyne, S.J., a Jesuit with a Ph.D. in astronomy, was sent to Rome to head the Vatican Observatory. One night he was working alone at the observatory and heard a door open. Not expecting anyone, he went to check on who this intruder might be. Standing in the hallway was Pope John Paul II. The Pope's summer residence is right next to the Observatory and he had strolled over to look at the Heavens.

Flat Italian Onion Bread

Susan Abbot and her husband, John, invited me to their home in Umbria, Castello di Polgeto. John is an architect and a very good cook. He shared with me one of his favorite recipes.

FOR THE BREAD

>   1 package active dry yeast
>   1 cup warm water
>   2 tablespoons honey
>   2 tablespoons olive oil
>   ½ teaspoon salt
>   4 cups bread flour
>   Cornmeal

FOR THE ONION TOPPING

>   2 tablespoons butter
>   2 tablespoons olive oil (more might be needed)
>   2 medium onions, thinly sliced and separated into rings
>   1 teaspoon chopped dried sage

Combine the yeast and water in a small bowl, stirring until dissolved. Add 1 tablespoon of the honey. Set aside for 5 minutes.

Mix in the remaining tablespoon of honey, the oil, and salt. Beat vigorously for 10 minutes, gradually adding flour until dough begins to pull away from the sides of the bowl.

Turn out on a lightly floured surface. Knead for 15 minutes, until dough is smooth and elastic, adding flour as necessary to prevent stickiness.

Lightly oil a large bowl. Place dough in bowl and turn to coat on all sides.

THE SECRETS OF JESUIT BREADMAKING

Cover with plastic wrap and let rise in a warm, draft-free place until doubled in bulk—about 1 hour.

Punch down the dough. Turn out again, cover with a tea towel, and let rest for 10 minutes.

While waiting for this last rise, sauté the onions in a skillet with the melted butter and olive oil until translucent. Add chopped sage, put aside and let cool.

Preheat the oven to 425 degrees. Grease a baking sheet or pizza pan and sprinkle with cornmeal.

Divide the dough in half. Roll into two 12-inch circles. Brush circles with oil from the frying pan and spoon half of the onion topping on each piece. Let stand until the dough looks puffy—about 15 minutes.

Bake for about 20 minutes. Cut into wedges like a pizza and serve hot.

VARIATION

Throw cheese on it, olives, or any kind of topping that sounds good to you.

YIELD: *Two loaves*

COMMON RULE

*I*t is not in keeping with poverty for Jesuits (Ours) to travel with several trunks.

Prosciutto Bread

osalie Mundo Breslin is married to a former novice who was my best
friend at Wernersville, Michael Breslin. This is her family's recipe.

> *1 package active dry yeast*
> *1½ cups water*
> *3 cups unbleached all-purpose flour*
> *½ teaspoon salt*
> *Cornmeal*
> *5 or 6 thin slices prosciutto, chopped into 1-inch-square*
> * pieces (about ½ cup lightly packed)*
> *Olive oil*

Combine the yeast and ¼ cup of the water in a large bowl, stirring until yeast
is dissolved. Set aside for 5 minutes.

Add 2 cups of the flour, the rest of the water, and the salt. Beat for 10 minutes, gradually adding flour until the dough begins to pull away from the sides of
the bowl.

Turn out on a lightly floured surface. Knead for 8 to 10 minutes, until
dough is smooth and elastic, adding flour as necessary to prevent stickiness.

Lightly oil a large bowl. Place dough in bowl and turn to coat on all sides.
Cover with plastic wrap and let rise in a warm, draft-free place until doubled in
bulk—about 1½ hours.

Grease a baking sheet and sprinkle with cornmeal or line one with kitchen
parchment.

Punch down the dough. Turn out again and press into a ½-inch-thick rectangle. Work into a tight round ball. Cover with tea towel and let rise until doubled in bulk—about 30 minutes.

To incorporate the prosciutto, flatten the dough, layer some prosciutto over the dough, and gently knead it in. Repeat this process until all the prosciutto has been incorporated. (The prosciutto will start popping out of the dough when it's well incorporated.) Shape into a loaf and place on the baking sheet. Cover with a tea towel and let rise until doubled in bulk—about 1 hour.

Preheat the oven to 400 degrees. Brush the loaf with olive oil and make three diagonal slashes. Bake for 20 minutes.

YIELD: One loaf

Jesuit Easter Bread

This recipe for Jesuit Easter bread was given to me by Brother Joseph Fee, S.J., at Loyola College in Baltimore. Brother Fee was in charge of the altar boys at the Church of the Gesu in the 1950s and was such a good example to them that many claim his influence as the reason they entered the priesthood and the religious life.

> 3 tablespoons active dry yeast
> 8 cups unbleached all-purpose flour
> ½ cup wheat bran
> ½ cup raisins, soaked and drained
> ½ cup finely chopped apricots
> 1 cup chopped walnuts
> 1 cup brown sugar
> 2 tablespoons sea salt
> 1 tablespoon ground cinnamon
> ½ cup low-fat buttermilk
> 1½ cups water (see note)

Combine the yeast, flour, wheat bran, raisins, apricots, walnuts, brown sugar, salt, and cinnamon in a large bowl. Add the buttermilk. Beat vigorously for 10 minutes, gradually adding enough water to form a kneadable dough.

Turn out onto a lightly floured surface. Knead for 8 to 10 minutes, until dough is smooth and elastic, adding flour as necessary to prevent stickiness.

Lightly oil a large bowl. Place dough in the bowl and turn to coat on all sides. Cover with plastic wrap and let rise in a warm, draft-free place until doubled in bulk—about 1½ hours.

Grease two 9 x 5-inch loaf pans.

Divide in half, shape into loaves, and place in the pans. Cover with a tea towel and let rise in a warm, draft-free place until doubled in bulk—about 45 minutes.

Preheat the oven to 300 degrees. Bake for 45 minutes. Transfer to a wire rack to cool.

NOTE: This is a crazy recipe in that the amount of water can vary drastically. One day it may take 1½ cups of water and on another day, 3 cups.

Yield: Two loaves

After Holy Saturday night Mass, we went into the dining room where an unbelievable amount of quick breads were put out for us. But there was also an arrangement of ethnic Easter breads. The Brothers from various cultures had each contributed their special Easter loaf to the event. Years later I learned that these Brothers spent part of Good Friday and Holy Saturday in the bakery celebrating their own ethnic history by baking traditional breads from their homes. As a result, Easter became a nationalistic holiday, a patriotic waving of the flag—or, in this case, bread. Each proud Brother would hover around us as we ate, wanting to know which bread we liked the best and hoping of course that our favorite was his.

Loyola Center's Easter Bread

Compliments of Brother Fitzgerald.

½ tablespoon active dry yeast
4 tablespoons warm water
½ cup skim milk
2 tablespoons butter
2 tablespoons sugar
½ teaspoon salt
2 to 2½ cups unbleached all-purpose flour
½ teaspoon ground cardamom
1 egg
Cornmeal
1 raw egg dyed red with Easter dye
Milk
Sugar

Combine the yeast and water in a small bowl, stirring until dissolved. Set aside for 5 minutes.

Heat the milk, butter, sugar, and salt. Cool to warm.

Combine 2 cups of the flour, the yeast, milk mixture, and cardamom in a large bowl. Add the egg. Beat for 10 minutes, gradually adding flour until the dough begins to pull away from the sides of the bowl.

Turn out on a lightly floured surface. Knead for 8 to 10 minutes, until dough is smooth and elastic, adding flour as necessary to prevent stickiness.

Lightly oil a large bowl. Place dough in bowl and turn to coat on all sides. Cover with plastic wrap and let rise in a warm, draft-free place until doubled in bulk—about 1 hour.

Grease a baking sheet and sprinkle with cornmeal or line one with kitchen parchment.

Punch down the dough. Divide into thirds. Roll each piece into a 15-inch rope and braid. Place on the baking sheet. Put the raw dyed egg in the center of the braid (see note). Cover with a tea towel and let rise in a warm, draft-free place until doubled in bulk—about 30 minutes.

Preheat the oven to 350 degrees.

Brush braid with milk and sprinkle with sugar. Bake for about 40 minutes. Cool on a wire rack.

NOTE: I don't put the egg in until after the bread is baked because, as the bread rises, the egg gets knocked. Also, when I do braid this dough, I shape it into a circle and put the egg in the center as if it were in a nest. The egg, of course, in the center symbolizes the resurrection of Christ.

YIELD: One loaf

Polish Easter Bread

Brother Leikus gave me this Polish Easter bread.

1 package active dry yeast
¼ cup warm water
¼ pound (1 stick) butter
½ cup honey
4 egg yolks plus 1 egg yolk, beaten
1 teaspoon salt
1 tablespoon grated lemon rind
4 cups unbleached all-purpose flour
1 cup scalded milk, cooled
1 cup raisins

Combine the yeast and water in a small bowl, stirring until yeast is dissolved. Set aside for 5 minutes.

Cream butter and honey in a large bowl. In another bowl, beat the 4 egg yolks and salt until thick. Add these egg yolks to the butter mixture. Stir in the yeast, lemon rind, and 2 cups of the flour. Beat for 10 minutes, alternately adding the milk and additional flour until the dough begins to pull away from the sides of the bowl. Stir in the raisins.

Turn out on a lightly floured surface. Knead for 5 minutes, until dough is smooth and elastic, adding flour as necessary to prevent stickiness.

Lightly oil a large bowl. Place dough in bowl and turn to coat on all sides. Cover with plastic wrap and let rise in a warm, draft-free place until doubled in bulk—a good 1½ hours.

Punch down the dough and let rise again for another hour.

THE SECRETS OF JESUIT BREADMAKING

Preheat the oven to 350 degrees. Grease a 10-inch fluted tube pan or 1 large 12 × 5-inch loaf pan.

Turn out again. Shape into one long roll or divide into three sections, rolled into equal lengths and braided. Place in the pan and brush the top with the remaining egg yolk.

Bake for 30 minutes. Transfer to a wire rack to cool.

YIELD: One loaf

COMMON RULE

—

Our brothers do not wear the Roman collar. At home they wear the cassock, unless the nature of their work interferes. When they go out of the house, they wear a black suit of modest cut.

139. Let superiors see to it that all are provided with the clothing that they need, taking into consideration both our state of poverty and the variety demanded by differences in climate. Let subjects take care not to have more clothing than they need, or clothing that is not suitable for religious men.

Brother Bandera's
Italian Easter Bread

Brother Bandera served this at the Curia in Rome every Easter.

FOR THE BREAD

4½ cups flour
1 tablespoon active dry yeast
1 teaspoon salt
½ cup sugar
½ teaspoon nutmeg (preferably freshly ground)
¼ teaspoon allspice
½ teaspoon grated lemon peel
⅔ cup skim milk
3 tablespoons butter
3 eggs, lightly beaten
⅓ cup chopped fruit peel

FOR THE EGG WASH

1 egg
1 tablespoon water

Combine 2½ cups of the flour, the yeast, salt, sugar, nutmeg, allspice, and lemon peel in a large bowl.

Warm the milk and butter in a saucepan until the butter is melted. Stir to melt the butter. Add the milk mixture to the flour mixture. Stir in the eggs. Beat vigorously for 10 minutes, gradually adding flour until the dough begins to pull away from the sides of the bowl.

Turn out on a lightly floured surface. Flatten dough and knead in the fruit peel. Knead for 8 to 10 minutes, until dough is smooth and elastic, adding flour as necessary to prevent stickiness.

Lightly oil a large bowl. Place dough in the bowl and turn to coat on all sides. Cover with plastic wrap and let rise in a warm, draft-free place until doubled in bulk—about 1 hour.

Oil a 10-inch-round cake pan

Punch down the dough. Divide into 4 pieces, roll each into a tight ball, and place in the cake pan. Cover with a tea towel and let rise again until doubled in bulk—about 30 minutes.

Preheat the oven to 350 degrees. To make the wash, beat the egg with the water. Lightly brush on the top of the dough.

Bake about 45 minutes, until nicely browned. Transfer to a wire rack to cool.

YIELD: One loaf

Cologne Coffee Cake

Hermann Breulmann, S.J., a German Jesuit who with his colleague, Eva Marie Streier, made a film on our Theatre Workshop a number of years ago, was my host in Cologne. While I was there he made this bread for me. It's a walnut coffee bread and he baked it in an angel food cake pan.

> 1 package active dry yeast
> ¼ cup warm water
> ½ cup sugar
> ¾ cup warm milk
> 1 teaspoon salt
> 1 teaspoon vanilla extract
> ¼ pound (1 stick) butter
> 3½ to 4 cups unbleached all-purpose flour
> 3 egg yolks

FOR THE WALNUT FILLING

> 2 cups chopped walnuts
> ½ cup sugar
> 1½ teaspoons ground cinnamon
> 1 teaspoon vanilla extract
> 4 tablespoons butter, melted
> 1 egg, slightly beaten

FOR THE ICING

> 1 cup confectioners' sugar
> ¼ teaspoon vanilla extract
> 1 teaspoon butter
> 1½ to 2 tablespoons warm water

Combine the yeast and water in a large bowl. Add 1 tablespoon of the sugar and stir until dissolved. Set aside for 5 minutes.

Add the milk, the remaining sugar, salt, vanilla, and butter. Add 2 cups of the flour and beat vigorously for 5 minutes. Add the egg yolks, one at a time. Beat for another 5 minutes, gradually adding flour until the dough begins to pull away from the sides of the bowl.

Turn out on a lightly floured surface. Knead for 12 minutes, until dough is smooth and elastic, adding flour as necessary to prevent stickiness.

Lightly oil a large bowl. Place dough in bowl and turn to coat on all sides. Cover with plastic wrap and let rise in a warm, draft-free place until doubled in bulk—about 1¼ hours.

To make the walnut filling, spread the walnuts in a shallow pan and bake at 375 degrees until they are golden brown and smell fragrant. (Baking the walnuts takes some of the bitterness out of them and leaves a sweet flavor.) Let them cool slightly. Finely chop the walnuts in a food processor or blender. Reserve 1 tablespoon of the walnuts for decoration.

Combine the sugar and cinnamon in a medium bowl. Mix in the walnuts, vanilla, and butter. Blend in the egg.

Punch down the dough. Cover with a tea towel and let it rest for 10 minutes.

Grease a 10-inch angel food cake pan.

Turn out again and roll into a 15-inch square. Spread the surface with walnut filling, leaving a 1-inch margin on all sides. Roll like a jelly roll and pinch the ends to seal them. Cut the roll into 1-inch slices.

Place the slices on edge in the cake pan, overlapping the slices. Press the slices into both the outside and inside edges of the pan. Cover with a tea towel and let rise until almost doubled in bulk—about 45 minutes.

Preheat the oven to 375 degrees. Bake for about 40 minutes. Cool in the pans on a wire rack for about 10 minutes. Remove from the pans and finish cooling.

To make the icing, combine the sugar, vanilla, and butter. Gradually blend in the water until the icing is smooth and a good consistency for drizzling. Put it in a pastry bag and drizzle on bread when cool. Sprinkle the reserved walnuts on top of the icing.

YIELD: One cake; serves eight

FRANCIS GARATE

———

Francis Garate was born in 1857 and grew up next to the castle where Ignatius had lived as a boy. As a young Brother, Garate was an infirmarian and tirelessly worked at the College of La Guardia near the Portuguese border for ten years. He spent the next forty-one years in Deusto, Spain, as a porter, very similar to his patron, St. Alphonsus Rodriguez. He died when he was 72. He was beatified in 1985 and I was able to attend part of the proceedings. When I stayed at the Curia, I was delighted to see the glorious breads that were served to celebrate the Beatification.

INDEX

Abbot, Susan and John, 218
accomplishment, excellence in, 11
activation of yeast, 15
adjustments to recipes, 15
Advent, 29
Advent breads:
   Buttermilk Biscuits, 41
   Date and Walnut Bread, 36–37
   French Bread, 31–32
   Mincemeat Bread, 56
   Pan de Sal, 49
   Poppy Seed Braid Loaf, 38–39
   Potato Bread, 34–35
   Rick's Cranberry-Walnut Buttermilk
      Loaf, 46–47
   St. Alphonsus Rodriguez's Raisin
      Bread, 43–44
   Sweet Potato Bread, 53–54
almonds, in St. Peter Canisius's Stollen,
   83–84
Alphonsus Rodriguez, Saint, 42
   Raisin Bread, 43–44
Altar Bread, 191
America House, 149
America magazine, 72
American Jesuits, and food, 64
Andrews, Steve, 184
anonymity of Jesuit Brothers, 114
apple bread, Holy Thursday, 128–29
apples, on Good Friday, 132
applesauce, in Oatmeal Quick Bread, 87
apricots, dried:
   in Apricot, Orange, Cranberry Bread, 50–51
   in Christmas Morning Bread, 79
   in Christmas Panettone, 90–91
   in Hot Cross Buns, 120–21

   in St. Peter Canisius's Stollen, 83–84
artisans, Jesuit Brothers as, 1–2, 68
Ashley, Ralph, 129
Ash Wednesday, Hot Cross Buns, 120–21
Ateneo de Manila, 49
Atkins, Carter, 101

Bagels, 124–25
baguettes, 21, 31–32
bakeries:
   at Center for the Working Child, 200
   Jesuit, 13, 196–97
      Wernersville novitiate, 2
baking of bread, 20–21, 31
   French bread, 30
   industrialization of, 5
Baltimore, Maryland, 74
bananas, in Christmas Morning Bread, 79
Bandera, Raphael, 24, 210
   Focaccia, 211–12
   Italian bread, 213–14
   Italian Easter Bread, 228–29
bannocks, oatmeal, 186–87
barley flour, 6
Barnstable Patriot, 131
Barth, Fred, 172
Basic Corn Bread, 66
Basic Refrigerator Rolls, 104–5
Basic Sourdough Bread, 168–69
Bath Buns, 198–99
beard, St. Joseph's bread shaped like,
   141–42
Beatification of Francis Garate, 232
beating of dough, 15
Bennett, Barbara, 190
Benny, Brother (Biniakiewicz), 52

Nickolas Owen, Saint, 180
noon examination of conscience, 171
North American martyrs, 48
notes about recipes, 21–22
Novices, Jesuit, 28, 55
Novices, Jesuit (cont.)
    and baking, 159
novitiate, Jesuit, 1–4. *See also* Wernersville,
       Pennsylvania, novitiate
nuts, 10
    in Christmas Morning Bread, 79
    in Christmas Panettone, 90–91
    in Zucchini Bread, 194–95
    see also walnuts

oatmeal:
    in Whole Wheat and Oatmeal Bread,
       136–37
    in Oatmeal Bannocks, 186–87
    in Oatmeal Quick Bread, 87
    in O'Brien's Oatmeal Bread, 138–39
O'Brien, John, 138
O'Donnell, John, 2
O'Hare, Joseph A., 149
Oils, 9
    for coating dough before rising, 17–18
O'Keefe, Vincent J., 202
Oldcorne, Father (Reformation martyr), 129
Olive Bread, 122–23
Olive oil, 9
O'Malley, Tom, 147
One-Bowl Hard Rolls, 101–2
100% Whole Wheat Bread, 135
Onion Bread, 192
Onion Rolls, 112–13
Orange, Apricot, Cranberry Bread, 50–51
order, in daily routine, 179
Overnight Basic Italian Bread, 160–61
Owen, Saint Nickolas, 180

pan centro, 200
Pan de Sal, 49

Pane di San Giuseppe, 140, 141–42
panem aurelium, 59
Pan Maraqueta, 201
Panettone, 89
    Christmas Panettone, 90–91
pans, 13–14
    cleaning of, 173
    for Panettone, 91
    preparation for baking, 9, 19–20
Paramananda, Swami, 152
Paris, Jesuit Community, brioche from,
      208–9
Parker House Rolls, 108–9
Parsons, Robert, letter from, 196–97
Paul III, Pope, 1
    and St. Ignatius, 45
Paul VI, Pope, 180
peasant bread, 143
Pelcin, Craig, 201
penance, 123
    of Lent, 117
Pennington, Basil, 189
Peru, Center for the Working Child, 200
    Pan Maraqueta, 201
Peter Canisius, Saint, 82
pineapple, in Zucchini Bread, 194–95
Pius XI, Pope, 61, 180
Poilâne bakery, Paris, 30
Polish Easter Bread, 226–27
Pont–St. Esprit, France, 7
Poor Clare Monastery, New Orleans, 187
    Oatmeal Bannocks, 186–87
poor people, feeding of, 4
poppy seeds, 38
    Brother Brennan's Three-Seed Bread,
      203–4
    Poppy Seed Braid Loaf, 38–39
Potato Bread, 34–35
Potato Rolls, 110–11
poverty, religious, 183, 219
    St. Ignatius and, 145
powers of corn bread, 67

Pozzo, Andrea dal, 107
praepos, 173
prayer, x, 3–4, 6–7, 11, 12–13
   by St. Ignatius, 28
   see also blessings
preparation:
   for breadmaking, 14
   of food, rituals of, viii
priest day, 128
priest holes, 129, 180
priests, martyred, 129, 180
problems with breads, 22–24
Prosciutto Bread, 220–21
Pumpernickel bread, 183
   Brother Andrews's, 184–85
punching down the dough, 19

Queen Elizabeth II, recipe from, 50

raised bread, discovery of, 5
raisins, 10
   in Brother Andrews's Pumpernickel Bread,
      184–85
   in Brother Brennan's Three-Seed Bread, 204
   in Brother Leikus's Oatmeal Quick Bread, 87
   in Christmas Morning Bread, 79
   in Christmas Morning Cinnamon Buns, 92–93
   in Christmas Panettone, 90–91
   in Cinnamon Raisin Walnut Bread, 88–89
   in Holy Thursday Apple Bread, 128–29
   in Irish Soda Bread, 148
   in Polish Easter Bread, 226–27
   in St. Joseph's Bread, 141–42
   in St. Peter Canisius's Stollen, 83–84
   in Sweet Potato Bread, 53–54
ratio studiorum, 12
recipe book, Wernersville novitiate, 25, 127
recipes:
   notes, 21–22
   reading of, 14–15
   sources of, 24–25
Reformation, martyred priests, 129

refrigerator:
   bread rising in, 18
      Basic Refrigerator Rolls, 104–5
      Brother Bandera's Italian bread, 214
      Overnight Basic Italian, 160–61
     Date and Walnut Bread stored in, 37
     Potato Bread dough stored in, 35
refugees, prayers for, 28
regional differences in corn breads, 59
religion, and food, viii–ix
religious life, St. Ignatius and, 145
religious poverty, 219
   purpose of, 183
Religious Sacred Heart order, 215
Réné Goupil, Saint, 48
repetition, learning by, 12
resting the dough, 20
rice flour, 6
Rick's Cranberry-Walnut Buttermilk Loaf, 46–47
rising of dough, 17–19, 22, 23
rivalry, Boston College and Holy Cross, 134
Rodríguez, Alphonsus, Saint, 42
   Raisin Bread, 43–44
rolls. *See* dinner rolls
Romans, ancient, 5
   sourdough bread, 164
Rosemont's Bread, 158–59
Rule of St. Benedict, 13
rules:
   blessings and thanksgivings, 51
   cleanliness, 175
   of the cook, 102–3
   craftsmanship, 68
   dress, 227
   morning rising time, 85
   noon examination of conscience, 171
   order, 179
   penance, 123
   property, 70
   travel, 219
rye bread, Swedish, 181–82
rye flour, 7

The
Good Apple
BIG BOOK
of
Bulletin Boards
by
Robyn Freedman Spizman

illustrated by Janet Armbrust
and
Veronica Terrill

Cover by Dan Grossmann

Copyright © Good Apple, 1993

ISBN No. 0-86653-742-2

Printing No. 987654321

Good Apple
1204 Buchanan St., Box 299
Carthage, IL 62321-0299

A Paramount Communications Company

Dedication

This book is dedicated with thanks and appreciation to the many teachers who have created the hundreds of bulletin boards that I have designed over the past ten years for Good Apple. A great big, make that enormous, thanks to the amazing art director, Tom Sjoerdsma, and talented artists, Janet Armbrust and Veronica Terrill. My sincerest appreciation also goes to all the wonderful folks at Good Apple. And a special thanks to my wonderful husband, Willy, who has been my source of inspiration and determination and to our children, Justin and Ali, who fill my life with love and happiness.

Table of Contents

To the Teacher

Here it is! *The Good Apple Big Book of Bulletin Boards* is filled with ideas that should last for years to come. A labor of love, this book is jam-packed with clever boards to liven up your classroom and captivate students.

Whenever possible, involve students in the creation of these boards. I'll never forget when I was in the third grade, and my teacher Mrs. Watson put me in charge of one of the bulletin boards for our classroom. It was a springtime board, and I vividly remember loving every minute of it. So much in fact, I have never stopped making bulletin boards and have had the pleasure of writing over a dozen bulletin board books for Good Apple.

So go to it, and I hope you will enjoy making the bulletin boards in this book as much as I did creating them. And be sure to remember how proud students will feel after they've added their personal and unique touches to the finished product!

Best wishes always,
Robyn

GA1457

SEPTEMBER

1

September Events

September–First Monday, Labor Day

September 19–Mickey Mouse first appeared in a talking cartoon in 1928.

September 23–First day of autumn

September–First Saturday after the full moon, American Indian Day

September 25–First American newspaper was published in 1690.

September 26–Johnny Appleseed was born in 1774.

Additional Special Days and Weeks in September

National Sight-Saving Month

Read a New Book Month

American Newspaper Week

Sukkot, The Feast of Tabernacles–Jewish festival occurring in September or October

Simchat Torah–A Jewish holiday that falls the day after Sukkot. It is the "Rejoicing with the Torah" and is a very festive day.

WORLD-CLASS KIDS

Use this bulletin board to welcome students in September. Each student's name should be added to a star reproduced from the pattern below. This bulletin board can also introduce a wonderful unit on studying the world or the planets. The stars can be colored, laminated and recycled for future bulletin boards.

3

A WORLDLY WELCOME TO MRS. SMITH'S CLASS!

Welcome your class to school in September with an out-of-this-world theme! Duplicate a world for each student. Write their names on them. Laminate each world and use as a name tag all year. Use the award on the next page to praise a student for doing great work or improving in any area.

Name

4

THE GREATEST WORK ON EARTH!

Each time you hand in your homework or an assignment on time, color in a star. When the entire page is completed, you have reached your destination!

Reach for the Stars

5

GA1457

_____'s

WORK

IS OUT OF THIS WORLD!

_____

GA1457

Use this bulletin board to ignite student participation in any subject or skill area. Duplicate a race car for each student. Have students color the cars and add their names. Then place each car on the bulletin board. As students rev up their motors and improve in an area or show progress, give them stickers to add to their cars or move cars one space each time around the racetrack. To build class teamwork, the goal of this bulletin board could be that as soon as every car has reached its destination, the entire class earns a special treat.

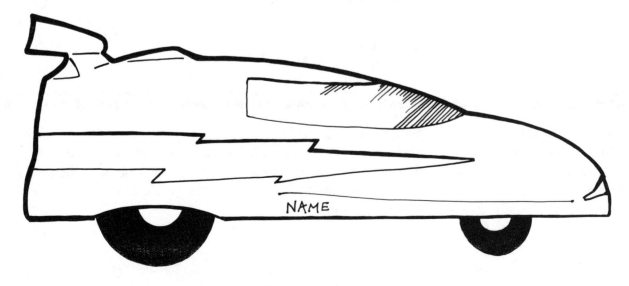

GA1457

SUMMER FUN!

I read 50 new books! Ali

I went to Palm Beach! Gabrielle

I got to visit my cousin in Florida. Bettye

I went to camp Blue Star and had a great time! Justin

I went to New York and saw the statue of Liberty. It was awesome! Kip

I went to soccer camp and had a blast. Bud

I learned how to skate. Kimberly

Use this bulletin board to highlight the activities each student did during the summer months. This will also provide great ideas for a creative writing lesson. This bulletin board can be used graffiti style by letting students write their summer fun-filled memories directly on the bulletin board background paper. Students can then choose to write stories on what they did, or interview fellow students about their summer fun.

TEACHER FEATURE

LIKES

DISLIKES

Mrs. Kassey

BOOKS

PEACH PIE

DISNEY MOVIES

RAIN

LEMON SHAKE UP

LATE HOMEWORK

MEXICAN FOOD

CORN DOGS

DIRTY DISHES

TRAVEL

ART

RADISHES

Teacher: Introduce information about yourself by creating a bulletin board that highlights your family, interests or things about you that will help students get to know you better. Consider ways, from photographs when you were their age to your favorite hobbies and food, that will allow students to learn about you.

TALK ABOUT IT: Have a class discussion about the things you have in common with your students. This is also a wonderful opportunity to discuss likes, dislikes and how we differ and can appreciate each other. Perhaps you like jogging, or spaghetti is your favorite food. Ask your students what things you have in common.

GA1457

Use this bulletin board to motivate students to build specific skills such as listening, cooperating, or following directions. Each child could choose one thing to work on. Each time students accomplish something, they get to write their names on stars and add them to the bulletin board. Duplicate stars from the star pattern on page 3, and let students keep a supply on hand. Present the all-star award shown below when each student gets a specific number of stars on the bulletin board.

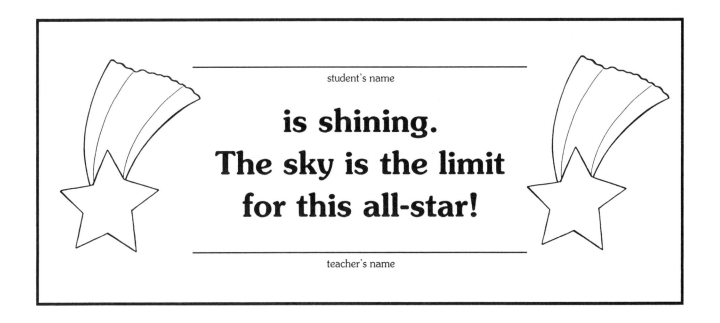

GA1457

LOOK WHO'S ART SMART!

This bulletin board will encourage younger students to explore writing numbers and alphabet letters, while older students will get a kick out of using them to make clever designs. Instruct students to use the numbers and letters of the alphabet to create designs and pictures. Which numbers or letters could be used to make a face, a truck or a butterfly? Refer to the examples below for ideas.

GA1457

MAKE SENSE FROM CENTS!

Meredith I saved 23 ¢!

Eric I saved 48 ¢!

Sally I saved 17 ¢!

Sam I saved 51 ¢

Justin I saved 50 ¢!

This bulletin board will encourage students to use addition and subtraction skills to see how much they can save by using grocery store coupons. Have students begin coupon files for the items they use at home and supply Mom or Dad with these coupons when they go shopping. Compare the actual cost with the amount saved and compute the difference. Each time students use coupons and save, let them add their names and how much they helped save to the bulletin board. Use the "cents"ible coupon shown below to award students whose names appear at least five times on the board. Create a colorful border with real coupons. Pin or staple them to the board.

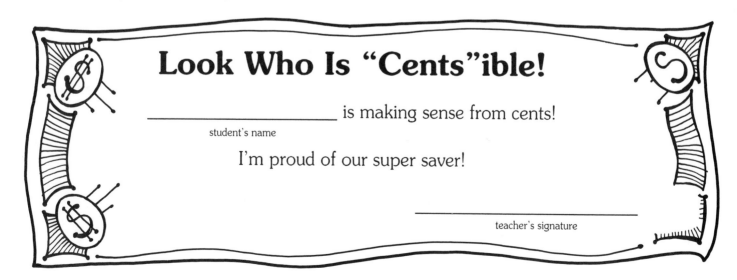

Look Who Is "Cents"ible!

_____ is making sense from cents!

student's name

I'm proud of our super saver!

_____

teacher's signature

12

GA1457

S IS FOR SEPTEMBER . . .

SPACE

SMALL

SCHOOL

SHOWER

SUPER

Use this bulletin board to introduce a new letter of the alphabet. You could begin with *A* IS FOR AUGUST IS OVER, *B* IS FOR BACK TO SCHOOL, *C* IS FOR CLASS! Let the class vote on the letter of the week, and then have a class-wide activity where students bring in magazine pictures or photographs of objects or items or even people they know that begin with that letter.

ALTERNATE ACTIVITY:
CREATE A STORY by instructing each student to write a story based on the alphabet.
Begin with the letter *A*.
A rabbit visited my house.
Buddy was his name.
Can you guess what he wore?
Did you get to see him?
Everyone who did thought he was so funny.
(Continue with each letter.)

ADD SOME CLASS! This can also be a classroom activity, and each student can add a sentence to build the story. With younger children, try this activity out loud and record the story on the board or a large pad of paper.

ADD SMART! A perfect art activity to go with this bulletin board would be to illustrate the story. Ask the students to answer the questions who, what, when, where and why. Students can choose one of these questions and illustrate the answer.

13

GA1457

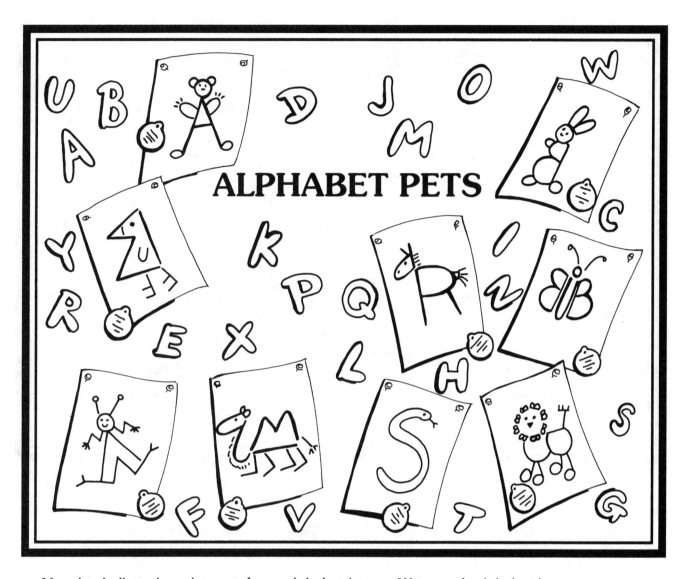

ALPHABET PETS

Use this bulletin board to reinforce alphabet letters. Write each alphabet letter on a piece of construction paper with a black marker. Encourage students to turn the alphabet letters into wild and wonderful pets. These alphabet pets could be funny, from outer space or resemble real animals. Have students also think of silly names that start with their letters and make name tags for their pets from the pattern below.

14

GA1457

ADD UP THE FUN IN SEPTEMBER

Here's a fun way to introduce a math unit and reinforce basic math skills. Give each student a paper plate and write a math problem on it. Next, have an art activity and let students decorate their paper plates by transforming them into funny characters. Odds and ends, scraps of paper, bits of yarn and glue will turn the paper plates into appealing creations. Add all of the faces to the bulletin board and instruct students to write their characters' names on index cards and staple or pin next to their artwork. Once all of the characters are in place, have the class try working all of the math problems. Each child can be involved in checking the answers by calling out his or her name and the correct answer of the math problems.

When students show significant progress in math or can add or subtract all of the problems successfully, acknowledge their efforts with this award.

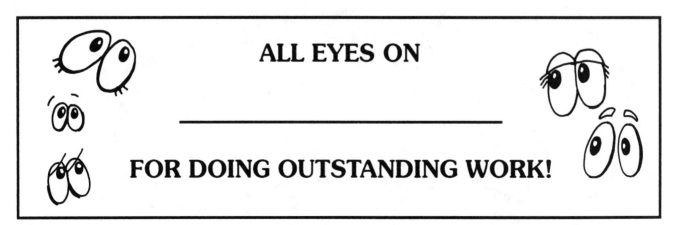

ALL EYES ON

_____

FOR DOING OUTSTANDING WORK!

GA1457

WE'RE SOARING IN SEPTEMBER

(Jill, Tim, David, Donna, Rob)

Use this bulletin board to launch a new unit or welcome students to school in September. Duplicate rockets from the rocket pattern below for students and instruct them to add their names. Have an art activity in which students decorate the rockets with colorful designs using crayons, markers, etc. The decorated rockets can all be placed in a row at the base of the bulletin board. As students do good deeds, listen to directions, or improve in any one specific skill area, they get to advance their rockets either one full space or an amount such as 6" (15.24 cm). This is also a great way to give students practice using a ruler.

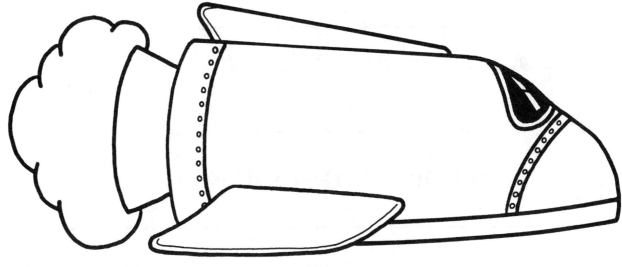

16

GA1457

_____is
soaring with great work!

_____

_____

_____

_____

_____ **IS**
AIMING FOR
NEAT WORK!

_____

_____

_____

_____

**September
sends us with
good manners**

Hooray for_____

_____

_____

_____

_____

_____

**September
All Star**

_____

_____

_____

_____

_____

_____

17

WHERE IN THE WORLD DO YOU LIVE?

Use this bulletin board to make sure students know their city, state and address. This bulletin board will also be useful to help identify cities and states, while using sorting skills. Cover the entire bulletin board with white paper and draw an outline map of the United States. Label each state. Instruct students to write their names and addresses on index cards. Add the cards to the bulletin board to form the border. Instruct students to begin saving return addresses from mail from family members or even "junk mail" and display these on the bulletin board in the correct states. Have students identify which state has the most mail coming from it and which one has the least.

WHAT IN THE WORLD ARE YOU LEARNING?

Choose a faraway place that interests you and search for information about your worldy location. List what you learn about it on this page.

_____

_____

_____

_____

_____

_____

_____

_____

_____

_____

_____

_____

_____

_____

_____

_____

Where in the world are you learning about? _____

GA1457

BIRTHDAY COUNTDOWN

This bulletin board is perfect for highlighting students' birthdays. List the students' birthdays on index cards, or instruct students to bring in recycled birthday cards and add their names and birthdays to the fronts of the cards in large letters. This will make the display even more colorful. Each month put the birthday students' cards in the spaceship. (There will probably be more than one student each month.)

20

GA1457

GET BOOKED FOR SEPTEMBER

Use this bulletin board to promote reading. Try choosing a specific theme that you are working on, such as space or science. Add suggestions to the board by displaying book jackets which are possible choices. Duplicate the Passport to Reading Record on page 22 and encourage students to record each new book that they read.

_____ is hooked on BOOKS!

Passport to Reading Record

_____'s Reading Passport

Books that I have read include: _____

_____

_____

_____

_____

_____

_____

_____

_____

_____

_____

_____

_____

_____

_____

_____

_____

_____

_____

22

WE'RE ALL CAPS!

Use this bulletin board to illustrate words that begin with capital letters. Duplicate the cap pattern below and give one to each student. Talk about which words begin with capital letters. Have each student write his or her name on a cap since it is a proper noun and starts with a capital letter. Instruct students to search for words that begin with capital letters and record them on their caps. Add the caps to the bulletin board.

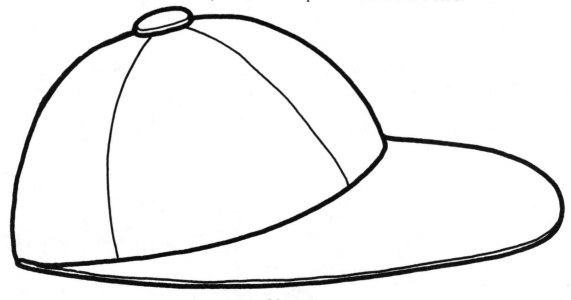

23

GA1457

LOOK WHO IS SHAPING UP!

Here's a fun bulletin board for encouraging any study habit or new skill. Duplicate smiling faces from the pattern on the right and give one to each student to color and finish. Add button eyes, yarn hair and any details to liven up those smiling faces. Have students write their names on the bow ties and add the faces to the bulletin board. Have an art activity where students cut out a variety of triangles, squares, rectangles and circles. Add the paper shapes to an envelope attached to the bulletin board. As students improve a skill, listen or do anything positive that you want to reinforce, allow them to select shapes and add them to the bulletin board to begin creating a shaped-up person!

name

GA1457

ME, MYSELF AND I!

Use this bulletin board to encourage creative writing skills and a way to get to know each student. Students should complete the work sheet on page 26. Add the students' work to the bulletin board. Invite students to bring photographs of family, pets, or any photos that tell something about them. Add the photographs to the bulletin board.

GETTING TO KNOW ALL ABOUT YOU!

Help us get to know you better. Fill in the blanks and finish each sentence.

Hi. My name is _____

_____

I like to _____

_____

I live _____

_____

My favorite food is _____

_____

My favorite thing to do is _____

_____

My least favorite thing to do is _____

_____

My favorite subject at school is _____

_____

The one thing that I really like about myself is _____

_____

I am really good at _____

_____

My birthday is on _____

 GA1457

HERE'S THE SCOOP!

Use this bulletin board to welcome students to your class. Duplicate an ice-cream cone for each student and add his or her name. As each day goes by, you can add assignments to the bulletin board or use it for special announcements. This bulletin board also makes an excellent place for students to display special accomplishments, awards, pictures of new siblings, etc. Students can color their cones to represent their favorite flavors. Count on this bulletin board for a fun math lesson and have students add up the total amounts of each flavor shown.

27

GA1457

I'VE GOT THE SCOOP ON _____

Get the scoop on someone you would like to know more about. Write this person's name on the ice-cream cone and find out information about him or her. List what you learn on the cone.

Mrs. Storne

Bettye loves to cook.

She's great at everything!

She's 40 years old.

28

THE SCOOP ON ME

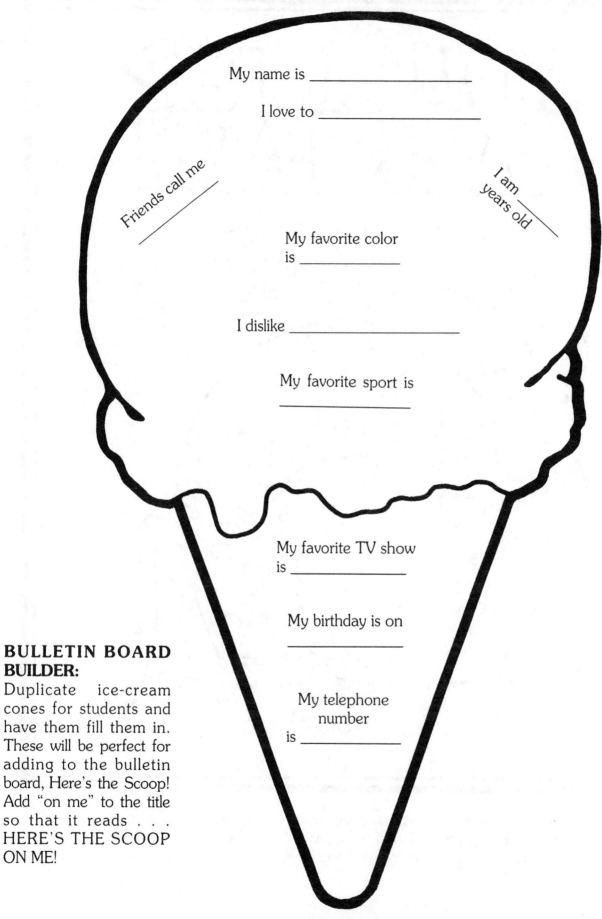

My name is _____

I love to _____

Friends call me _____

I am years old _____

My favorite color is _____

I dislike _____

My favorite sport is _____

My favorite TV show is _____

My birthday is on _____

My telephone number is _____

BULLETIN BOARD BUILDER:

Duplicate ice-cream cones for students and have them fill them in. These will be perfect for adding to the bulletin board, Here's the Scoop! Add "on me" to the title so that it reads . . . HERE'S THE SCOOP ON ME!

GA1457

Use this bulletin board to excite students about all the events that are happening at school in the fall. Display this bulletin board at P.T.A. activities and special events. This is also a great bulletin board for posting community happenings.

30

GA1457

REACH FOR GREAT WORK!

Use this bulletin board to point students in the right direction and highlight work that you are proud of. Give students copies of the hand pattern below, or let them trace their own arms and hands on construction paper and cut them out. Add all of the arms to the bulletin board with the students' names on theirs. Add student work to the center of the bulletin board for the finishing touch.

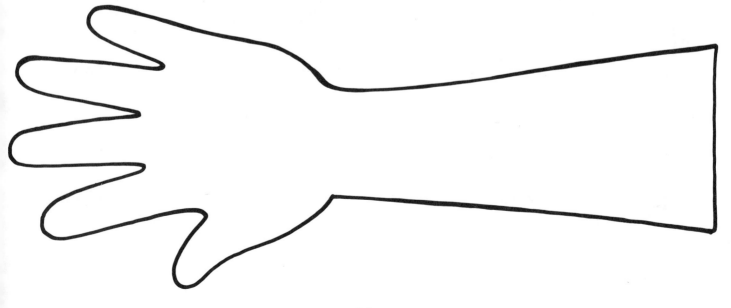

LOOK WHOSE HANDS ARE HELPING

Use this bulletin board to encourage students to help each other. Students should trace their hands on construction paper and cut them out. Add the hands to the bulletin board. Each time students do good deeds and help other classmates, add stars to the hands or let them write their signatures on the bulletin board.

BULLETIN BOARD BUILDER: Build onto this bulletin board by changing the title to "Hands Helping Hands." Have all the hands connected to each other so that they appear to be holding hands. Each time a student does a good deed and helps the environment, add a hand to the chain of hands. See how long the class can make the holding hands chain.

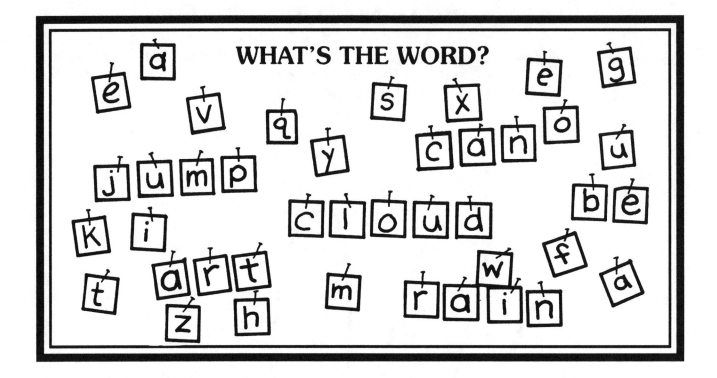

WHAT'S THE WORD?

Pin duplicates of alphabet letters on the bulletin board and encourage students to learn to spell new words or reinforce ones they already know. Each student can take a turn and create words. Play a game called Have You Heard the Word? Give each student a five-minute turn at the bulletin board and challenge him or her to make as many words as possible and spell them correctly. A point is earned for each correctly spelled word. As each student takes a turn, have classmates look the words up in the dictionary to make sure they are spelled correctly. Students can record their lists of words and the new ones they learn in their own word dictionaries and look up the definitions. Award students for super spelling with the certificate below.

HERE'S THE WORD ON

_____

CONGRATULATIONS
FOR BEING A SUPER SPELLER!

GA1457

A BIG HAND FOR . . . .

Observe people who are helping make your environment and school a better place. Write a name on each hand and how that person has given a hand to help! Add the hands to those with student names on them to a Look Whose Hands Are Helping bulletin board (page 32).

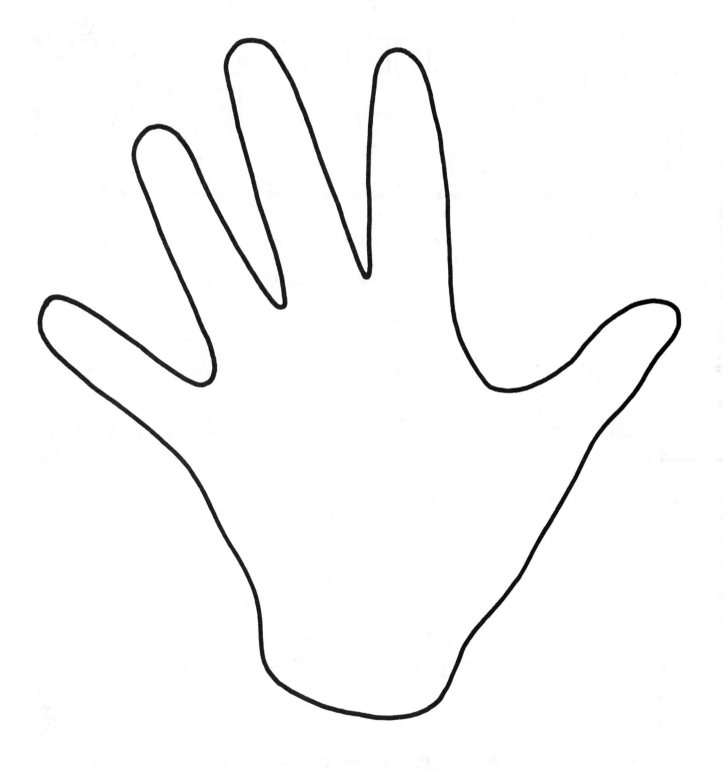

Use this bulletin board to display work students have created that you are proud of. Involve students in helping name the classroom "seal" and use this bulletin board to motivate students to improve in any area. This bulletin board is ideal for spelling, handwriting, creative writing or any other subject area. Duplicate the Seal of Approval Award below and use it to praise students' work.

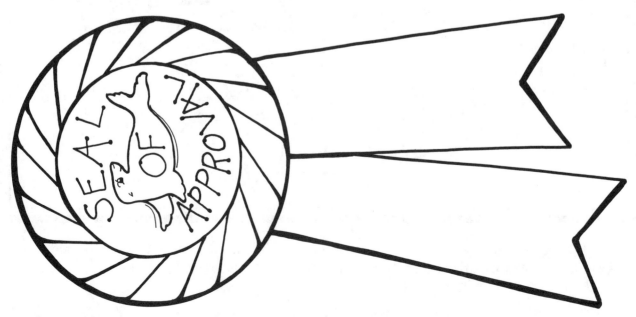

35

GA1457

OPPOSITES ATTRACT

HOT

FAST

UP

HELLO

HIGH

BIG

AWAKE

GOOD-BYE

SHORT

SALT

PEPPER

DOWN

SLEEPY

SOFT

HARD

COLD

TALL

LITTLE

SLOW

LOW

Use this bulletin board to encourage students to learn antonyms. Write words and their opposites on index cards and challenge the students to match the antonyms.

WE'RE NUTS ABOUT SCHOOL

Use this bulletin board to welcome students to the first day of school. Copy the pattern below to make acorns to use on the bulletin board. Add subject areas or topics that you and the students will be studying during September. Explain to the students that just as squirrels store nuts, they will be storing information that they learn in class.

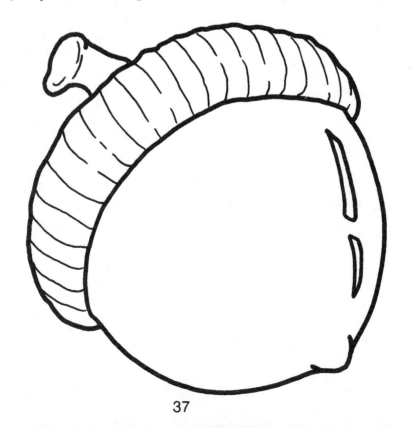

GA1457

SEPTEMBER PATTERNS

GA1457

SEPTEMBER PATTERNS

SCHOOL BUS

39

GA1457

40

October Events

October 1–First World Series played in 1903

October 3–Child Health Day

October 9–Leif Ericson Day

October 12–Columbus Day

October 15–National Poetry Day

October 24–United Nations Day

October 28–Dedication of the Statue of Liberty, 1886

October 31–Halloween

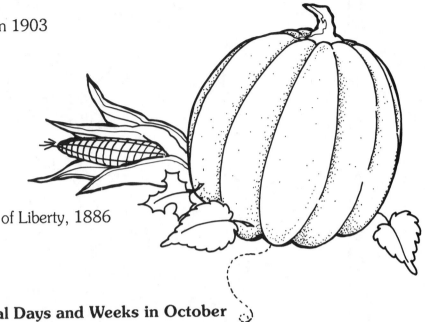

Additional Special Days and Weeks in October

Rosh Hashanah–Jewish holiday occurring in September or October. It ushers in the Jewish New Year.

Yom Kippur–Jewish holiday occurring in September or October. It is called The Day of Atonement and is a day of fasting and prayers.

International Letter Writing Week

Fire Prevention Week

National Stamp Collecting Month

41

GA1457

FAR OUT FUN

Use this bulletin board to introduce a unit on outer space. Each student can choose a planet to be in charge of and responsible for. What changes would he or she make, who would live on the planet, and what laws would be created to help care for it? This will make a wonderful creative writing lesson and also encourages students to learn about outer space. Display the stories on the bulletin board for some out-of-this-world student work.

42

BRIGHT IDEAS

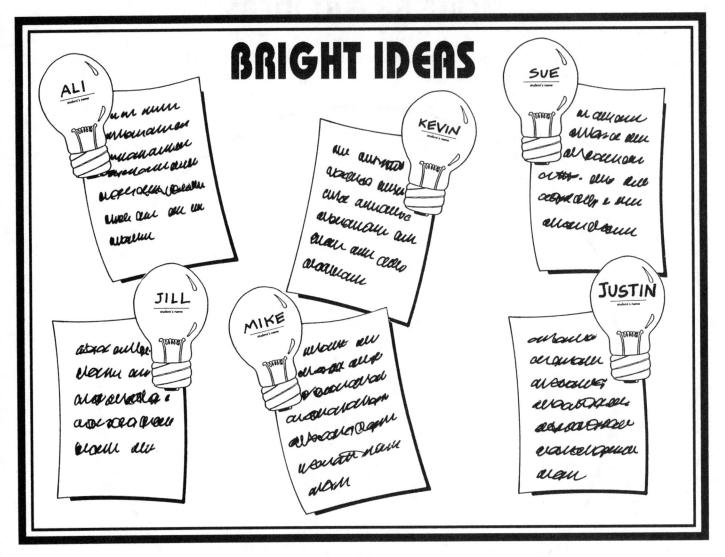

Use this bulletin board to encourage creative writing. Attach a paper bag to the bulletin board and have students write interesting or funny titles for stories. Put all of the titles in the bag. Students can choose story titles and complete them for extra credit. Display the creative writing on the bulletin board, with light bulbs containing names of students. Place these beside the stories to show the students' thinking lights are on.

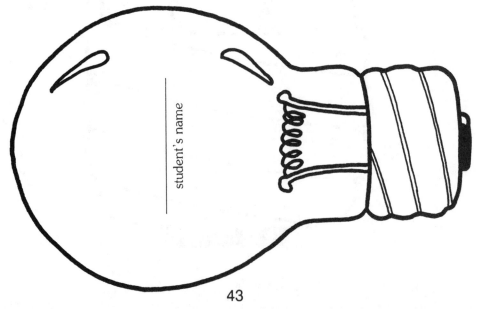

MORE BRIGHT IDEAS!

Use this light bulb to show off your bright ideas. Anytime you think of a clever idea, invention or special thought you think is terrific, list it on the light bulb.

44

LEARN HOW = KNOW HOW

Use this bulletin board to highlight students' achievements in any area and to encourage learning new skills and information. This bulletin board will also help build students' awareness of how to learn something new. It can also help reinforce students' self-esteem, so feel free to change it and add to it as often as possible. Feature what your students already know and stimulate new ideas they are interested in. Have students bring photographs of themselves involved in particular sports or activities. For students who do not have any extracurricular activities, let them cut out pictures from magazines of things that they would like to learn how to do.

SUPER SEARCH: Encourage all students to search in magazines and newspapers for articles or pictures of things that we can learn how to do or stories about individuals who have accomplished something. Also include pamphlets of activities in your community that are available for children.

WISH LIST: Have students make lists of all the things they would like to learn how to do. Add the lists to the bulletin board, and have a class discussion about where you might go to learn how to do any of these things.

I WISH I COULD....

45

LOOK WHO KNOWS HOW!

Interview someone who knows how to do something you would like to know how to do one day. Use these questions to get your conversation started.

How did you learn to _____?

_____

_____

When were you first interested in it?

_____

_____

_____

Were there any helpful books that you read on the subject?_____

_____

_____

Do you like what you do?_____

_____

_____

What is your favorite thing about it?_____

_____

_____

Who helped you learn how? _____

_____

_____

If you could learn how to do something new right now, what would it be? _____

_____

_____

_____

_____

GA1457

WE'VE GOT YOUR NUMBER

Use this bulletin board to reinforce math skills. Duplicate telephones for students and have them write their telephone numbers on the telephones. Instruct students to add up each number and see who has the biggest number, the smallest, the same, an even number, an odd number, etc. Each student can also make a class telephone directory by recording each student's name and number. This will be very helpful for exchanging homework information or for getting in touch with classmates.

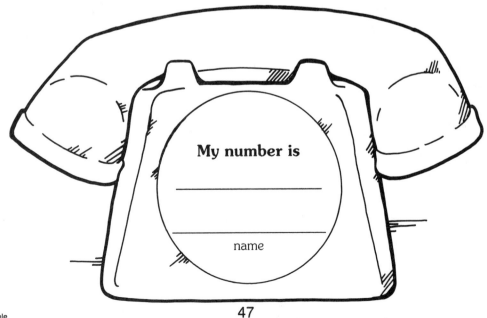

My number is

_____

name

CALLING ALL KIDS

Keep a diary of the telephone calls your family receives in one week. List the people who called, and see if you can find out why they called. Add up the calls and list the sum on the telephone.

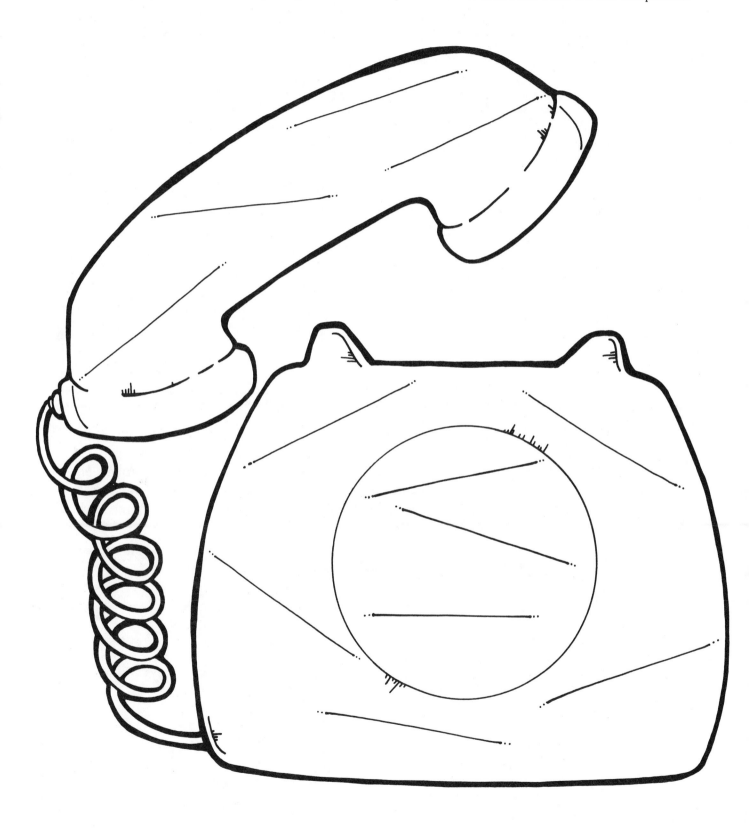

48

OCTOBER "WHO'S WHOOOOOO" OF FAME

Use this bulletin board in October to expose students to famous individuals you wish to study. Duplicate an owl for each famous person, add his or her name and place on the bulletin board. Duplicate a corresponding owl. On it list what the person is famous for. Have students try to correctly match the pairs of owls after studying who is who!

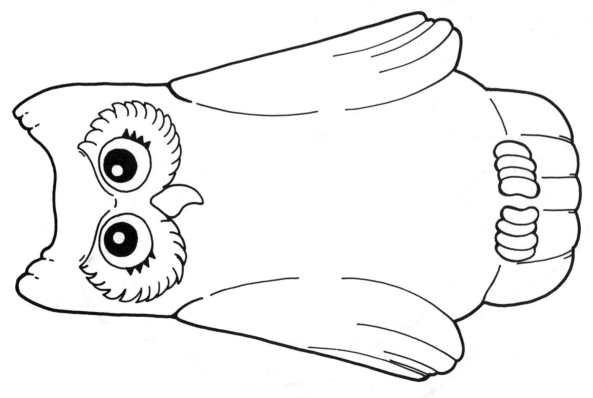

GA1457

WHOOO KNOWS THESE FACTS?

Duplicate ghosts for students and have them list particular facts they have learned in school. Students can decorate their ghosts and turn them into wild and wonderful characters. Using scraps of construction paper and odds and ends, encourage students to dress up their ghosts.

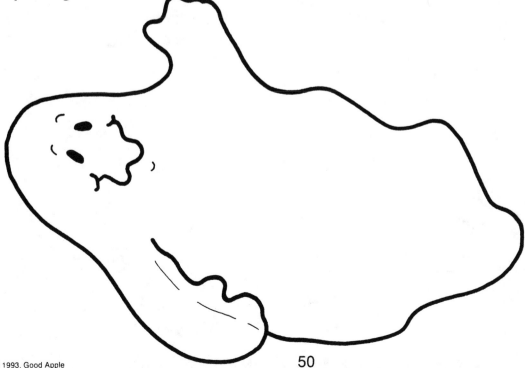

GA1457

WE'RE SPELLBOUND IN OCTOBER!

Using the letters in the word *Halloween*, challenge students to create as many different words as they can. Have students write their words on index cards or scraps of construction paper and add their words one by one to the bulletin board, with no repetitions. See which student has the most words and is the last one to add a word to the board.

HALLOWEEN:

halo	whale	awe	whole
hall	law	all	hole
how	lean	allow	howl
we	wall	new	who
owe	well	won	ewe
one	noel	hen	alone
when	wheel	no	lone
eel	heel	low	lane
hello	hoe	loan	own
lawn			

SHOW 'N' TELL: Students can draw pictures of these words made from the letters in the word *Halloween* and play a game called Show 'n' Tell. In this game, show the picture and have students guess how to spell the word correctly. This is a fun way to create flash cards useful for learning to spell new words.

FACE TO FACE

Here is a great way to learn about different cultures. Instruct students to search through magazines and newspapers and cut out as many different faces as they can find. Staple the faces on the bulletin board, challenging the class to cover the entire board. This bulletin board provides a wonderful opportunity to talk about different cultures and backgrounds.

GA1457

GOOD WORK HABITS TO DEVELOP

Use this bulletin board to illustrate work habits you wish to reinforce. Duplicate cameras from the pattern below for students and have them add their names. Place the cameras on the bulletin board. Each time a student demonstrates a good work habit, let him or her add a star to the camera.

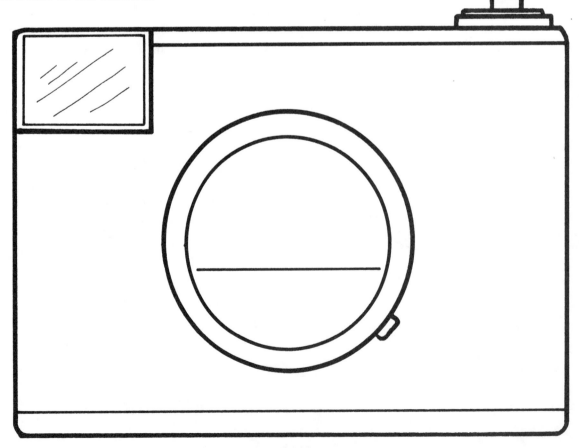

GA1457

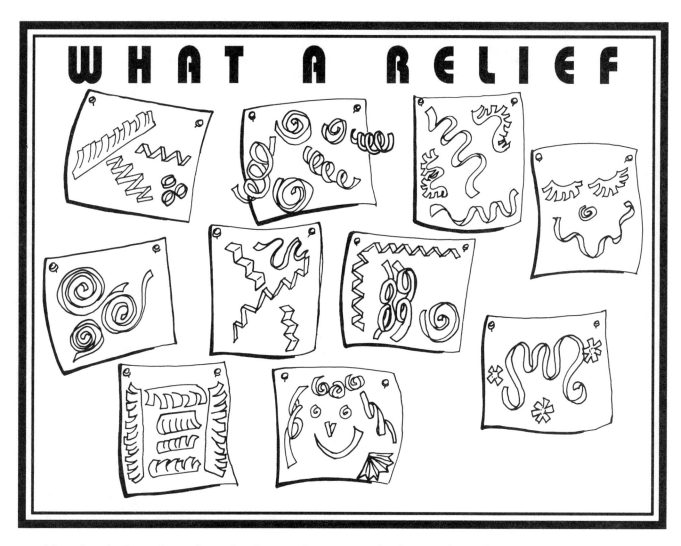

WHAT A RELIEF

Use this bulletin board to display student artwork that is three-dimensional. Teach students a variety of techniques for folding and curling strips of construction paper. Glue or tape them to a flat piece of cardboard or another piece of paper. Challenge students to see how they can vary their relief by twisting, accordion folding and curling the paper. Display the reliefs when completed on the bulletin board.

RELIEF TECHNIQUES:

curl paper

fanfold paper

cut a spiral

fringe paper

54

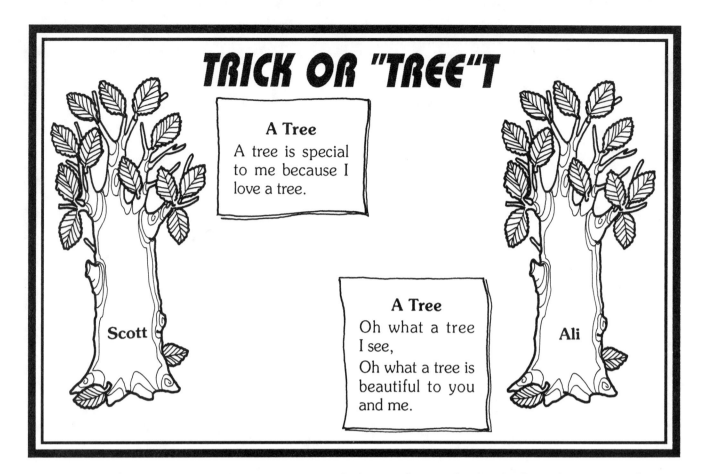

TRICK OR "TREE"T

A Tree

A tree is special to me because I love a tree.

Scott

A Tree

Oh what a tree I see,
Oh what a tree is beautiful to you and me.

Ali

October features National Poetry Day and also Halloween! This bulletin board is a fun way to recognize both of these events and also focus on the environment. Have students write poems about trees and add them to the bulletin board. Have a class discussion about how trees are treats for the earth and how they are helpful to the environment. What kinds of tricks can your class think of to help save more trees and also help the earth? Perhaps your class will help pick up litter and candy wrappers or trash thrown on the ground on Halloween night. Or see how your class can cut down on paper use by writing on both sides or erasing mistakes instead of wadding up paper and throwing it away. Duplicate trees for students and add to the board next to their poems. Every time students demonstrate that they are helping the earth or cutting down on wasting paper, reward them with leaves cut from construction paper to add to their trees.

WHICH MAKES MORE CENTS?

Duplicate the trees from the previous bulletin board pattern and add a money amount to each tree. Challenge students to add up the sum of each tree and see which one has the greatest value and the smallest value. Change this bulletin board as often as you wish, and involve students by letting them be in charge of adding new amounts daily.

GA1457

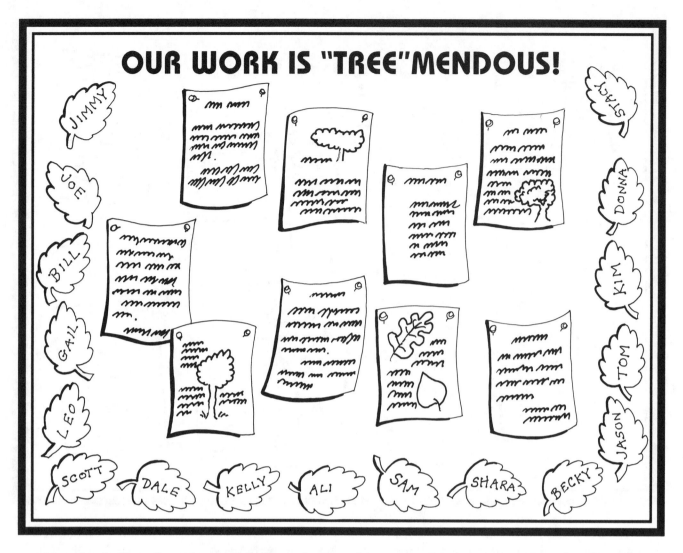

Use this bulletin board to highlight student work in any area that you want to reinforce or praise. Duplicate a leaf for each student. Each time a student improves in a specific area or subject, add his or her name on the leaf to the bulletin board border.

GA1457

Use this creative bulletin board activity to encourage students to express their feelings in a positive way. Instruct students to write about what bugs them. Display the work on the bulletin board. Turn this project into an art lesson and give students construction paper, glue and scissors, and let each design a bug. Add each student's bug by his or her work, and have a class discussison about feelings. This is also a great opportunity to role-play situations that will help students get along better.

Choose two students to role-play a situation. Have a class discussion about how the students reacted and what might be appropriate responses. Encourage students to learn how to work out their differences in constructive ways.

IDEAS TO ROLE-PLAY:
- A student trips you.
- Someone tells a secret and you think it's about you.
- Your lunch is missing and someone played a practical joke on you.
- Someone rips up your homework by accident.
- You are left out of a game on the playground.
- You get blamed for something you didn't do.
- You have to clean up a mess and it wasn't your fault.

DO YOU BE"LEAF" IT?

Write a "Believe It or Not" story about something that really happened to you or really didn't! Think of something that really happened that was out of the ordinary or hard to believe. If you can't think of any real story, make one up! Classmates must guess if the story really happened or if you made it up!

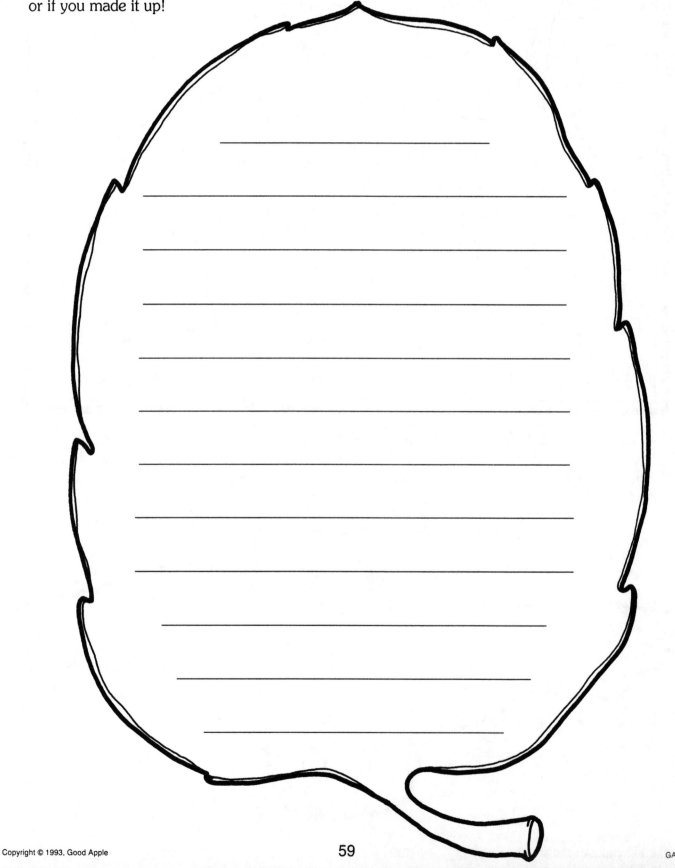

"OWL" BELIEVE IT WHEN I SEE IT!

Display your Halloween artwork on this bulletin board. Have students think of things they know they really can't see on Halloween. From monsters to spooky creatures, display their creations on this board. Duplicate the owl pattern below for a colorful border or added appeal.

GA1457

BUG BORDER

Duplicate these bugs and students can color them for a border that is certain not to bug anyone!

61

GA1457

RED ROVER, RED ROVER, SEND OCTOBER OVER!

Use this bulletin board as a fun way to study seasons, reinforce matching and sorting skills, and for challenging students to observe their environment during the month of October. Pin a piece of colorful yarn down the center of the bulletin board. On one side place the name of the month that you are using, such as October; leave the opposite side blank. Add photographs, magazine pictures, seasonal symbols, events, etc., to the blank side, and challenge students to place the things that relate to October on the correct side. Add new things daily to the wrong side and encourage students to sort them correctly and bring in additions for the bulletin board.

As this bulletin board fills up, the challenge is to see who can find the daily additions that are out of place.

BULLETIN BOARD IDEAS:

leaves
clothing articles
events happening in October
pictures that don't belong:
    clothing articles like a swimsuit, earmuffs, fan, valentines, holiday items, etc.

Halloween items
masks
PTA night

DO YOU READ ME?

Use this bulletin board to encourage students to develop reading skills and gain a love of learning.

63

MISSION: GOOD NUTRITION

Use this bulletin board to study the four basic food groups. Have students cut out pictures of healthy food and display on the board. Encourage students to keep a daily record of the foods they eat in each food group, and have a class discussion of what makes a balanced diet.

GA1457

HEY DIDDLE, DIDDLE...
TRY OUT THIS RIDDLE!

Use this bulletin board to encourage students to think and ask questions. Divide the class into teams, and let teams create riddles to display and answer.

65

GA1457

TACKLE THESE SPORTS

Use this bulletin board to display various sports. Instruct students to bring sports-related pictures and add them to the bulletin board.

66

GA1457

COLOR MY WORLD

Use this bulletin board to teach students the primary colors. Have students create designs from the primary colors and then experiment by mixing and making new colors. Display the colorful creations on this board.

A RHYME EVERY TIME

Use this bulletin board to encourage students to make rhymes. Have students write words on index cards and place the cards on the bulletin board. Play a class game where each student gets to choose a word from the board and say a word that rhymes with it. You can also play round-robin by seeing how many words your class can think of that rhyme with each particular word.

68

GA1457

A RHYME EVERY TIME

Record your rhyming words on this page.

(lines for writing, left column)

_____

_____

_____

_____

_____

_____

_____

_____

_____

_____

_____

_____

_____

_____

_____

_____

_____

_____

_____

_____

_____

(lines for writing, right column)

_____

_____

_____

_____

_____

_____

_____

_____

_____

_____

_____

_____

_____

_____

_____

_____

_____

MY TIE LIE PIE BYE

~RHYME TIME CLIMB

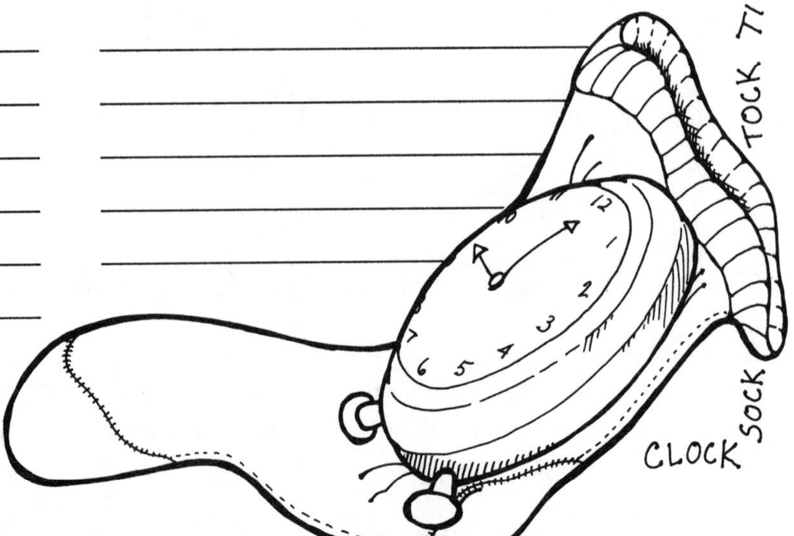

COW WOW SEE ME KEY TEA PEA BEE APPLE DAPPLE GOOD WOULD SHOULD HIGH SKY FLY

RHYME TIME CLIMB ALL TALL MALL HALL BALL FALL COY TOY JOY BOY KICK PICK SLICK TICK TOCK SOCK CLOCK

HOW MAT SAT BAT RAT CAT FAT

CLOCK

69

GA1457

ROUND UP THESE SOUNDS

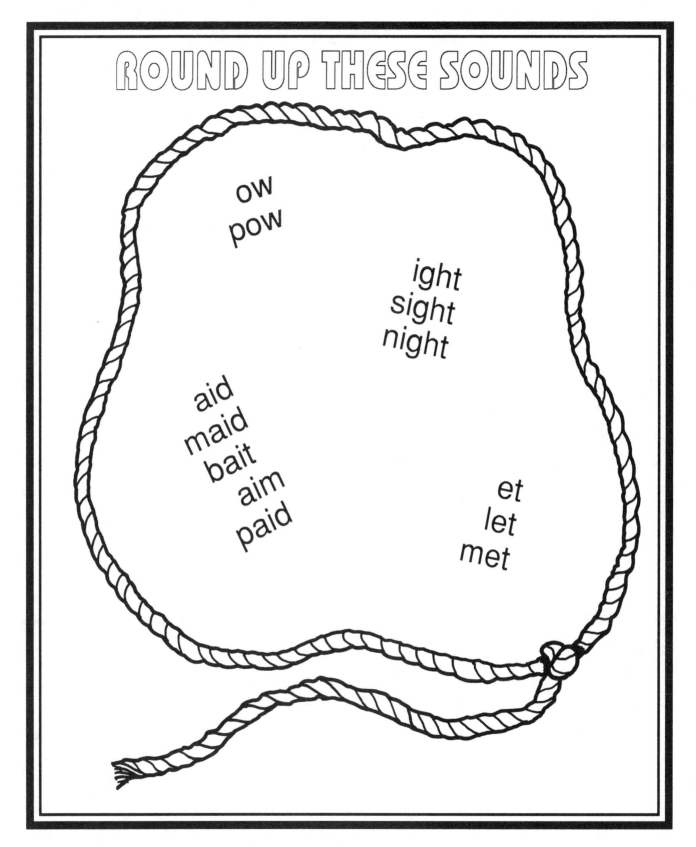

ow
pow

ight
sight
night

aid
maid
bait
aim
paid

et
let
met

Use this bulletin board to encourage students to learn to recognize word sounds. Give each student a try at this bulletin board. Instruct students to name and print words that match each sound displayed in the word roundup. See how many words can be added to the word corral.

ABOUT FACE

Here's a great activity for October. Instruct students to cut out facial features from magazines and newspapers and start a collection of as many details as they can find. Once students have an assortment, create paper plate faces by gluing the features to complete faces. Challenge students to create fabulous faces and, if desired, enhance them with odds and ends to turn them into clever characters.

WRITE ABOUT IT! Inspire a creative writing lesson with this bulletin board by instructing students to write stories about their characters. Make sure they give details about how their paper plate characters look. Mix up the stories and have a student read one and instruct the class to guess which character the story is about. Display the stories on the bulletin board.

OCTOBER PATTERNS

72

GA1457

OCTOBER PATTERNS

GA1457

NOVEMBER

GA1457

November Events

November–Election Day

November 9–Sadie Hawkins Day

November 13–Peanut butter invented, 1890

November 14–Favorite Author's Day

November 18–Mickey Mouse's birthday

November 22–Assassination of President John F. Kennedy, 1963

November–Thanksgiving Day, fourth Thursday in November

Additional Special Days and Weeks in November

Children's Book Week

International Cat Week–Begins first Sunday in November

Good Nutrition Month

American Education Week

GA1457

NO-NO'S IN NOVEMBER

Use this bulletin board to highlight ways that students can help the environment. Instruct each student to draw a picture of something that doesn't help the earth, from littering to wasting water. Discuss how we can help the earth. This bulletin board also offers a great opportunity for learning about the world of advertising. Students could create posters or slogans that would sell others on helping Mother Earth.

GA1457

EARTH WATCH

Encourage students to keep their eyes on the earth and watch for ways they can help preserve the earth's treasures. Duplicate a pair of glasses for each student and have him or her record ways to help the environment. Add students' watchful words to the bulletin board and challenge students to focus on ways that they can make a difference.

NAME ⎯⎯⎯⎯⎯⎯⎯⎯⎯⎯⎯⎯

GA1457

SUPER "BEE"HAVIOR!

Use this bulletin board to get students buzzin' with good behavior. Duplicate, color and label a bee for each student. Display the bees on the bulletin board. Duplicate honey jars for students. Every time they exhibit positive actions or demonstrate behaviors you want to encourage, have them color a row on the honey jar found on the next page.

78

GA1457

FILL IT UP!

79

DIRECTION PERFECTION

Use this bulletin board to help students learn the international directional signs. Put a series of signs on the bulletin board and encourage students to learn all of the signs and their meanings. Students can search for actual signs and make duplicates of the signs on construction paper. Add their signs to the bulletin board.

80

GA1457

OUR BUNCH IS THANKFUL

Here's a wonderful bulletin board for encouraging students to be thankful as the Thanksgiving holiday approaches. Duplicate bananas and add a student's name to each banana. Place the bananas on the bulletin board and encourage students to bring photographs and pictures of people or things that they are thankful for. Add the items to fill the bulletin board with thanks!

OUR HANDFUL OF THANKS

Instruct students to trace their hands on orange, brown, yellow or red construction paper. Cut out the hand shapes and create the tail of the turkey by overlapping and stapling all of the hands to the bulletin board. Add the turkey's head. Have students search for pictures of their favorite food items and add them to the bulletin board.

GA1457

NOVEMBER KNOW-IT-ALLS!

Use this bulletin board to display work that students are proud of. Ask students to choose work that they feel good about and add it to the bulletin board. The purpose of this board is to encourage students to have a sense of pride about their work and to be involved in evaluating what they have done. Whether they made a great score on a test, wrote a creative poem, printed a story neatly or created a terrific work of art, this bulletin board is a place where they can show it off!

KEY IN ON LEARNING

Encourage students to unlock math problems displayed on the bulletin board. Duplicate several locks from the pattern below and write a math problem on each. Duplicate keys and list the answers. Give students turns at trying their hand at the bulletin board, matching the right answer with the correct math problem.

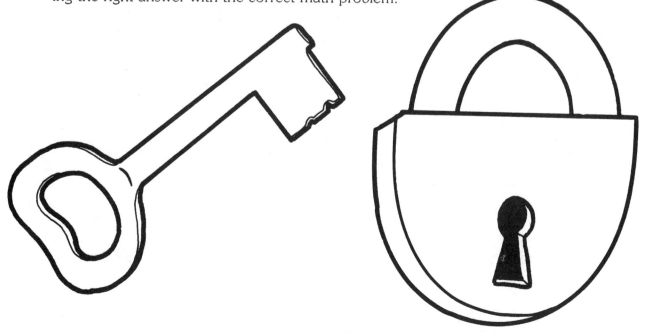

84

KEY PROBLEMS TO SOLVE!

Unlock each math problem by solving the math sentence and writing the correct answer.

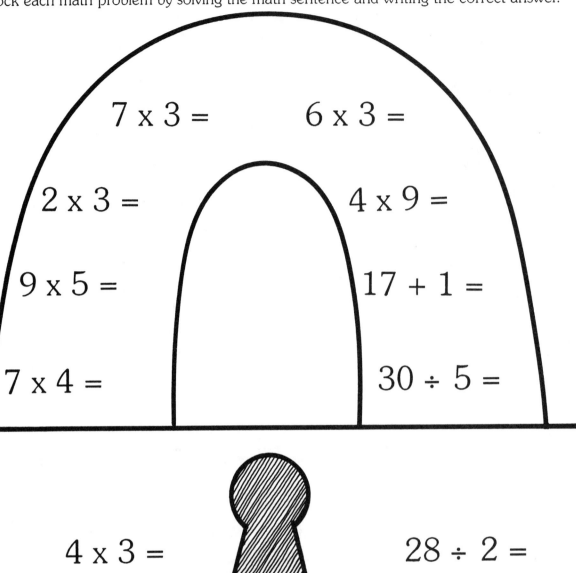

$7 \times 3 =$ $6 \times 3 =$

$2 \times 3 =$ $4 \times 9 =$

$9 \times 5 =$ $17 + 1 =$

$7 \times 4 =$ $30 \div 5 =$

$4 \times 3 =$ $28 \div 2 =$

$4 + 1 =$

$6 + 10 =$ $6 \times 12 =$

$9 \times 3 =$ $4 \times 6 =$

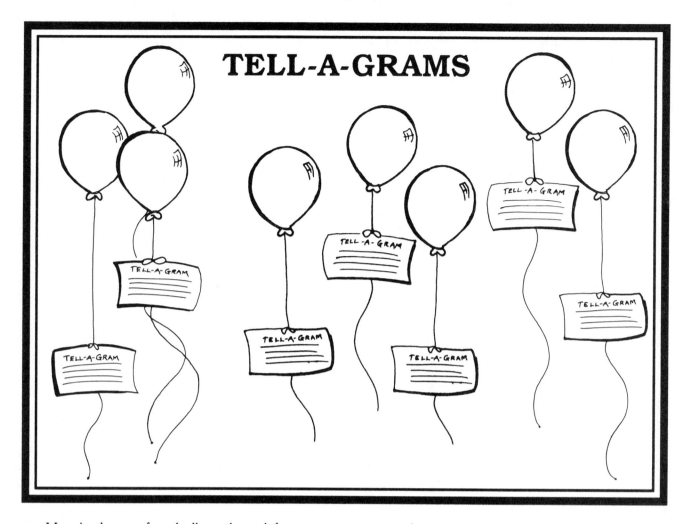

TELL-A-GRAMS

Here's the perfect bulletin board for encouraging students to get along better. Duplicate the "tell-a-gram" from the pattern below. Each time students want to tell something positive to other students, they can write a tell-a-gram and add it to the bulletin board.

TELL-A-GRAM

TO: _____
FROM: _____

86

GA1457

ALPHA-PETS

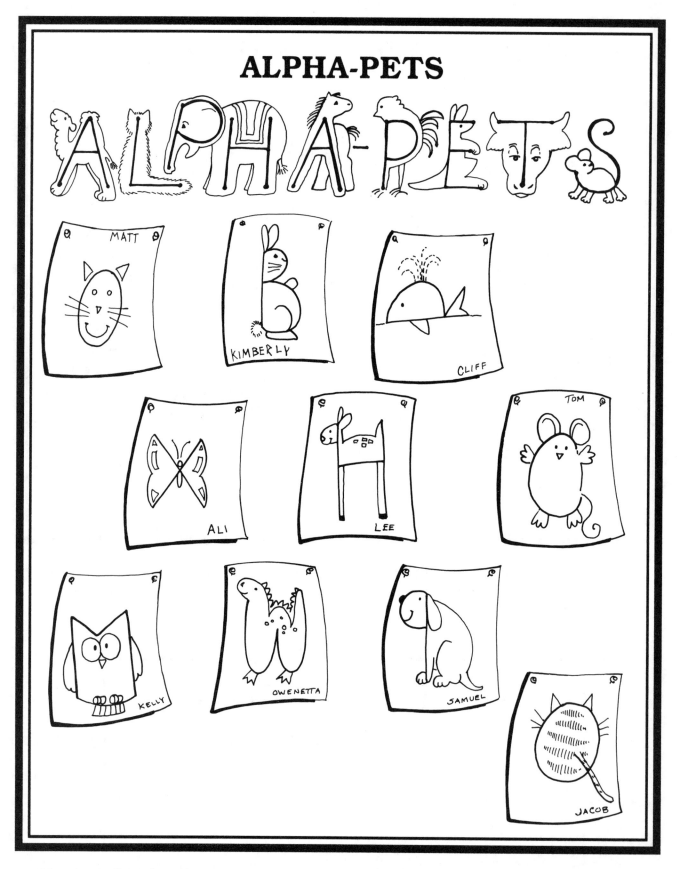

Use this bulletin board as an art activity. Turn alphabet letters into favorite pets by adding shapes to the letters and coloring them. Display the alpha-pets on the bulletin board.

87

ONE GOOD DEED DESERVES ANOTHER!

Lisa   GAIL   Dustin

Josh   Ali

Kevin   Jared

Gabrielle   Ali

Justin

Bettye   Jeffrey   Josh

Use this bulletin board to inspire students to do good deeds. When students accomplish good deeds, they get to sign their names directly on the bulletin board. Use the pattern below to award students with well-deserved praise.

GOOD DEED AWARD

This award certifies that

_____

has done a good deed! We are so proud!

GA1457

JEWEL OF AN IDEA!

Bedazzle students with a jewelry-making art lesson, perfect for any month of the year. Challenge students to recycle odds and ends and transform trash into treasures, using anything from crushed aluminum foil to paper chains to glittered bottle top earrings.

Title Waves:
Jewel of a Mom
Jewel of a Dad
Jewel of a Student
Priceless Artwork
Ready, Set, Recycle
Trash to Treasures

Odds and Ends:
pizza box
bottle tops
aluminum foil
cardboard paper tube

BUDDING ARTISTS

Give each student a paper plate and cover the top side of the plate with paint. Let the plates dry, and then teach students how to fringe the edges by cutting slits around the rim of the plate. Add stems and leaves and display the work of your "budding" artists on this bulletin board.

1. Paint paper plate right-side up. Let dry.

2. Fringe rim of plate.

3. Cut out stem and leaves from construction paper and glue or staple to flower.

4. Add details to make a face and glue in place.

90

GA1457

BONE UP ON MATH

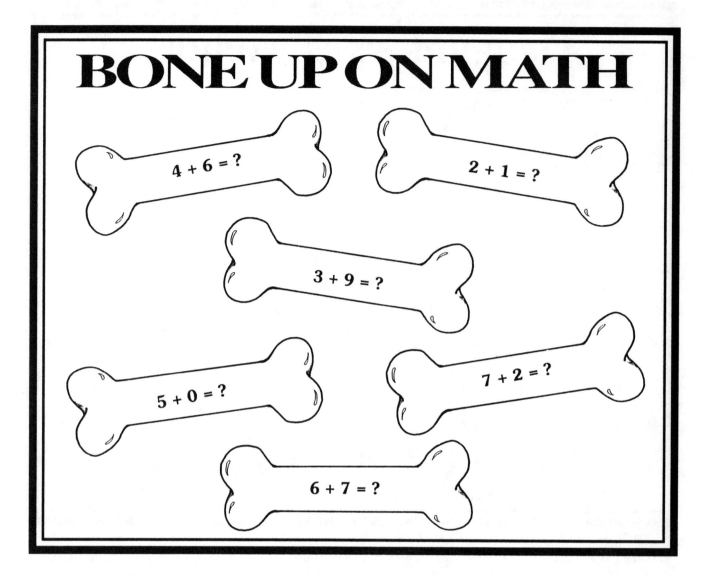

4 + 6 = ?

2 + 1 = ?

3 + 9 = ?

5 + 0 = ?

7 + 2 = ?

6 + 7 = ?

Here's a fun bulletin board that is great for encouraging students to bone up on a certain subject. Duplicate a bone for each math problem and display the bones on the bulletin board. Challenge students to try answering the problems correctly. Change the problems often. Also consider using this bulletin board for boning up on spelling or any other subject area.

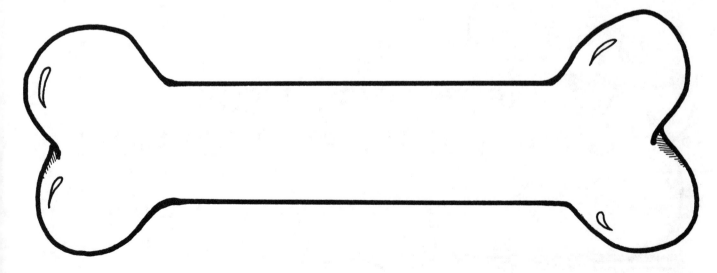

PURRRR-FECT WORK!

Here's a bulletin board to display student work that you are proud of. Award students who are making progress with the cat's meow award below.

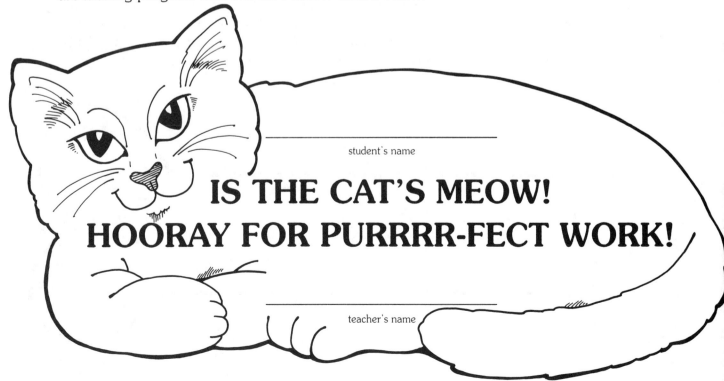

_____
student's name

IS THE CAT'S MEOW!
HOORAY FOR PURRRR-FECT WORK!

_____
teacher's name

92

GA1457

FISH FOR FACTS

Go fishing with this bulletin board and display facts about any subject that you want your students to learn. Each student can keep a record of facts on a copy of the fish pattern below. From who, what, when, where and why to science facts, this bulletin board can be recycled week after week to teach and reinforce new ideas!

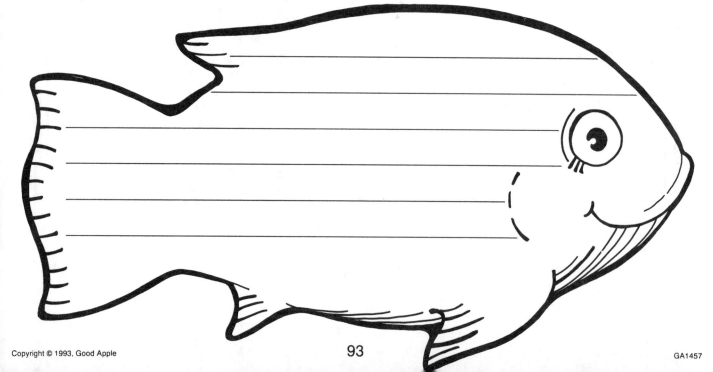

GA1457

HERE'S WHAT'S UP

Students will love looking for pictures and words that have to do with the concept of up. From spaceships to rockets to airplanes to things we see in the sky, this bulletin board will be an unlimited activity that has high hopes for learning. Have students search for related pictures and display them on the bulletin board.

94

UP IN THE CLOUDS

Instruct students to observe cloud formations and see what they can see up in the clouds. From mountains to castles to animals, students can draw pictures of their findings and display them on this bulletin board.

HOOK A BOOK

Hook a Book

Display books that you want students to read on this bulletin board by adding the book jackets directly to the board. Add a hook on a piece of yarn and encourage students to get hooked on each book and read it by a specific date. Duplicate a Hook-a-Book Record from the pattern below and have students record each book as they hook it!

I've hooked these books:

Hook-a-Book Record

GA1457

ANTONYM . . . FILL IT IN!

Use this bulletin board to teach students about antonyms. Write a variety of opposite words on index cards and place them in the envelope on the bulletin board. Write their mates on the magnet pattern below and display them on the bulletin board. Have each student choose a card from the envelope and try to find its match. Pin the pairs in place.

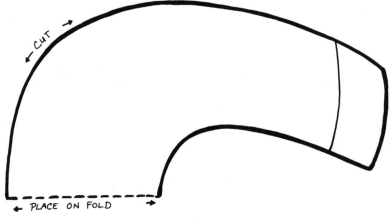

GA1457

THE GAME'S THE SAME

Use this bulletin board to teach students about homonyms. Homonyms are words that sound the same, and may even be spelled the same, but differ in meaning. Place these words on the bulletin board and have students find their matches, saying the meanings of the two different words.

CATCH A MATCH

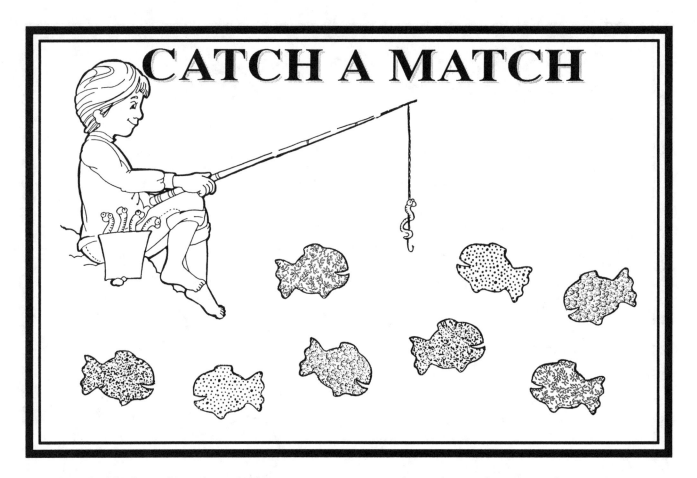

Use this bulletin board as an activity center to teach students about matching patterns. Using the fish pattern, create pairs that match. Mix them on the bulletin board. Have students match the pairs correctly. Patterns may be taken from wallpaper books or patterned fabrics.

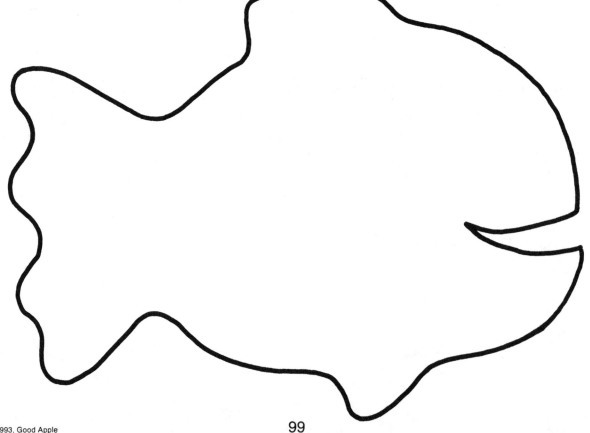

GA1457

BOWL US OVER

Use this bulletin board to encourage student inquisitiveness and reinforce any subject area in a fun way. Instruct students to display answers on the pin pattern and, in Jeopardy style, have students answer them in the form of a question. When they answer all the questions correctly, they have knocked down all the pins and have achieved a strike.

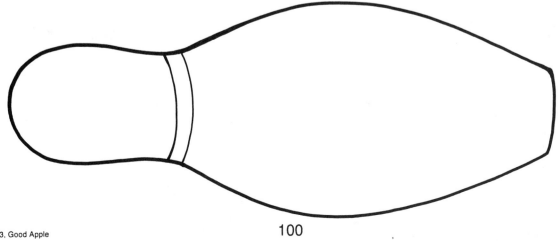

GA1457

FRAME UP

Use this bulletin board as an activity. Instruct students to cut out the center of a paper plate leaving the border as a frame. Encourage students to decorate their "frames" with lively patterns and colors.

We are Thankful

GA1457

NOVEMBER PATTERNS

103

DECEMBER

104

December Events

December 2–Georges Seurat, French painter, born 1859

December 7–Pearl Harbor Day, 1941

December 8–Eli Whitney, inventor of cotton gin, born 1765

December 16–Ludwig van Beethoven, born 1770

December 25–Christmas Day

Additional Special Days and Weeks in December

Hanukkah–Begins on the eve of the 25th day of the Hebrew month, Kislev. The holiday is known as the Festival of Lights.

The first human heart transplant was performed in Capetown, South Africa, by Dr. Christian Barnard on December 3, 1967.

The first Nobel Prizes were awarded December 10, 1901.

Illinois, Indiana, Alabama, Mississippi, Iowa and Texas were admitted to the Union.

Harry S. Truman, former President of the United States, announced the official end of World War II on December 31, 1946.

TRIM THE TREE WITH GREAT IDEAS

Use this bulletin board to encourage students to think of new ideas on any subject, from ways to help the earth to things they can do for others. This bulletin board can be recycled by adding new thoughts daily. Duplicate ornaments from the pattern below and instruct students to write their ideas on them, color with markers or crayons and add them to the bulletin board to trim the tree.

106

GA1457

WRAPPING UP DECEMBER

TARRA	Craig	Heather
Rode a two wheeler.	to ride a bike	soccer

Joseph	Mary	Larry	Brooke
ABC's	addition	to ski	Hit a baseball

Maggie	Ivan	Henry	Shirley
jump rope	whistle	Yo Yo	do a cartwheel

Use this bulletin board to highlight creative writing and help build self-esteem. Duplicate a package for each student from the pattern below. Ask students to list their favorite things that they wrapped up or learned this past year, from riding a two-wheeler to learning to recite the alphabet to playing a new game. The packages are waiting to be filled with their accomplishments and newly learned skills.

107

GA1457

WE'RE POETS AND WE SURE KNOW IT!

Use this bulletin board to display poetry written by the students. These poems can also make a wonderful holiday gift for a family member or a special friend. Talk about the importance of expressing your thanks and how words have always played an important part in the holiday spirit.

108

GA1457

DECEMBER DE"LIGHTS" US!

Duplicate light bulbs for students and have them write the ideas that delight them during the month of December. Display the lights on the bulletin board, and show your students' shining examples of neatness, creative writing and clever brainstorming.

109

GA1457

WHAT WOULD YOU DO IF . . .

Use this bulletin board to encourage a creative writing unit. Have students write wild and crazy ideas that finish this sentence: What would you do if . . . ? Place all the ideas in an envelope attached to the bulletin board, and display the creative writing examples when they are complete.

Some examples:

What would you do if . . .
    a monkey moved in as the pet next door?
    you had to ride a giraffe to school?
    there was no such thing as candy?
    you could visit someone who lived long ago?
    you could go anywhere in the world tomorrow?

MENTION OUR INVENTION!

Challenge students to create new inventions that would make better use of their time. Students should illustrate their inventions and write a page about how they work. Display the inventions on the bulletin board, and discuss which ones might really work.

INVENTION IDEAS:

homework machine
a meal in a minute
instant art
cleanup machine
instant bath

GA1457

WE'RE ART SMART

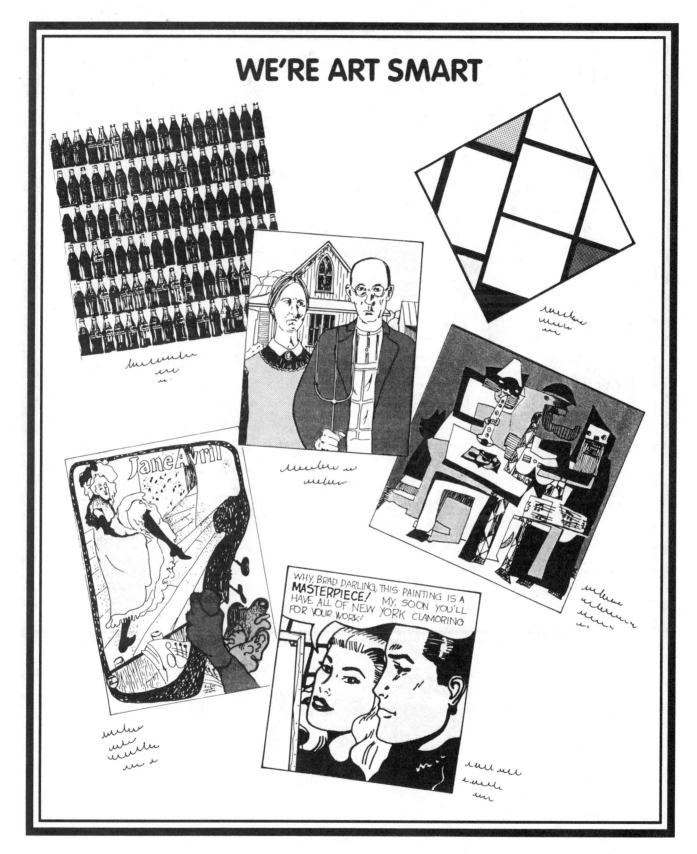

Use this bulletin board to study a variety of famous artists, periods and famous works. Display reproductions on the bulletin board with the names of the artists. Encourage the students to pick specific artists' styles and create pictures that relate to them.

GA1457

DIG INTO THE DICTIONARY

deliver

design

determine

deposit

deceive

decide

depart

delinquent

depend

deplete

"De-cember" is the perfect time to have your students dig into the dictionary and find words that begin with *de*. They will enjoy going on a treasure hunt for words from *de-ter-mined* to *De-cember* to *de-liver*. This bulletin board can be changed easily by searching for new letters. Students can write the words that they find on index cards and display them on the bulletin board.

113

GA1457

GRAND IDEAS

This bulletin board offers you a wonderful display for featuring student work in any subject, from creative writing to spelling, sentences to book reports. Assign each student a week to be in charge of collecting work and displaying it on the bulletin board. Encourage more "grand ideas," and allow students to add musical notes or any decorative additions to the board.

114

GA1457

IT'S A HANUKKAH HAPPENING!

Use this bulletin board during the month of December to focus on Hanukkah. Hanukkah is the Festival of Lights, an eight-day Jewish celebration. The Hanukkah holiday begins on the eve of the twenty-fifth day of the Hebrew month of Kislev, which usually falls in the month of December. It is the celebration of God's deliverance of the Jews in 165 B.C. This was when the Jews won their first struggle for religious freedom by defeating the Syrians who wanted them to give up Judaism. After the victory, Judah Maccabee, the Jewish leader, proclaimed a festival to be observed by Jews. It was to be called Hanukkah, which in Hebrew means "dedication."

Use this bulletin board to teach these terms:

dreidel: a spinning top used in the customary game played on Hanukkah. One Hebrew letter appears on each of the four sides of the dreidel and stands for the words *A Great Miracle Happened There.*

menorah: When the Jewish people won their victory, they returned to dedicate their temple and rekindle the eternal light in the temple lamp. When they arrived they found only a small jar of oil, which meant the light would burn for only one night. But the oil burned in the menorah, the candelabrum, for eight days. The menorah is lit on each night of Hanukkah to reenact the miracle of lights.

latke: a potato pancake and a traditional food eaten on Hanukkah

shamos: The menorah has eight branches and one extra for the helper candle which is called the shamos. The shamos is used to light the other candles on each night of Hanukkah.

GA1457

HOLIDAYS ARE HAPPY DAYS!

Use this bulletin board to display student-made greeting cards or cards made from recycled store-bought cards. Have students bring old greeting cards to class. Discuss various styles and examples. Students can cut up the cards and the messages, and then recycle them into new cards they create themselves. Add the cards to the bulletin board to display.

116

DIGEST THESE FACTS

The purpose of this bulletin board is to encourage students to learn the information you choose to display in any subject area. For an additional activity, duplicate "Food for Thought" found on the next page and display student work on the bulletin board.

117

FOOD FOR THOUGHT

List the things that you enjoy thinking about, from your favorite sports to books you like to read. Record your ideas on this page.

_____

_____

_____

_____

_____

_____

_____

_____

_____

_____

_____

_____

GA1457

LOOK WHAT'S COOKING IN DECEMBER

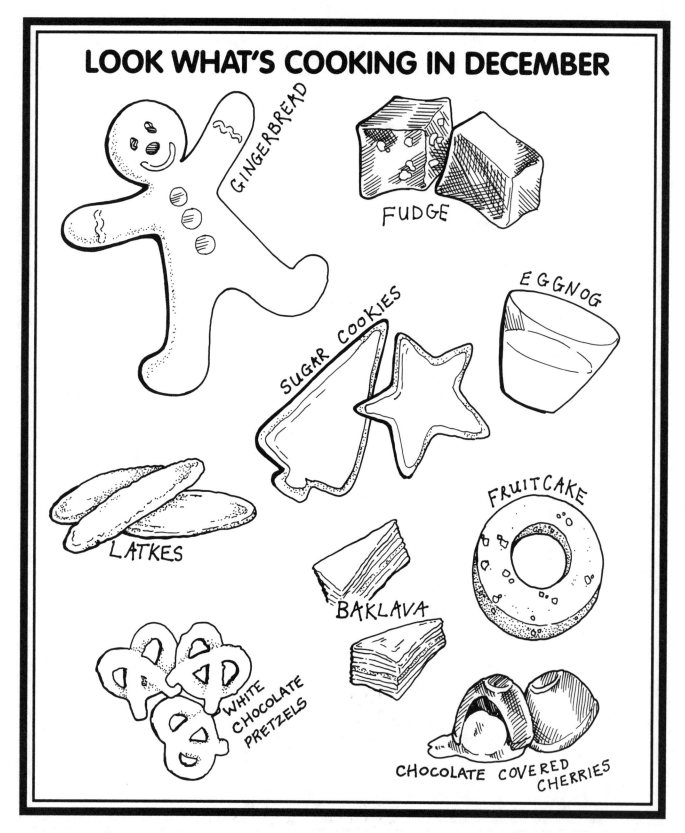

GINGERBREAD

FUDGE

EGGNOG

SUGAR COOKIES

FRUITCAKE

LATKES

BAKLAVA

WHITE CHOCOLATE PRETZELS

CHOCOLATE COVERED CHERRIES

Here's a great bulletin board for celebrating the holiday season by displaying pictures of traditional and enticing holiday dishes. Some of these dishes represent special family traditions, so encourage a class discussion and learn all about one another's delicacies during the holiday season. A fun class activity would also be to have a taste test and invite parents in to help students prepare a few of the dishes.

REMEMBER DECEMBER

Schoolwide play Dec. 3!

Remember Trim-the-Tree Dec. 10!

Chorus Practice Tuesdays!

Hanukkah!

Christmas!

Use this bulletin board to list events that occur in December. Involve students by challenging them to look up or recall historical events, special family occasions and dates. This is also an ideal bulletin board for posting school activities and other events that occur in the month of December.

GA1457

WARM UP TO READING

Use this bulletin board to encourage students to read books for pleasure over the holidays. Display actual book jackets on the bulletin board as an example of the kinds of books you recommend.

121

MATH REALLY ADDS UP

Use this bulletin board to encourage math skills. Instruct students to cut out numbers from magazines and the newspapers and bring them in and staple them to the bulletin board. Challenge students to record the numbers and keep a running tally of what this bulletin board adds up to!

122

IT'S "S-NOW" OR NEVER

Use this bulletin board to ignite a cool art activity. Have students imagine or recall a scene that shows what happens when it snows. Use household objects like cotton balls or plastic packaging materials to simulate snow and have an art activity where students create snowmen or any snow scene on paper. Display the finished artwork on the bulletin board.

GA1457

BREAK THE ICE

Use this bulletin board to encourage students to get to know one another better and work as a team in the classroom. Have students write something about themselves on paper plates. Students should not put their names on their plates. Display the plates on the bulletin board and let the other students try to guess who's who.

GA1457

"ELF" YOU'RE WISE, YOU'LL LISTEN

Use this bulletin board to encourage good behavior and cooperation in the classroom. Every time students listen, cooperate or show positive behavior, instruct them to sign their names on this graffiti style bulletin board.

125

THE REASON FOR THE SEASON

Use this bulletin board to teach the class about the different holidays that each classmate celebrates. Instruct students to interview one another and learn about the different holidays. Students can write about what they learn and display the finished work on the bulletin board.

126

WORK OUT FOR WINTER

Use this bulletin board to teach the students about the various activities they can do during the winter months. Have students search for pictures of activities in newspapers and magazines, as well as draw pictures to be added to the bulletin board.

DECEMBER'S DANDY

Have a class discussion about how the holidays make you feel. Instruct students to write poems about their feelings and display them on the bulletin board.

128

"TREE"MENDOUS WISHES FOR A HAPPY HOLIDAY

This seasonal bulletin board is perfect for students to create by themselves. Cut out a large Christmas tree for them to decorate, and challenge students to recycle throwaways; be resourceful and use a variety of materials. Encourage a variety of art activities, from ornaments made from egg cartons to bottle cap miniature frames, that can go on all month. Students can take down this board and then wrap up their ornaments before the holidays and give them to their families as holiday presents.

GA1457

RECYCLED WREATHS

Use this bulletin board as a holiday art activity. Have students save a paper plate, bows and scrap ribbon and reuse them to embellish their creations. Begin this activity by cutting out a circle from the center of the paper plate. This will leave a wreath shape. Students can collage the plate with a variety of colorful odds and ends to create the wreath. Add the finished products to the bulletin board to display.

ENTER WINTER

This bulletin board is perfect to feature student artwork illustrating winter activities. You've heard of brainstorming; well now it's time to snowstorm with your class. Then create characters and objects that depict a winter scene. Encourage students to investigate what animals do when it gets cold and how we can help them.

GA1457

DASH INTO DECEMBER

Play Pin the Nose on the Reindeer. Write a math problem on each reindeer's antlers, and the correct answer on each reindeer's nose. Have the students match the correct answers by pinning the reindeer noses on the correct reindeer. You can also assign students to work as a team and time each team as they play Pin the Nose on the Reindeer.

DECEMBER PATTERNS

GA1457

DECEMBER PATTERNS

134

DECEMBER PATTERNS

135

JANUARY

136

GA1457

January Events

January 1–New Year's Day

January 1–Betsy Ross, born 1752

January 4–Louis Braille, born 1809

January 15–Martin Luther King, Jr., born 1929

January 20–Inauguration Day. The President of the United States takes the oath of office on this day following each general election.

January 27–Wolfgang Amadeus Mozart, born 1756

January 30–Franklin D. Roosevelt, born 1882

Additional Special Days and Weeks in January

Chinese New Year–may occur in December some years

Elvis Presley was born in Tupelo, Mississippi, on January 8, 1935.

GA1457

WE'RE IN GREAT SHAPE FOR A NEW YEAR

Use this bulletin board to teach different shapes such as squares, triangles, circles, etc. Students will love shaping up this bulletin board with their creative touches. Have an art activity and instruct students to put the different shapes together to make pictures or characters.

GA1457

NEW YEAR'S NEWS

Articles courtesy of the Hancock County Journal-Pilot Newspaper, Carthage, IL

Use this bulletin board to display current events. Have the students bring in newspaper clippings and add them to the board, making a collage of news.

139

GA1457

RING IN A NEW YEAR!

Use this bulletin board to display students' New Year's resolutions. Duplicate telephones for students and have them list the things they want to improve during the year. Display the telephones on the bulletin board.

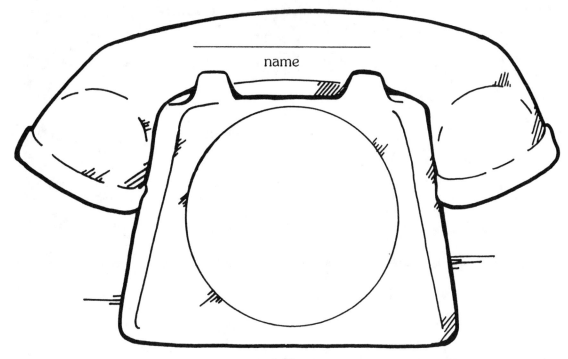

name

MAKE THIS A RECORD YEAR

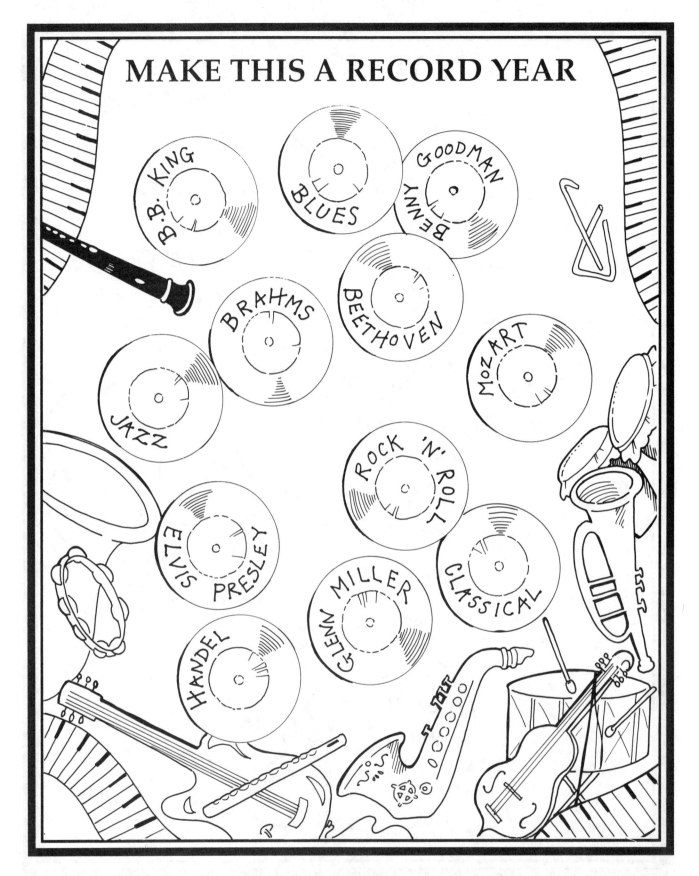

Use this bulletin board to teach students about the various kinds of music and the people who write and sing music. Also, display various instruments to familiarize students with them.

141

GA1457

NEW YEAR'S WISHES

Use this bulletin board to encourage students to make New Year's resolutions and write stories about their wishes for themselves and the world.

GA1457

TUNE IN THE NEW YEAR

Use this bulletin board to display events that are happening at your school for the upcoming year. Include holidays, field trips, special school events, closing days, etc.

143

JUMP INTO JANUARY

Use this bulletin board to encourage physical fitness during the winter months. Display illustrations of students' favorite activities. Encourage students to draw pictures of themselves in action.

144

WATCH OUT IN WINTER

Use this bulletin board to encourage safety during the cold winter months. Display the proper clothing, the right things to eat and drink and ways to avoid accidents. Students can make posters to encourage safety. Use this bulletin board to display pictures from magazines, student artwork or any other signs or warnings that will help students be safe, from looking both ways when crossing the street to avoiding thin ice.

"WONDER"FUL WINTER

Use this bulletin board to inform students about various activities that occur during winter. Why does it snow? Why is it cold? Why do birds fly South? This board can explain all the winter oddities and encourage your students to wonder about them and learn why they occur.

146

READY, SET, READ

Use this bulletin board to fight the winter doldrums by listing suggested book titles for students to read as winter approaches.

147

GA1457

Use this bulletin board to celebrate Martin Luther King Day. Discuss what Martin Luther King accomplished, and have the students display their own special dreams on the board.

148

CHILL OUT IN JANUARY

Use this bulletin board to encourage good behavior in the classroom. Have the students list appropriate behavior and define inappropriate behavior. Every time students do something that you want to encourage, award them with good behavior awards duplicated from the pattern below.

_____'s Good Behavior Is Showing!

           student's name

_____

           teacher's name

GA1457

JANUARY JAZZ

Use this bulletin board to motivate students after they return from the holidays. Choose ideas, topics or activities to display on the board.

150

KEYED UP ABOUT JANUARY

invented the lightning rod

invented bifocal glasses

refused to patent any of his inventions or use them for profit

"An ounce of prevention is worth a pound of cure."

Benjamin Franklin's birthday is January 17th. Use this bulletin board to encourage students to learn about him and all of his accomplishments and inventions.

GA1457

"SNOW" KIDDING! THIS CLASS IS COOL

Use this bulletin board to display students' work, photographs and special projects created during the month of January.

152

BE A WINNER IN WINTER

Use this bulletin board to encourage students to win raving reviews by displaying good penmanship.

153

GA1457

CAN YOU FIND WHAT'S MISSING?

Use this bulletin board to teach students to find the missing element in a series of events. Example: Justin opened the refrigerator, took an apple, got a glass of milk, put the milk back, and started eating his apple. The action that is missing is closing the refrigerator door. Have students write events in proper order except for one action or event on the board. Then have the rest of the class fill in the correct missing action or event.

154

ON YOUR MARK, GET SET, SNOW!

Use this bulletin board to encourage students to write creative stories about winter. Display the students' writing on the board.

155

GA1457

LOOK WHO TAKES THE CAKE

Mrs. Harris

Is the Icing on the Cake!

Use this bulletin board to highlight students, community helpers or anyone who helps others in some way. Feature a school helper or even a student or teacher who has done something special for another person or the entire community.

GA1457

ALL IS WELL WHEN YOU CAN SPELL

Use this bulletin board as a fun way to encourage students to learn to spell new words. Place pictures of objects that are on students' spelling lists on the bulletin board with the letters scrambled next to the pictures. Have students unscramble the words to identify the pictures.

157

A BETTER LETTER

Use this bulletin board to teach students writing skills and to learn to write a proper letter. Instruct students to collect letters from home and add them to the bulletin board. Point out which letters are easy to read and which ones are more difficult. Discuss the main parts of a letter. Have students write to someone famous or a person of their choice.

ELECTION SELECTION

Use this bulletin board to encourage students to plan a class election, including campaigns and speeches leading up to the inauguration (January 20th). Have students make promotional posters and display them on this bulletin board.

IT'S A TREAT TO BE NEAT

Use this bulletin board to promote neatness in the classroom. Have a class discussion about neatness. Invite students to write about how neatness makes them look great and why. Have a class discussion about what might have happened if an important document was written and no one could read it. Brainstorm a variety of documents, such as birth certificates or The Bill of Rights, for which neatness counts.

160

GA1457

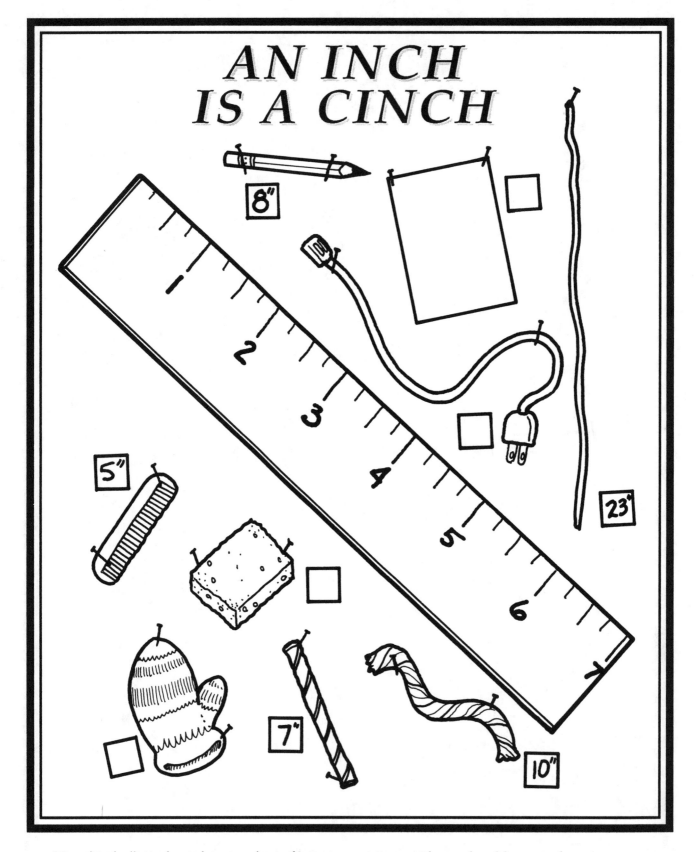

AN INCH IS A CINCH

8"

5"

23"

7"

10"

Use this bulletin board to teach students to measure with a ruler. Have students measure the objects on the bulletin board and other things around the classroom. Challenge students to measure objects of different shapes and sizes. Add the measurements of these objects to the bulletin board.

161

GA1457

Use this bulletin board to highlight monthly activities and promote excitement for what is happening at school.

162

JANUARY PATTERNS

163

GA1457

JANUARY PATTERNS

GA1457

FEBRUARY

GA1457

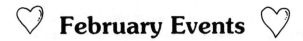 # ♡ February Events ♡

February 1–National Freedom Day

February 2–Groundhog Day

February 11–Thomas Alva Edison, born 1847

February 12–Abraham Lincoln, born 1809

February 14–Valentine's Day

February 22–George Washington, born 1732

February 29–Leap Year Day, occurs every four years

 ## Additional Special Days and Weeks in February

African American History Month

Purim–Jewish holiday that occurs in February or March on the fourteenth day of the lunar month of Adar. It is the Feast of Lots, a celebration of the casting of lots which showed Haman to be very evil and Esther to be good.

On February 3, 1876, the National League of baseball was organized.

National Wildlife Week–Begins the third Sunday in February

GA1457

FIRSTHAND LOOK AT FEBRUARY

Use this bulletin board to encourage students to plan events for the classroom, displaying these events on the hands. This bulletin board can also be used to display school events planned for the month.

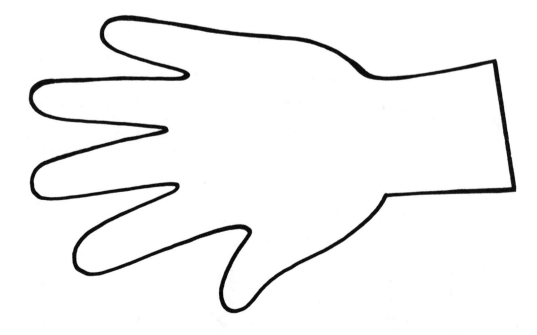

CAN YOU GUESS THIS PRESIDENT?
NEED A HINT?

Use this bulletin board to encourage the celebration of Lincoln's and Washington's birthdays which both occur in February. Have students write facts about Lincoln and Washington and other Presidents on flags duplicated from the pattern below. Display the flags on the board. Then have students identify who's who by the facts written on the board.

GA1457

A HEART OF GOLD

Use this bulletin board to inspire a creative writing story about a person with a "heart of gold." Have students write their stories on the heart pattern and display them on the bulletin board as well as give them to their favorite valentines.

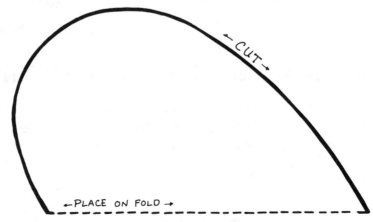

GA1457

SOUND OFF

Use this bulletin board to teach students to listen for, recognize, and identify vowel sounds. Display a variety of words with different vowel sounds on this bulletin board. Have a class-wide sound-off contest, and challenge students to correctly identify the vowels and their pronunciations.

FEBRUARY'S FINEST

Use this bulletin board to display students' outstanding work and achievements during the course of the month.

171

GO HOG-WILD IN FEBRUARY

Use this bulletin board to teach students about Groundhog Day which takes place on February 2. Take the students outside on that day to see if they can see their shadows.

172

GA1457

BRUSH UP ON DENTAL HABITS

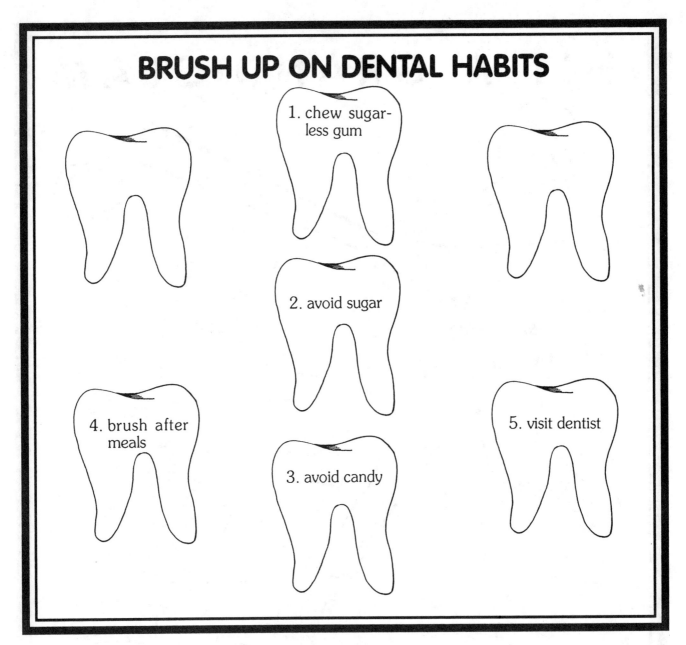

1. chew sugar-less gum

2. avoid sugar

4. brush after meals

3. avoid candy

5. visit dentist

Use this bulletin board to make students aware of Dental Health Week. Have a discussion with students about good dental health. Have students write their suggestions on teeth duplicated from the pattern below. Display the teeth on the board. Also, invite a dentist to speak to the class.

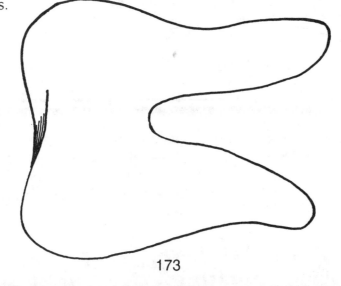

173

GA1457

HIT A GRAND SLAM

Use this bulletin board to make students aware of the founding of the National League of baseball on February 3, 1876. Have students gather facts about America's favorite pastime, bringing cards and memorabilia about their favorite players. Then invite students to write stories about their favorite ball players or sports heroes. Display the stories on the board.

GA1457

LEAP INTO FEBRUARY

Use this bulletin board to encourage students to discuss the calendar and to gather facts about leap year. Display the facts on index cards and add them to the bulletin board.

175

FAMOUS AFRICAN AMERICANS

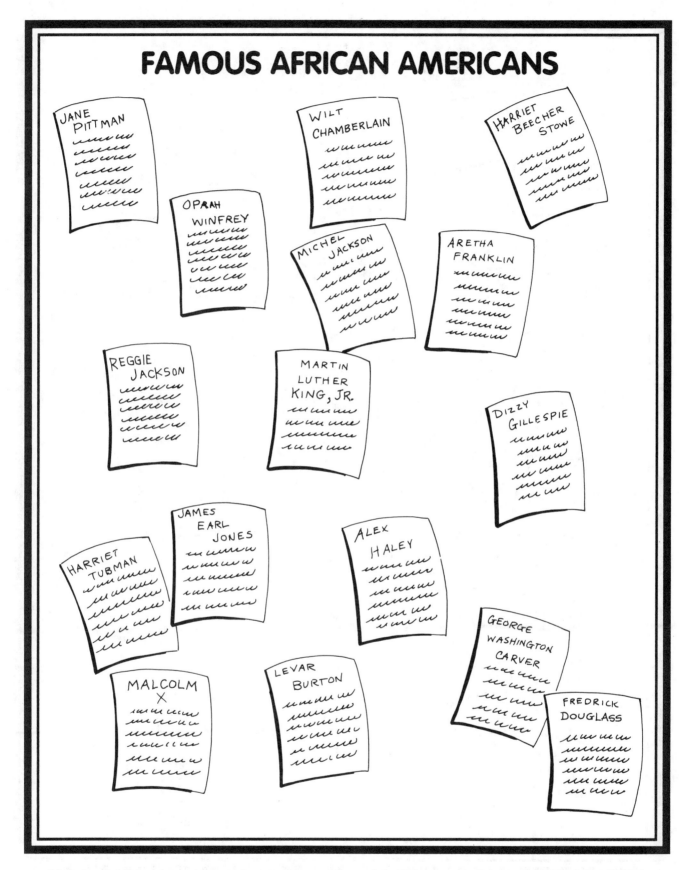

Use this bulletin board to make students aware that February is African American History Month. Have each student research a different African American and write about his or her achievements. Display the reports on the bulletin board.

GET FIT IN FEBRUARY

Use this bulletin board to encourage students to develop a physical fitness program for the class, taking a few minutes each day to exercise as a group.

GA1457

GOING WILD

National Wildlife Week begins on the third Sunday in February. Use this bulletin board to encourage students to gather facts about their favorite animals. Display them on the board. Contact a local zoo to have someone come talk to the students and bring some animals. Consider taking the class on a field trip to the zoo to observe the animals in action.

BE WISE AND ALPHABETIZE

Use this bulletin board as an activity center. Instruct students to put the owls in alphabetical order by pinning them in place. Use the owl pattern below and make an owl with each student's name on it. Mix up the owls so they are out of alphabetical order. Challenge students to pin them in their correct places.

179

YOUR ORDER, PLEASE!

d. e. ___, ___, ___, ___

A. a. B. b. ___, ___, ___, ___

a. ___, ___, ___, e. f. ___, ___

N. ___, ___, Q. R. S. ___, ___

Here's a terrific bulletin board to reinforce students' ability to place alphabet letters in order. On the bulletin board place hot dogs with letters of the alphabet in sequence. Some letters should be missing. It is the student's job to correctly supply the missing letters. Instruct students to number an answer sheet and write the correct sequence that should be given.

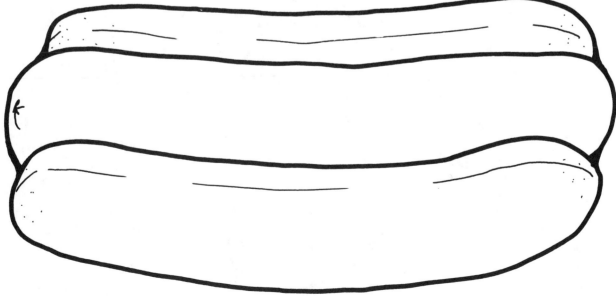

GET IN ACTION WITH A FRACTION

Use this bulletin board as an interactive activity for introducing fractions. Give students paper plates and have them divide them into fourths. Give students different fractions to cut out. For example, if cutting $\frac{1}{4}$, one piece should be removed from the plate. Instruct students to color the remaining pieces to look like a pizza or pieces of pie, and display their leftovers on the bulletin board.

GA1457

MATCH A BATCH

Use this bulletin board to teach students to recognize alphabet sounds and letters. Duplicate cookies and add alphabet letters to each and cut out a picture of an object that begins with that letter. Display the cookies on the bulletin board, and challenge students to match the words correctly with their beginning letters.

182

SOUND OFF

Use this bulletin board to teach students to identify sounds made by different objects or animals. Display pictures of the objects along with the sounds they make. Have students match the correct sounds to the objects. Example: train—chug; door slamming—bang; pencil breaking—crack; carrot—crunch; Rice Krispies™—snap, crackle, pop; dog—bark; cow—moo.

"AD" IT UP!

Use this bulletin board to teach students about the ways advertising slogans encourage us to purchase their products and services. Have the students match the slogan to the product.

ALTERNATE ACTIVITY: Have students come up with their own products and develop ad campaigns and slogans that will help sell the products. Students can also write jingles and songs to go with their products and perform them for the class.

YOUR HEALTH IS WEALTH

Eat a balanced diet.

Limit sweets

Brush your teeth three times a day, and floss at least once a day.

Exercise daily

Visit your dentist regularly.

Visit your dentist regularly.

Use this bulletin board to teach students about good health. Have students discuss what things they can do to keep themselves healthy. Point out to students that a lifetime of good health starts early and that by watching the little things now we can avoid bigger problems later on in life.

GA1457

GETTING TO THE ROOT OF THE MATTER

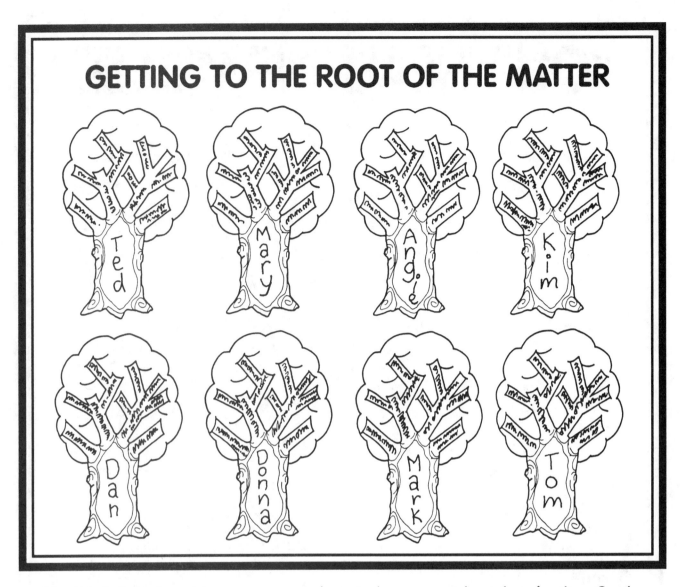

Use this bulletin board to encourage students to learn more about their families. On the limbs of the tree have students write names and places of birth of their families, tracking their origins. This will help students appreciate their roots and individual backgrounds.

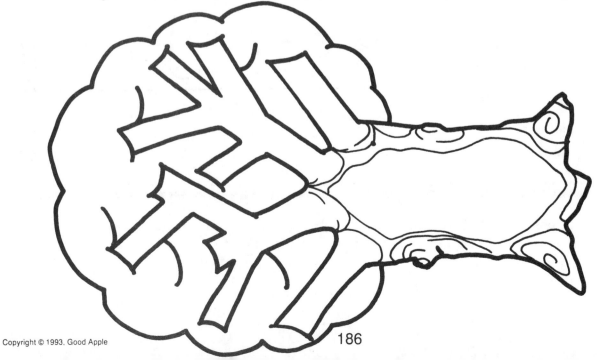

GA1457

IF THE SHOE FITS . . .

Use this bulletin board to encourage students to choose someone whose shoes they would like to be in–a famous sports star, a politician, an author. Encourage each student to do a research report about that person and display the work on the bulletin board. Duplicate shoe patterns from below, and add the students' names and persons they most admire by their reports.

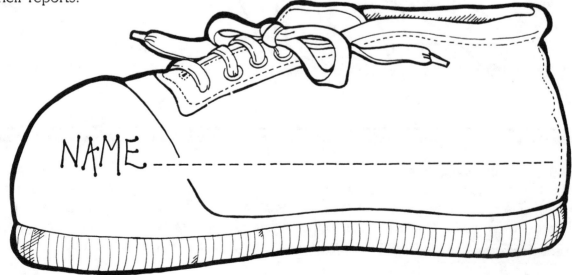

NAME _

187

GA1457

FACE THE FACTS

Use this bulletin board to help students learn research skills and to use reference materials in the library. Have students choose their favorite heroes or heroines and make collector cards of them. Draw or cut out pictures of their heroes or heroines to put on the top of the cards. Then invite students to go to the library, research facts about those people, and put the information below the pictures. Display the cards on the bulletin board.

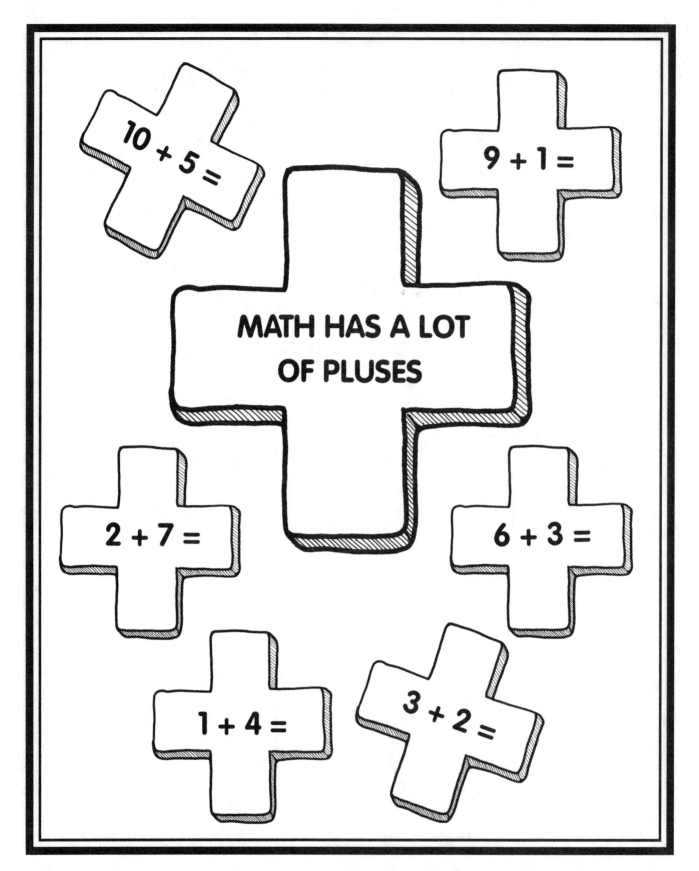

Use this bulletin board to teach students addition skills. On the plus pattern, fill out numerous addition problems. Divide the class into teams, having the teams fill in the answers displayed on the problems shown on the board.

IT'S F "AIR" TO SAY, BE CAREFUL!

Use this bulletin board to teach students about air pollution. Have the students research and make lists of pollutants, ways that the air is being polluted, and how each of these pollutants could specifically harm the environment. Display students' lists on the bulletin board.

190

LET'S MAKE A CLEAN SWEEP

Use this bulletin board to encourage students to help keep the classroom and the school neat and clean. On unannounced days have a classroom inspection for neatness. If the classroom passes inspection, students can earn certain privileges. Duplicate brooms for students and add their names. Place the brooms on the bulletin board border and recognize students with stars on the broom patterns every time they make an extra-special effort to keep the classroom clean.

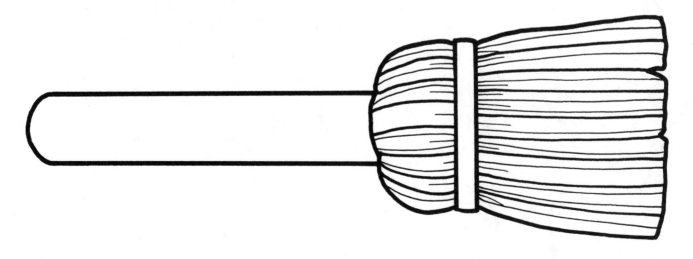

191

FEBRUARY PATTERNS

192

FEBRUARY PATTERNS

193

GA1457

FEBRUARY PATTERNS

194

MARCH

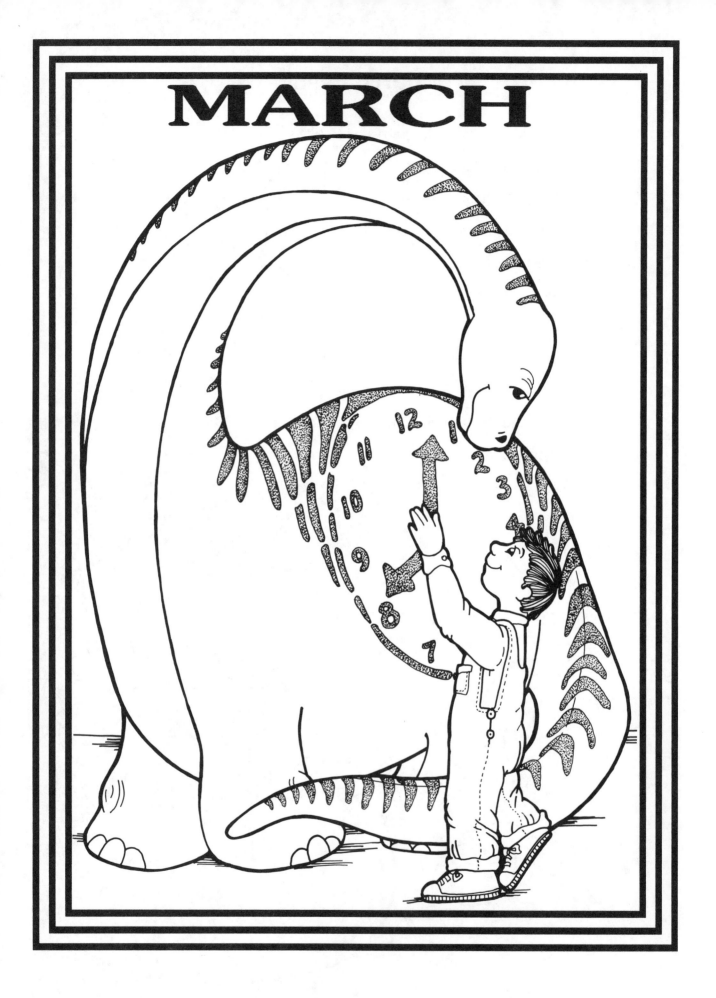

March Events

March 1–First United States bank established, 1780

March 3–Doll Festival in Japan

March 4–Dr. Seuss' birthday

March 6–Michelangelo's birthday, born 1475

March 17–St. Patrick's Day

March 21–First day of spring

March 24–Harry Houdini, born 1874

March 26–Robert Frost, American poet, born 1874

Additional Special Days and Weeks in March

National Nutrition Month

Save Your Vision Week

Camp Fire Girls Week

Red Cross Month

Youth Art Month

National Weights and Measures Week–Begins March 1

FORWARD MARCH

Use this bulletin board to display events and happenings in the classroom that will be taking place in March. This is also an excellent time to challenge your students to improve in a specific skill. Display student work that you are proud of on this bulletin board.

National Nutrition Week occurs in March. Use this bulletin board to make students more aware of eating nutritious foods. Invite the school dietician to discuss good nutrition with students. Have him or her talk about a balanced meal and what is required for a menu to be nutritious. Display pictures of proper meals on the board.

BE WISE WITH YOUR EYES

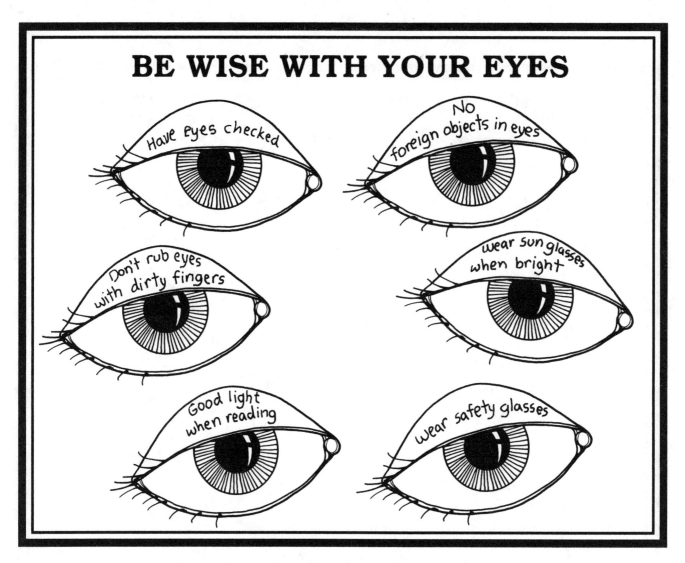

Save Your Vision Week occurs in March. Use this bulletin board to promote eye safety. Have an eye doctor come to class to discuss the proper ways to care for your eyes. Write these suggestions on the eye pattern and display on the board.

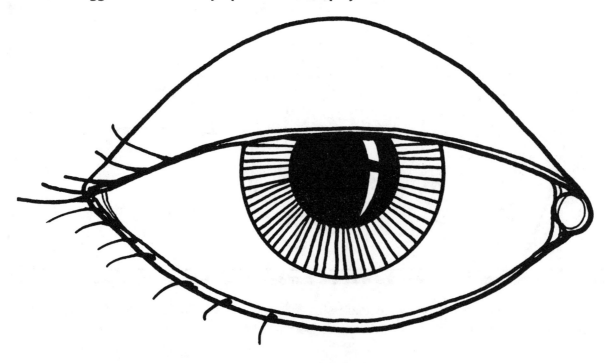

GA1457

WE REMEMBER DOCTOR SEUSS

March 4 is Dr. Seuss' birthday. Have each student make a birthday card for Dr. Seuss in the style and manner in which he wrote his books. Display these cards on the bulletin board.

GA1457

IT'S MARCH MADNESS

Use this bulletin board to display thoughts and messages of students in March. Encourage students to write positive comments, funny jokes or riddles. Compile this information for the month, and at the end of the month have the students award a prize for the most original comment, joke or riddle.

GA1457

FLY HIGH IN MARCH

Use this bulletin board to promote a feeling of excitement for the month of March. Suggest activities that are fun to do or that will strengthen writing and reading skills. Or consider displaying an art activity where your students make kites.

MARCH LINEUP

Use this bulletin board to encourage students to notice how they feel when they come to school. To promote an awareness of personal emotions, have students write how they feel on the people patterns and display on the bulletin board.

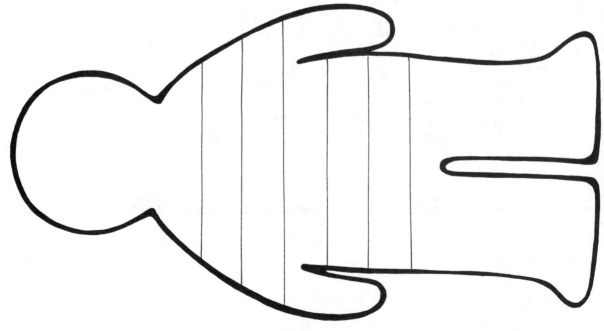

THE LUCK OF THE IRISH

March 17 is St. Patrick's Day. Use this bulletin board to celebrate this holiday by having students research and write about the origin and customs of St. Patrick's Day. Another activity could be to have students rename themselves in Irish by adding an "O" or "Mc" to the beginning of their last names. This will bring the Irish out in all of them.

GA1457

OUR ILLUSTRATIONS ARE SENSATIONS!

Use this bulletin board to promote an understanding of the job of an illustrator. Have students choose a series of words and then draw them with "feeling." Display the illustrations on the board. Words such as *fat, thin, smile* and *down* can be drawn to visualize the meaning. *Fat* could be written with wide lettering, *down* could be written vertically, etc.

GA1457

THERE'S MAGIC IN MARCH

On March 24, 1874, Harry Houdini, the famous magician, was born. Use this bulletin board to encourage students to learn magic tricks and perform them for the class. Invite a magician to class to share a few favorite tricks. This exercise is excellent for encouraging students to feel confident in front of a group and for trying their hand at something entertaining and fun.

MARCH ALONG IN MATH

Use this bulletin board to teach addition skills. Display various numbers on the bulletin board, and have the students list all the ways problems can be made to add up to the numbers displayed.

207

GA1457

Use this bulletin board to build students' map skills. Have them choose a city and learn facts about that city such as population, historic sites, famous citizens, professional sports teams, etc. This bulletin board can also be used to help students learn about distances between cities.

208

IT'S ABOUT TIME

Use this bulletin board to teach students to tell time and to help them understand the concept of time. Have them pick out important occasions in their lives and find out what times they occurred. Use the "It's About Time" work sheet on the next page. Display the students' completed work sheets on the bulletin board.

209

GA1457

IT'S ABOUT TIME WORK SHEET

1. What time do you do your homework every night?
   _____

2. What time does your favorite TV show come on?
   _____

3. What time do you eat dinner?
   _____

4. What time do you use the telephone the most?
   _____

5. What time do you wake up for school?
   _____

6. What time do you wake up on the weekend?
   _____

7. What time are you usually the hungriest?
   _____

GA1457

TIME MARCHES ON

Use this bulletin board to teach creative writing skills. Have students pick out particular periods in time and write imaginative stories set in those time periods. Display the stories on the bulletin board.

211

MARCH ROUNDUP

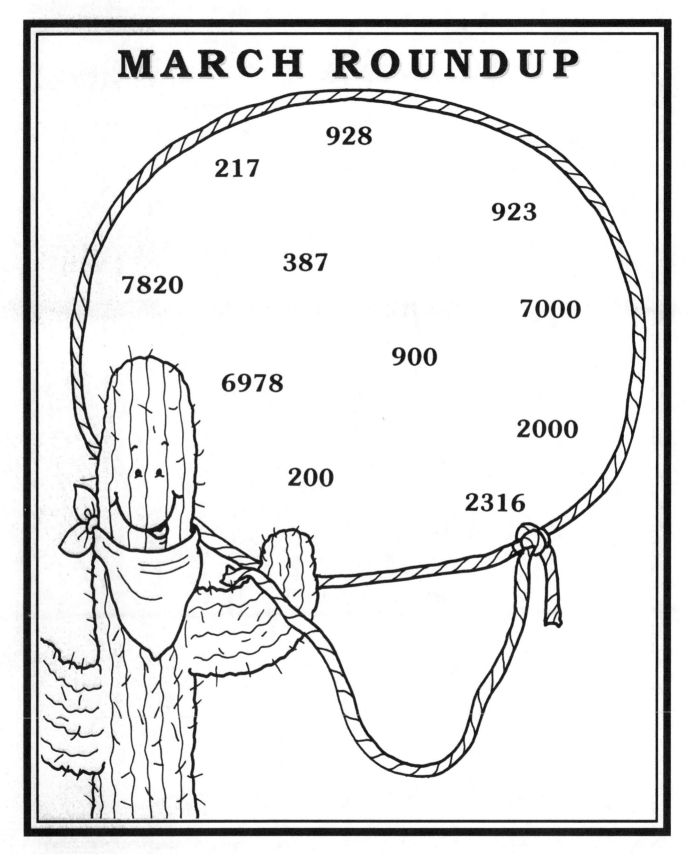

Use this bulletin board to teach students the concept of rounding off numbers. Have students look up statistics in the encyclopedia or almanac and round off these numbers to the nearest hundred or thousand. Display the actual number and the rounded off number on the bulletin board, as well as numbers you want your students to round off.

GET ON THE BALL IN MARCH

Use this bulletin board to display students' work as they improve in the classroom. Encourage students to choose areas they want to concentrate on, and have them complete the contract on the next page with their goals in mind.

213

LOOK WHO IS ON THE BALL!

I, _____,

am dedicating my time and effort to improve in the following area(s):

_____

_____

To improve, I will _____

_____

Signed _____

Date_____

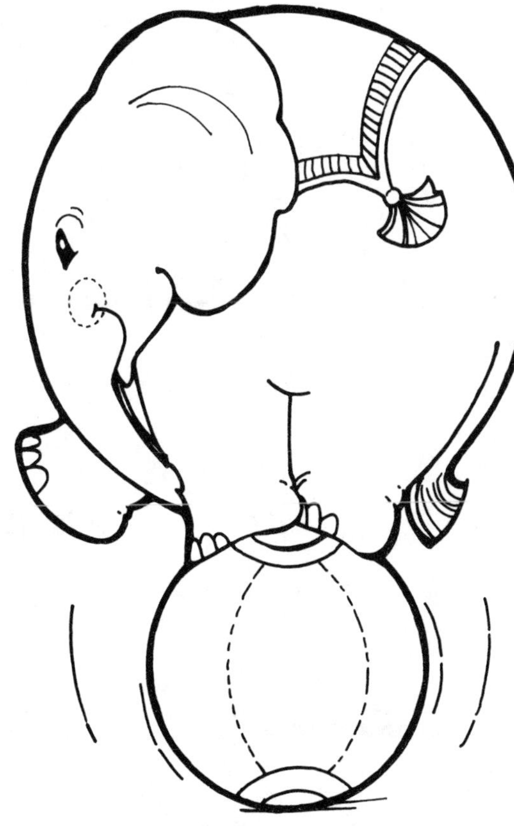

THE TEMPERATURE'S RISING

Use this bulletin board to encourage an awareness of fire prevention and fire safety. Have students research Fire Prevention Week. Discuss examples of dangerous situations and what could be done to prevent them. Invite a fire fighter to talk to the class or visit a fire station.

ALL ABOUT AIR

Use this bulletin board to teach students about air. Develop questions about air and have each student research and answer the question. Example: Can we see air? Do fish need air? What kind of air makes a balloon fly? If we can't see air, how do we know it's dirty? Challenge students to illustrate their ideas about air and display them on the bulletin board.

GA1457

ALL SORTS OF SPORTS

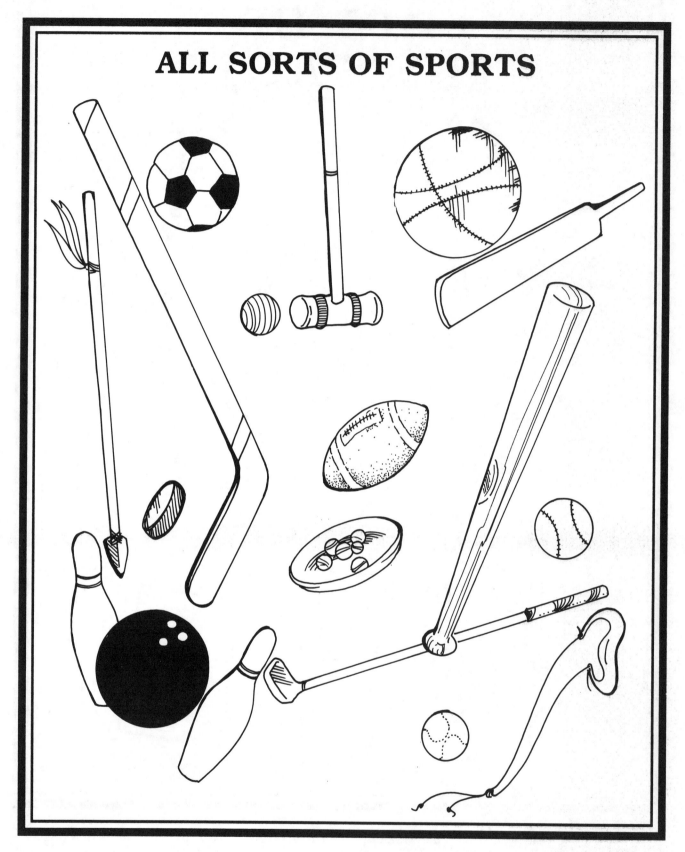

Use this bulletin board to teach students about the geography of the world. Have students pick countries and identify where they are in relation to home. Have them research and write reports about the sports that are played in those countries. Pictures of objects used in the sports can be displayed on the bulletin board along with the student reports.

DIG UP THE FACTS

Use this bulletin board to teach students how to use the library and resource materials. Have students pick topics and look up the facts to write short stories about their topics. Display students' finished work on the bulletin board.

218

"D" IS FOR DRAGON

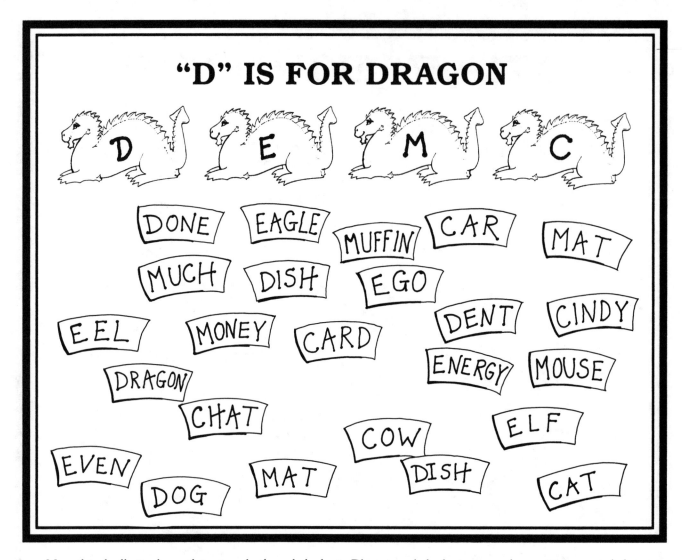

Use this bulletin board to teach the alphabet. Play an alphabet game by writing an alphabet letter on the dragon pattern. Write words on matching cards beginning with that letter, and let the students match the cards with their appropriate dragon mates.

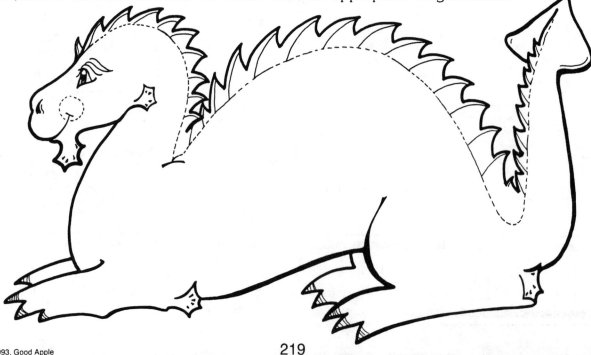

219

GA1457

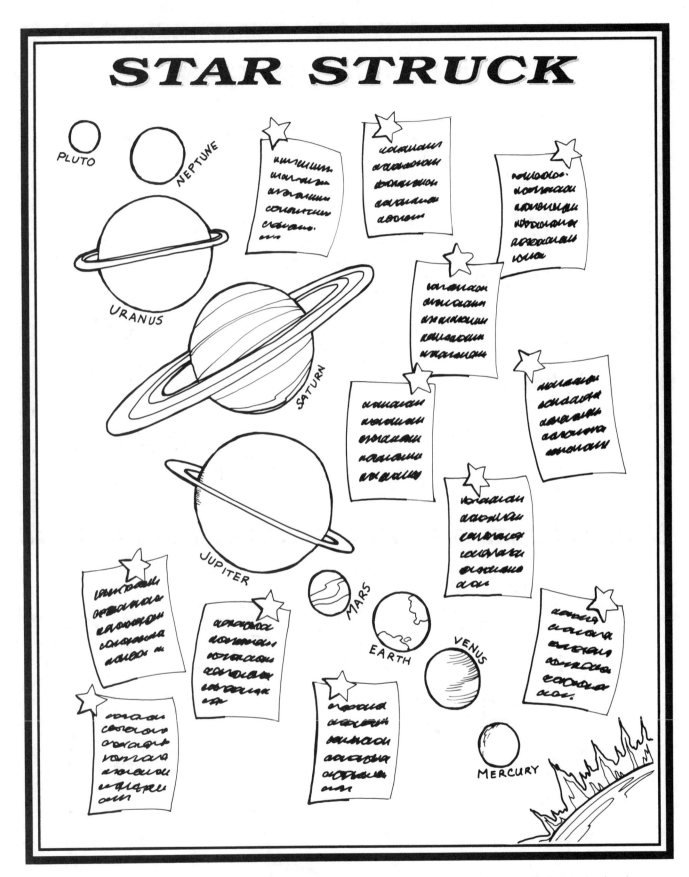

STAR STRUCK

Use this bulletin board to teach students about our solar system. Have students pick planets in our solar system, draw the planets, and research facts about the planets. Display the illustrated planets in correct sequence on the bulletin board.

220

SCIENCE SUPERSTARS

Use this bulletin board to display science reports that students have written. This bulletin board can show off students' work–anything from famous scientists to new discoveries. Have students create their own science experiments and explain them.

GA1457

DON'T BE SPELLBOUND

Use this bulletin board to teach students which words to capitalize when they write. On the magician's hat write words that need to be capitalized and words that do not need to be capitalized. The student uses the magician's wand to point to the words that need to be capitalized. This activity also develops dictionary skills.

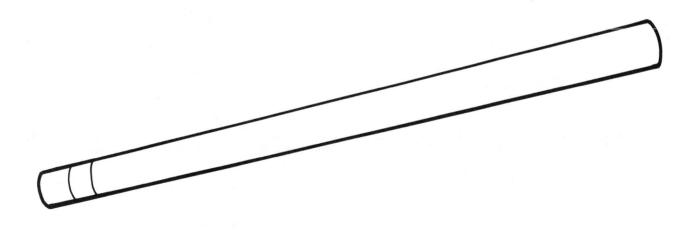

GA1457

A NOSE FOR NEWS

Use this bulletin board to encourage students to read the newspaper. Assign tasks for students to accomplish while reading the newspaper, such as copying the headline, identifying the byline, listing quotations, etc.

223

MARCH PATTERNS

GA1457

MARCH PATTERNS

GA1457

MARCH PATTERNS

226

GA1457

APRIL

GA1457

April Events

April 1–April Fools' Day

April 2–International Children's Book Day

April 10–First Arbor Day

April 18–Anniversary of Paul Revere's ride, 1775

April 22–Earth Day

April 23–William Shakespeare, born 1564

Additional Special Days and Weeks in April

Passover–The Feast of Unleavened Bread begins on the fifteenth day of Nisan and occurs in March or April.

Good Friday–Friday before Easter

Easter

National Automobile Month

Olympics began 1896–Athens, Greece

National Library Week–Begins second or third Sunday

GA1457

FOR OPENERS IN APRIL

Use this bulletin board to display student artwork in April. Have an outdoor art activity when flowers are opening and popping up. Have students draw what they see and color their flowers bright colors. Add events occurring in April to the board. Use the pattern below for flowering name tags or a budding border.

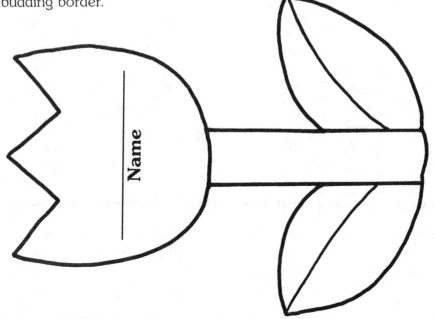

Name

229

GA1457

NO APRIL FOOLS IN THIS CLASS

Use this bulletin board to encourage students to write creative stories about April Fools' Day. Have them write about pranks that were played on them or come up with new pranks that they might play on their friends.

230

NO MORE SCHOOL
(APRIL FOOL)

Use this bulletin board as a graffiti and joke board. Have students write their favorite funny sayings and jokes on the board. Then have the class try to guess the punch lines of the jokes.

SHOWER YOURSELF WITH GOOD BOOKS

April 2 is International Children's Book Day. Encourage students to pick out their favorite books to read and write their choices on the umbrella pattern, displaying the umbrellas on the bulletin board. Have students fill the umbrellas with books they recommend to their fellow students.

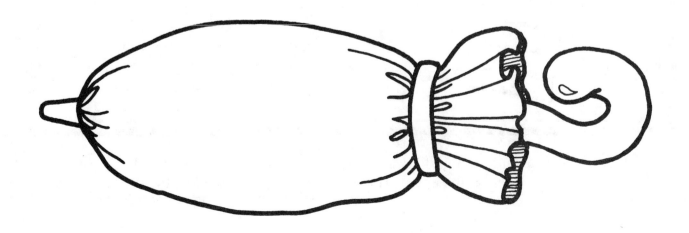

232

GA1457

WATCH OUR GARDEN GROW

Use this bulletin board as a hands-on art activity. Give students construction paper, scissors and glue and challenge them to make the bulletin board garden grow. Students could also cut out pictures of various varieties of flowers, placing them on the bulletin board and writing facts about the flowers below the pictures.

DROP IN ON APRIL

Mr. Smith's Birthday
April 2

Recycling Day
April 21

School Cleanup
April 24

School Play
April 26

Spaghetti Dinner
April 13

PTA Night
April 12

Paper Sale
April 8

Use this bulletin board to record facts, events, outings and other activities that occur in the classroom in April. Record this information on the raindrops, and display them on the board.

234

TO READ OR NOT TO READ?
THERE IS NO QUESTION.

William Shakespeare's birthday occurs on April 23. Use this bulletin board to learn all about Shakespeare. Display some of his favorite sayings and titles of his works on the bulletin board.

GA1457

APRIL ALL-STARS

Elizabeth

Beth

Rick

telephone

Know

John

circus

bicycle

Use this bulletin board to award students when they have done well in spelling. Have a classroom spelling bee and add the names of the spelling all-stars each day. Add additional words for students to learn, and have them use these new words in a creative writing exercise.

EARTH DAY BIRTHDAY

Use this bulletin board to encourage students to have a better appreciation for the earth. Duplicate a candle for each student from the pattern below. Have students write their hopes and wishes for a better planet and things that they have already done to improve the place they live. Display the candles on the bulletin board.

237

GA1457

BARK UP THE RIGHT TREE

Dear Students:
Here's your chance to register a complaint. Think of something that bothers you about the way people treat the earth, and write a letter with your concerns and ideas for changing it.

To whom it may concern:

_____

_____

_____

_____

_____

_____

_____

_____

_____

_____

_____

_____

_____

_____

_____

_____

Sincerely,

_____

GA1457

EASTER IS "EGG"CITING

Use this bulletin board to teach students about patterns. Have students combine lines and colors to decorate the Easter eggs. Display students' creations on the bulletin board. Have a class discussion first about pattern and color, and use what students are wearing to illustrate patterns–polka dots, stripes, plaids. Discuss how pattern adds interest and excitement to things that we wear or decorate with.

239

GA1457

PLANT A THOUGHT IN APRIL

JUSTIN IS A GOOD FRIEND. HE ALWAYS THINKS OF OTHERS.

I like it when someone gives me a compliment. Matthew

It makes me happy when I help someone else. Ali

Sharing Is Caring! Janet

GIVE SOMEONE A HUG TODAY. TIARA ♥

I Like to learn about others. Samuel

Plant a seed with love + watch it grow. John

Use this bulletin board to encourage students to write their feelings and thoughts. By "planting" good thoughts on the board, students can promote goodwill and think of others first in the classroom.

240

GA1457

OPENERS IN APRIL

Use this bulletin board to encourage students to create opening lines for creative story writing. Place these opening lines in an envelope on the bulletin board. Have students pick ideas and write stories using the story starters as openers. Display each student's story on the bulletin board.

241

GA1457

HOP TO IT FOR MATH

2 + 3 =

3 x 3 =

4 - 1 =

2 x 1 =

10 ÷ 2 =

4 x 2 =

Use this bulletin board to teach math skills. Display addition, subtraction, multiplication, division or word problems on the rabbit ears. Have the students solve these problems, displaying answers on the other rabbit ears.

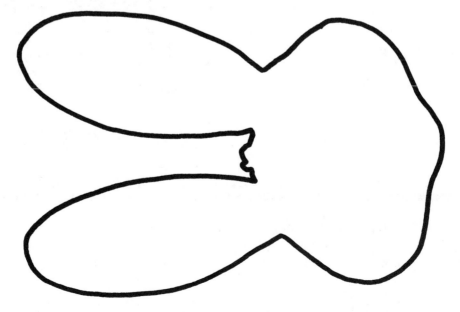

LOOK WHAT'S "HOP"PENING IN APRIL

Use this bulletin board to display school events and happenings. Display classmates' birthdays and special holiday dates, and encourage students to maintain and update the board during the month.

LOTSA MATZOH

Use this bulletin board to teach students about the holiday of Passover. This is a Jewish holiday that commemorates the freedom of the Jews from Egypt and the creation of their own homeland. Have students research different Passover words and their meanings, and encourage questions such as why matzoh (unleavened bread) is eaten.

GA1457

ART-O-MOBILES

April is National Automobile Month. Have students design and draw cars of the future, coloring and displaying them on the board. This is also an excellent time to encourage students to research who created the first car. You can also study how a car runs, what you need to know to avoid air pollution and how transportation has evolved over time.

GA1457

"EAR" YE, "EAR" YE, APRIL HAS ARRIVED

Use this bulletin board as an art activity during April. Have students create rabbits made from paper plates. Give each student two paper plates. Cut ears from one plate and add the ears to the other plate, making a bunny's face for a "hoppy" April activity. Display the rabbits on the bulletin board.

ART DISPLAY STEPS:

1. Cut out ears.　　2. Staple to plate.　　3. Add details.

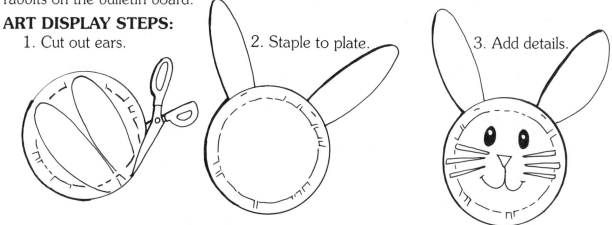

246

GA1457

OUR INTEREST IN MATH IS GROWING

Use this bulletin board to display students' math work during the month. This bulletin board could also be used to encourage interest in any other subject area. Have students add up all the numbers on the flowers on the board, and every day add a new flower so the total grows.

Use this bulletin board to teach students to put the alphabet to use in a clever way. List each letter of the alphabet, and have students list their interests and activities beginning with that letter.

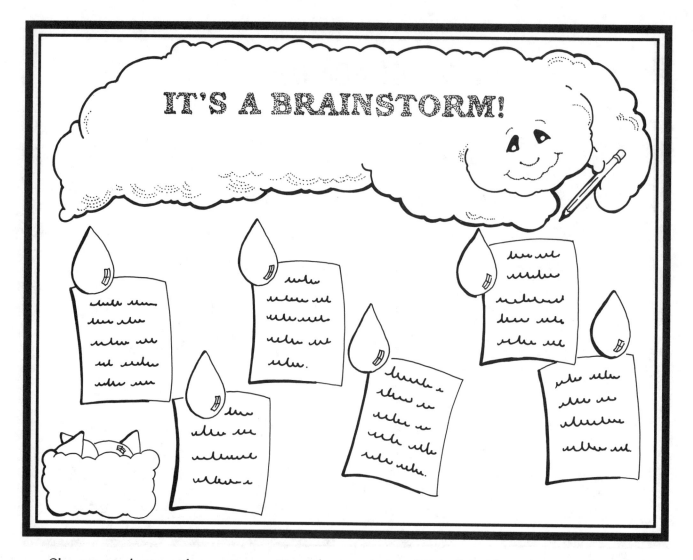

Shower students with creative writing ideas and use this bulletin board to inspire clever stories. Duplicate the raindrop pattern below and write a story idea on each drop. Add the raindrops to a pocket on the bulletin board. Instruct students to choose one story idea to write about. Display the creative writing on the bulletin board.

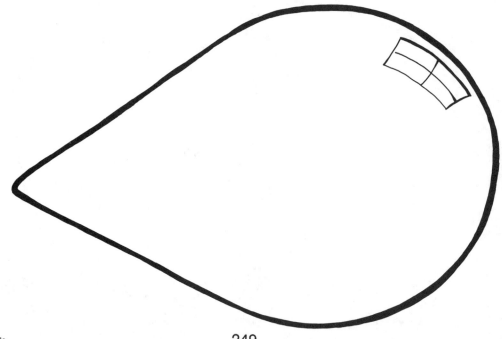

GA1457

QUACK UP

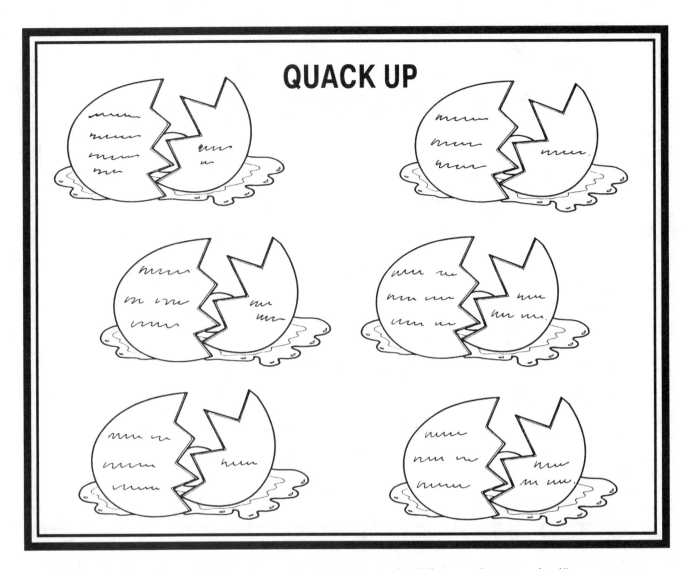

Use this bulletin board to display students' jokes and riddles on the "quacked" up egg pattern below. Make eggs for students and have them write their favorite jokes on the eggs. Display them on the board. Example: What happens when a duck flies upside down? He quacks up!

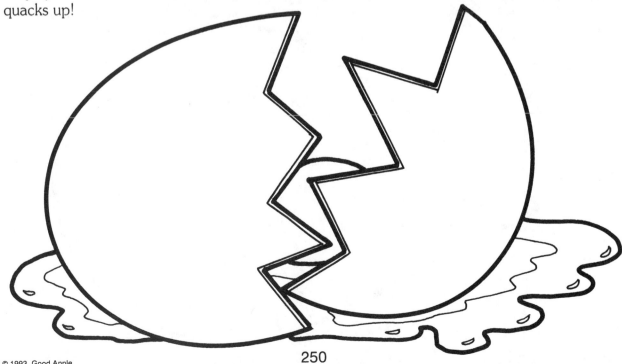

250

"EGGS"TRA SPECIAL KIDS

Use this bulletin board to focus on the students and praise them for being special. Have each student create an Easter egg, color it in and add his or her name. Display the eggs on the bulletin board. To further praise students, award them for some specific areas that they have improved in or achieved in with the "Eggs"tra Special Award on the next page.

251

"EGGS"TRA SPECIAL AWARD

_____ IS "EGGS"TRA SPECIAL

AND IS DOING GREAT IN_____.

KEEP UP THE GREAT WORK!

_____
Teacher

APRIL OPENERS

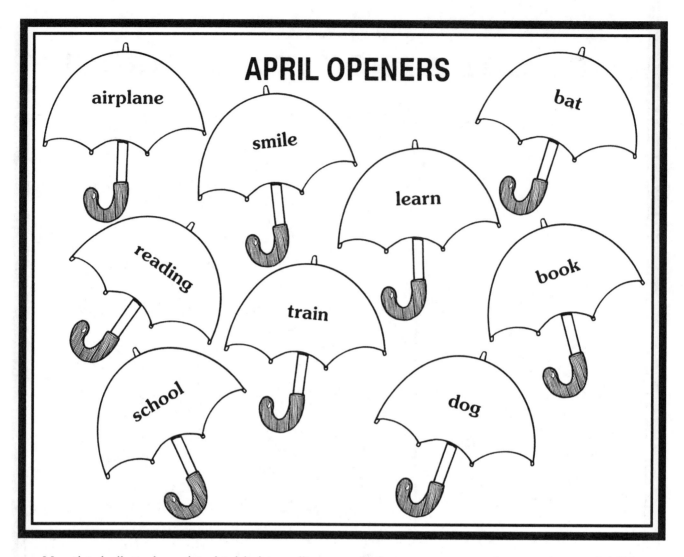

airplane
smile
bat
learn
reading
book
train
school
dog

Use this bulletin board to highlight spelling words that you want students to learn. Add the words to umbrellas duplicated from the pattern below.

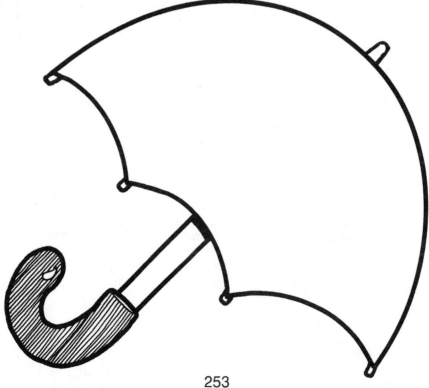

GA1457

HE'S GOT A FROG IN HIS THROAT

Use this bulletin board to teach students to recognize and use idioms. Have students compile a list of idioms, illustrating at least one of them. Examples include it's raining cats and dogs, barking up the wrong tree, once in a blue moon, sitting on pins and needles, hit the road, hit the sack, you take the cake and many more.

Instruct each student to color a pattern on an egg, and then cut the egg in half in a broken fashion. Place both halves of the egg in the envelope on the bulletin board. Play a game where each student gets to choose two halves from the envelope. The object of the game is to try to make a match.

APRIL PATTERNS

GA1457

APRIL PATTERNS

257

GA1457

APRIL PATTERNS

GA1457

APRIL PATTERNS

GA1457

MAY

GA1457

May Events

May 1–May Day

May 6–World's first postage stamp issued in 1840

May 7–Red Cross Day

May–Mother's Day, second Sunday in May

May 15–L. Frank Baum, born 1856

May 21–Clara Barton, founder of the American Red Cross, born 1881

May–Memorial Day, last Monday in May

Additional Special Days and Weeks in May

Be Kind to Animals Week

Cinco de Mayo

National Music Week–Begins first Sunday in May

GA1457

The world's first postage stamp was issued on May 6, 1840. Use this bulletin board to encourage students to learn more about the postal system and about stamps and stamp collecting. Have students collect stamps from around the world, displaying them on the bulletin board. This bulletin board can also be used as an art activity by having students design stamps that they feel would be meaningful to our country.

METER MAY'D

Use this bulletin board to teach students about the metric system of measurement. Have students display pictures of various objects on the bulletin board, measuring them first in inches and then converting them to centimeters and millimeters.

263

UP, UP AND AWAY IN MAY

May 1 is the birthday of Scott Carpenter, the second American to circle the earth in a spacecraft. Use this bulletin board to teach students about space travel and exploration. Have them research the space program and write famous events that occurred on rockets. Display the rockets on the board.

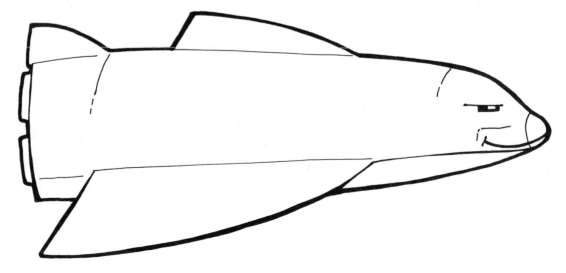

GA1457

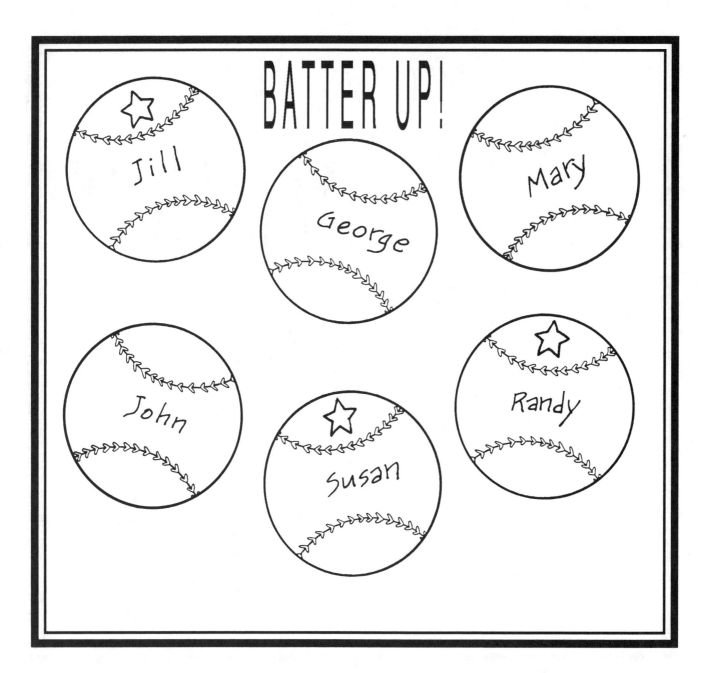

BATTER UP!

Jill

George

Mary

John

Susan

Randy

Use this bulletin board to encourage students to participate in school-wide activities such as newspaper drives, collecting food for the homeless or fund-raising. Place the students' names on baseballs made from the pattern on the right. Display the balls on the board. As the students accomplish their goals, add stars to the baseballs. Accomplishments could also be written on pennants and placed on the board.

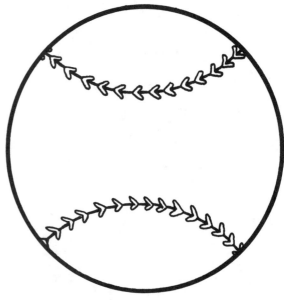

Use this bulletin board to feature school activities that occur in the month of May. Duplicate the cow pattern below, and add an event to each cow on the board.

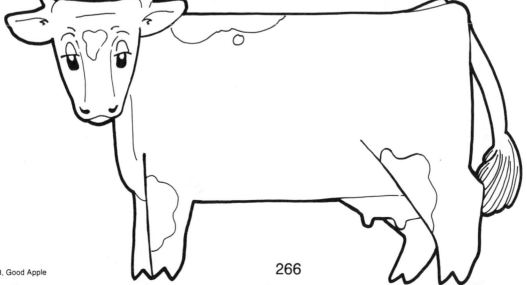

GA1457

SPLASH INTO SUMMER

This bulletin board is an art activity. Have students splash various colors of paint on paper, displaying their unique designs on the bulletin board.

267

GA1457

Use this bulletin board to teach students to rhyme. Pick a word of the day and have students display other words that rhyme with it on index cards. Students can keep a rhyming dictionary for future use.

268

MAY'S MASTERPIECES

Use this bulletin board to display students' artwork. This is a wonderful board that students can be in charge of and change as often as they want.

269

ON THE BALL IN MAY

Use this board to encourage physical fitness in the classroom. As the upcoming summer requires physical exertion, have students design a fitness program of daily exercises for May to get ready for the active summer break.

270

A BOOK A DAY IN MAY

Use this bulletin board to encourage students to make a list of reading material for the summer break. List books on the bulletin board, and have students pick their choices for the vacation.

271

HOLD THE MAY-O

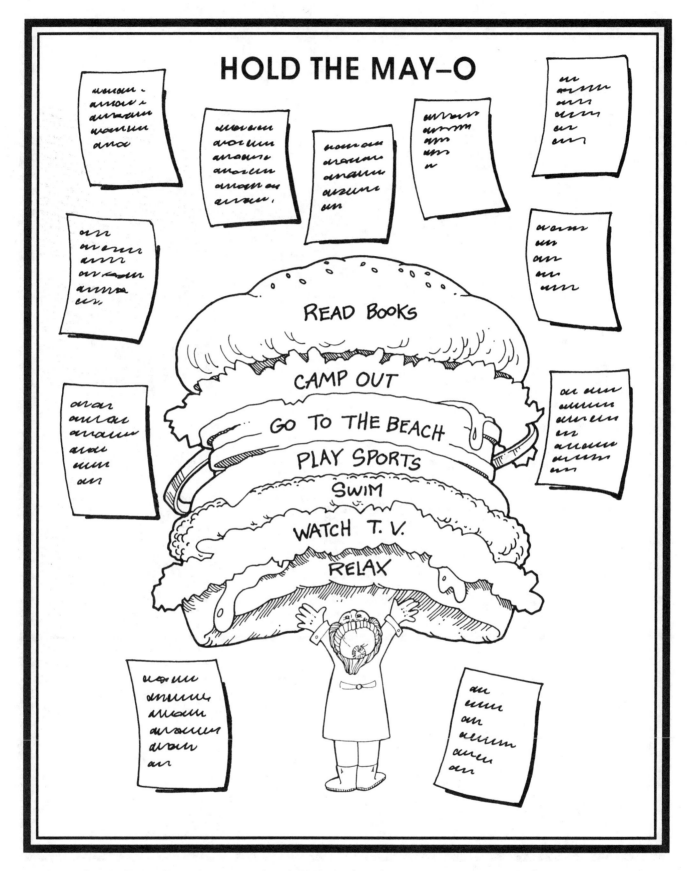

READ BOOKS

CAMP OUT

GO TO THE BEACH

PLAY SPORTS

SWIM

WATCH T. V.

RELAX

Use this bulletin board to "sandwich" ideas for the summer in poetry form. Have each student write a poem. Display the poems on the bulletin board, and give students the chance to recite their poems in front of the class.

GA1457

"MAY"BE YES, "MAY"BE NO

Use this bulletin board to teach the concept of opposites. Choose a variety of words, objects and colors. Display them on the board, encouraging students to match the opposites on the board.

273

Use this bulletin board to encourage good attendance the last month of the school year. Display students' homework or other activities completed during the month of May.

GA1457

FIX 'ER UP

timely

senseless

un   tion

Pre ly ment less in
              Con
        de   ex

deflate

prepay

conserve

Use this bulletin board to teach students about prefixes and suffixes. Prefixes come before another word, changing the meaning of that word. Suffixes come after another word. Have students list as many words as possible using the prefixes and suffixes shown on the board.

SURPRISE, SURPRISE, ALPHABETIZE

Use this bulletin board to teach students to put words in alphabetical order. On the gift box pattern write words, and have students put the boxes on the bulletin board in alphabetical order.

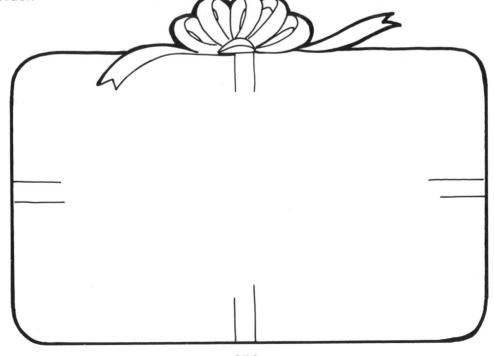

GA1457

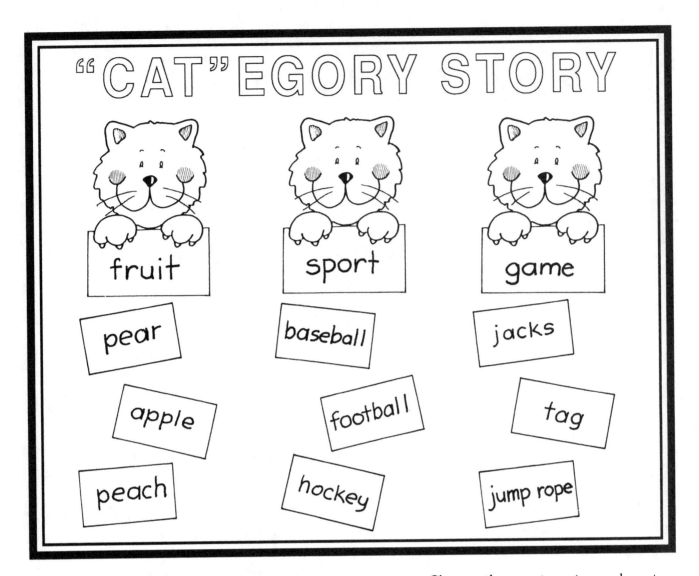

"CAT"EGORY STORY

fruit	sport	game
pear	baseball	jacks
apple	football	tag
peach	hockey	jump rope

Use this bulletin board to teach students to categorize. Choose three categories and post them on the cat patterns. Instruct students to write words on index cards and place them below the appropriate categories. Students can also use this as a creative writing exercise. Have them choose words from each category and then write stories.

GA1457

DON'T LET MATH COUNT YOU OUT

$5+8=$

$15\div5=$

$1\times17=$

$13-4=$

$10-3=$

$5\times9=$

$6\times3=$

$12\div4=$

$24\div3=$

$8\times3=$

$7\times4=$

$10\times2=$

$11+5=$

$9+12=$

$15\div3=$

$8+7=$

$17-9=$

Use this bulletin board to review math skills. Display a variety of math problems on the board, and encourage students to solve these problems in a certain time period.

BRANCH OUT IN MAY

Use this bulletin board to encourage students to plan for their summer vacations. Instruct students to write their ideas for summer activities and fun on index cards. Display their ideas on the "tree of learning."

279

GA1457

SUMMERTIME BLUES

Use this bulletin board as an art activity. Instruct students to draw various summer scenes incorporating the color blue in their work. These scenes could depict any subject from the ocean to the pool to the big blue sky. Display students' summertime blues on the bulletin board.

LOOK WHAT BUGS US

Use this bulletin board as a science project. Have students observe and study the insect world, and if possible, bring insects into the classroom for observation. Then be sure to let them go outside. Have students write short stories about their choices and display the work on this bulletin board.

MY BUG BOX

Dear Student:
Pretend you are going to catch a variety of bugs and put them in the box. Draw your collection here.

GA1457

OCEANS IN MOTION

Use this bulletin board as a science activity to introduce students to a whole new world under the sea. Encourage students to research topics related to the sea and write short stories about their topics.

283

ROCK ON

Use this bulletin board to teach students about rocks and rock formations. The earth's history can be learned from rocks, so encourage students to research questions about rocks and write reports, displaying them on the board. Use this bulletin board to interest students in collecting a variety of rocks to share with fellow classmates.

284

GA1457

SCRAMBLED EGGS

Use this bulletin board to encourage good spelling. On the egg pattern scramble a variety of words. Challenge students to unscramble the words, spell them correctly and add them to the frying pan. This board can be adapted to cities, countries, science terms or any other subject area.

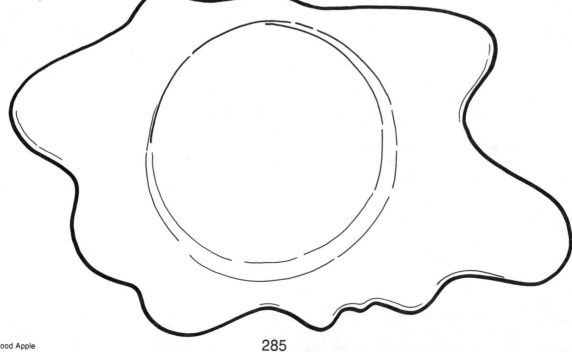

285

GA1457

IDEAS WE FIND A "PEEL"ING

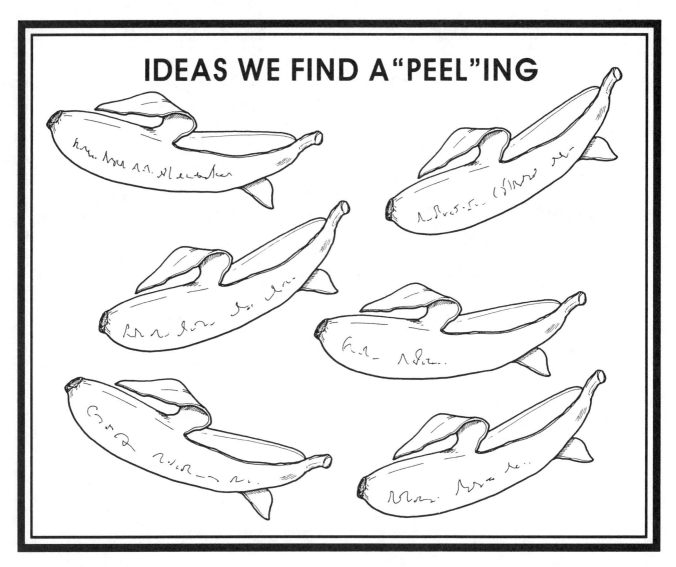

Use this bulletin board to encourage creative thinking. On the banana peel patterns, encourage students to write their good ideas for summer fun.

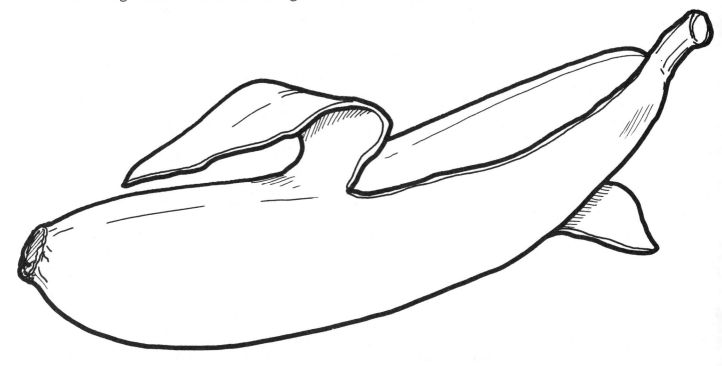

286

MAY PATTERNS

MAY PATTERNS

SCHOOL'S OUT!

288

Word Searches

Patterns

Awards

Work Sheets

289

WORD SEARCH

Mix up words on this page, and add letters of the alphabet to fill up the page. Exchange word searches, and circle the words that are listed.

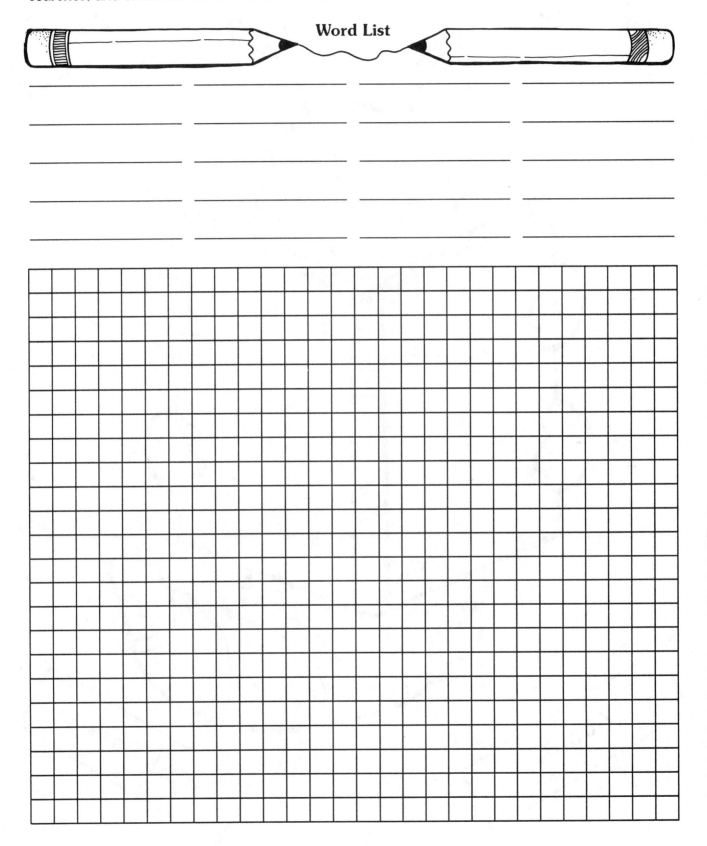

Word List

NO TELLING WITH SPELLING

Use this word search grid to hide spelling words. Fill in the remaining spaces with random letters. Give students copies of the word search, and ask them to circle the hidden words.

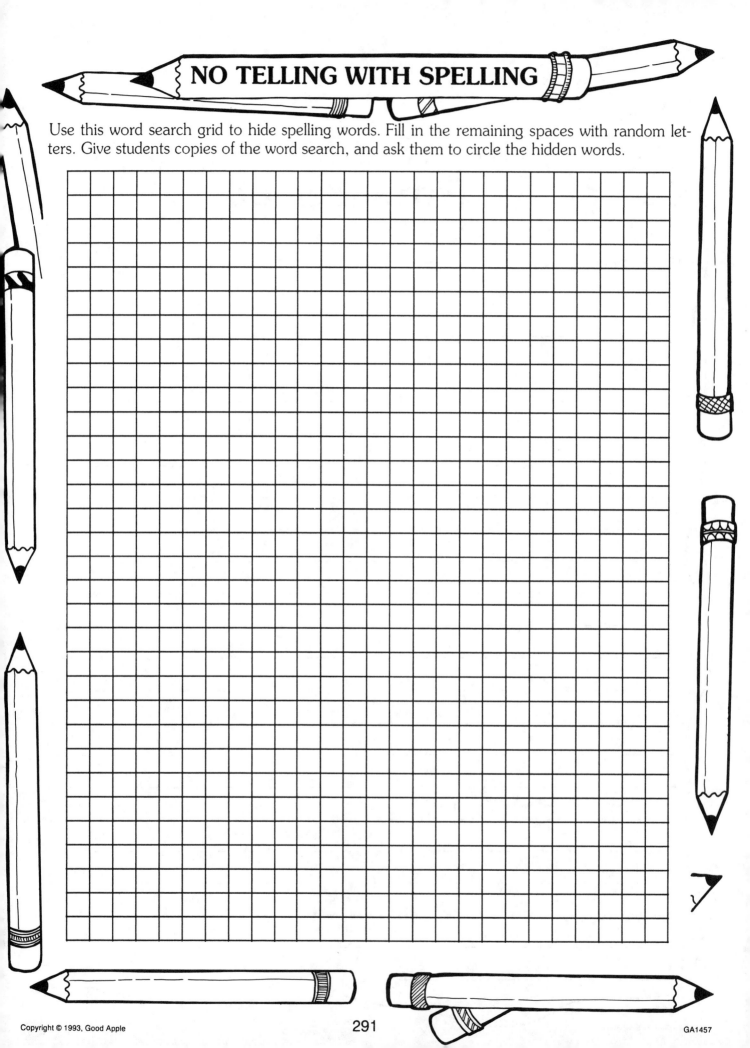

291

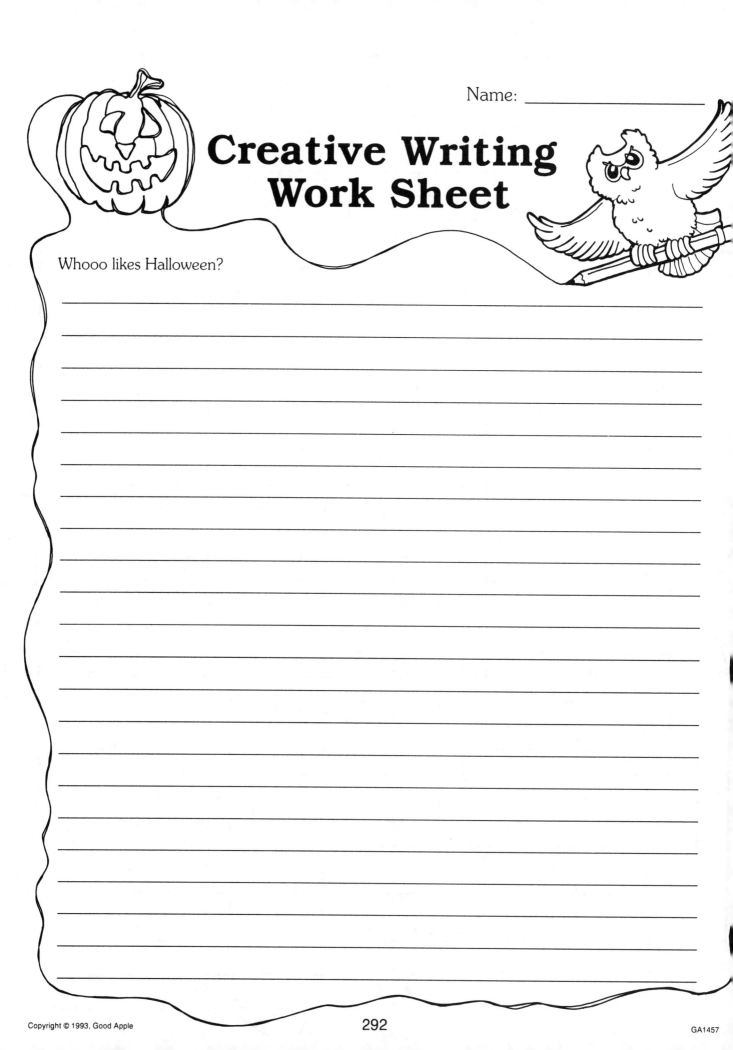

Name: _____

Creative Writing
Work Sheet

Whooo likes Halloween?

_____
_____
_____
_____
_____
_____
_____
_____
_____
_____
_____
_____
_____
_____
_____
_____
_____
_____
_____
_____
_____
_____
_____

Name: _____

Creative Writing
Work Sheet

Write a story about what you would do if you didn't have a form of transportation. How would this affect your life?

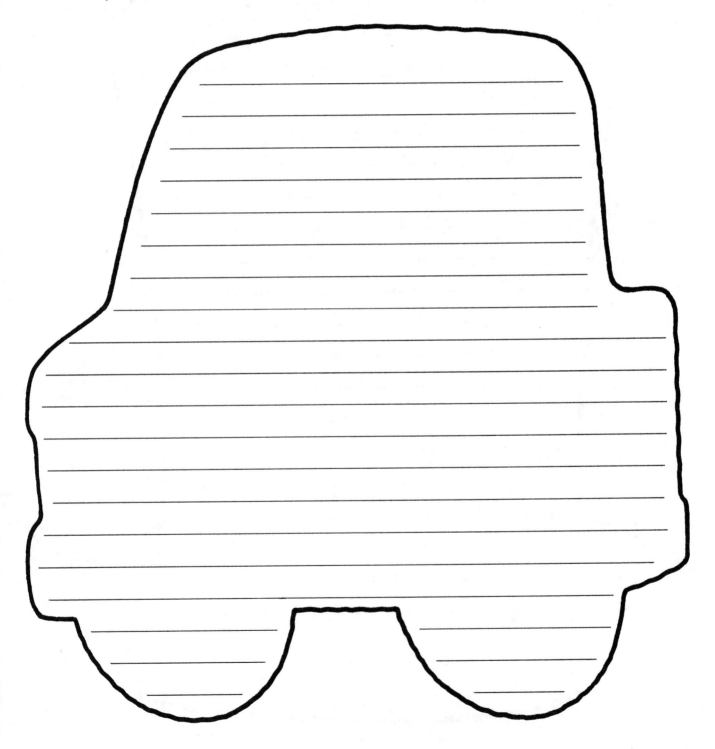

GA1457

Top Pop

Write a letter to your dad, grandpa or a top pop to tell him why he's special.

World-Class Mom

Write your mom, grandmother or a favorite mom a letter and tell her why you think she's special.

295

My Family Tree

Use this family tree to research your relatives. List their names on the tree.

Class Newspaper

GA1457

Calendar Pattern

Sunday	Monday	Tuesday	Wednesday	Thursday	Friday	Saturday

Patterns

299

GA1457

300

GA1457

U.S. MAIL

301

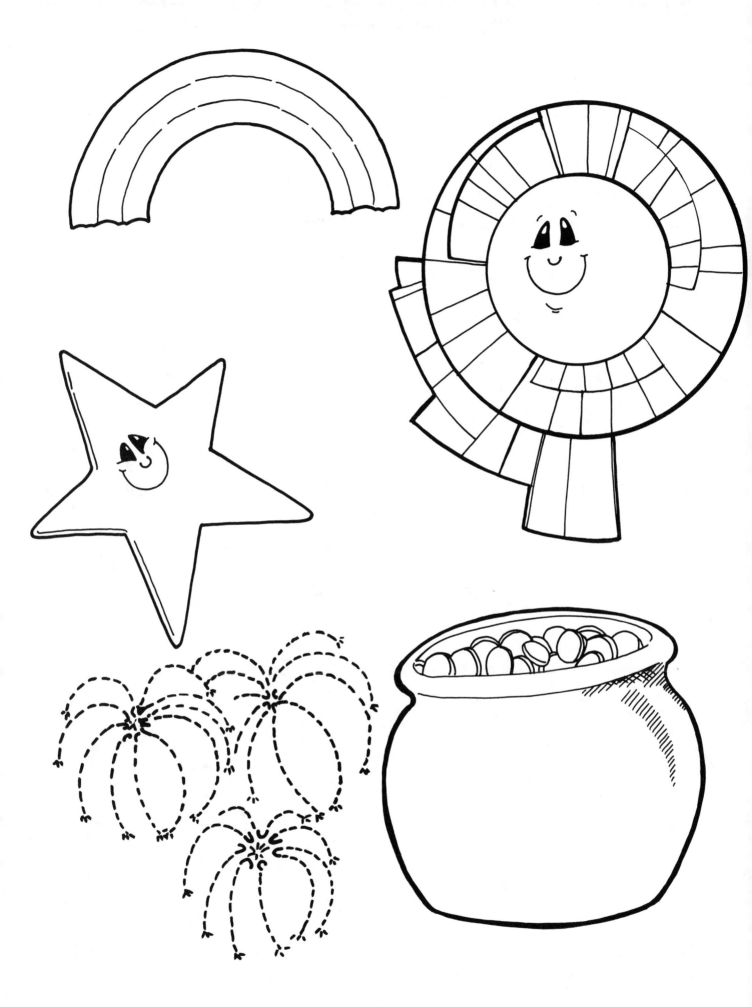

302

GA1457

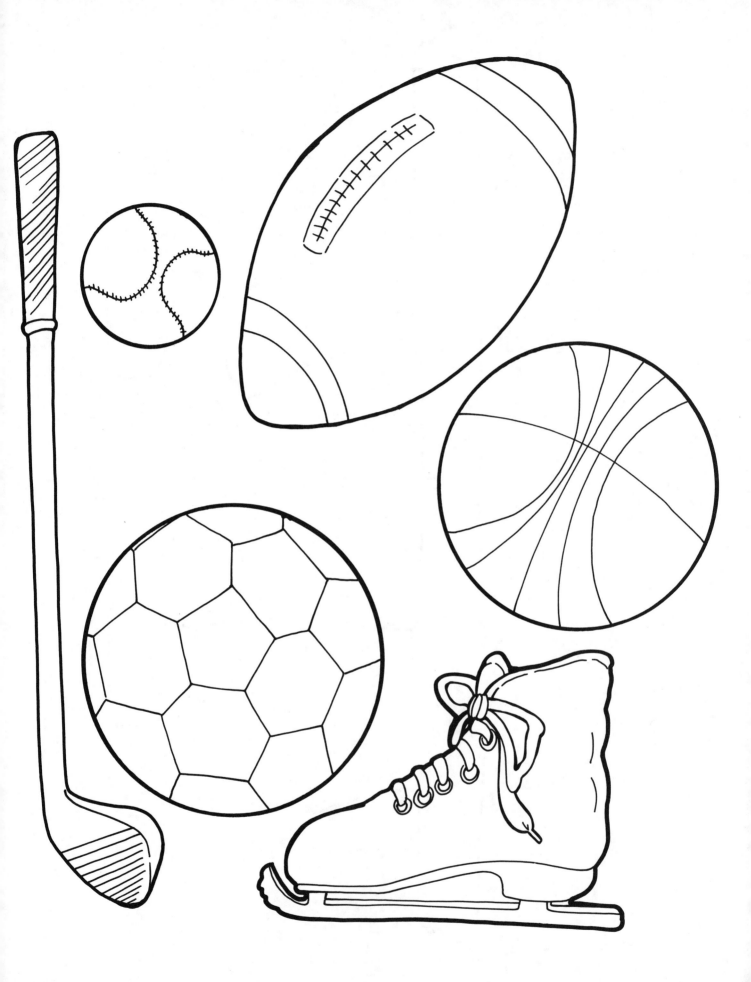

303

GA1457

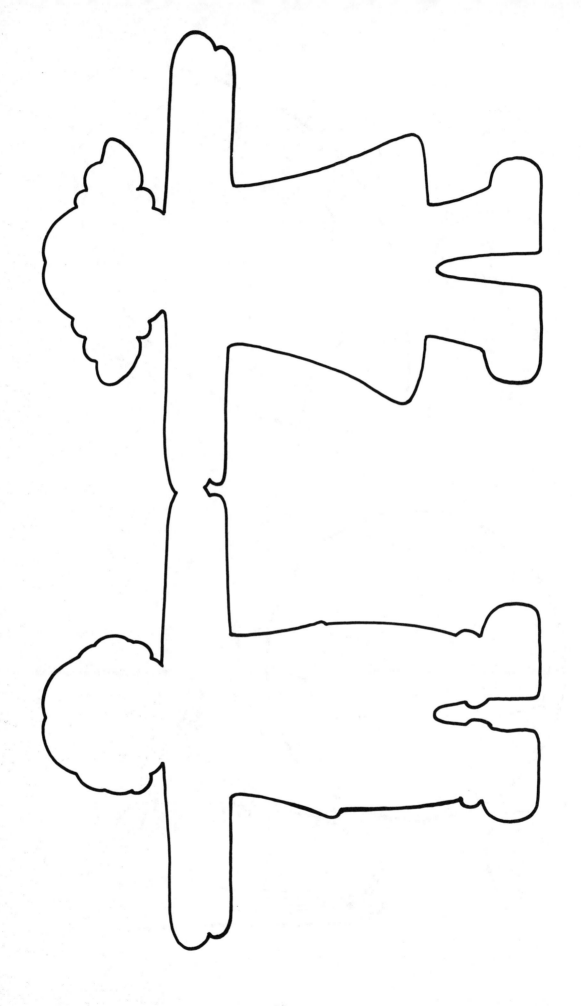

304

GA1457

305

GA1457

307

GA1457

308

GA1457

ONE TWO THREE FOUR FIVE SIX SEVEN EIGHT NINE TEN

310

GA1457

311

GA1457

GA1457

Awards

_____

is
a
winner!

TERRIFIC!

WINNER!

313

_____

student's name

is in
tip-top shape
in

_____

subject

_____

signed

314

_____
student's name

Is

Shining Brightly

in

_____

Hooray for _____
student's name

_____
signed

315

Happy Birthday to

_____
student's name

Have a "Tree"mendous Day!

_____
signed

GA1457

Happy Birthday to

_____
student's name

Have a Very "Hoppy" Day!

_____
signed

EXTRA! EXTRA!
Read All About It!

_____
student's name

has improved in

_____ !

_____
signed

318